Media and Politics in Pacific Asia

Media and Politics in Pacific Asia is the first book to provide a detailed account of the political influences exerted by both domestic and international media in Pacific Asia. Duncan McCargo argues that the media are political actors and institutions in their own right, and that as such they can play a variety of political roles, some of which support processes of democratic transition and consolidation, and some which do just the opposite.

Drawing on first-hand research in Hong Kong, Indonesia, Japan and Thailand – and employing comparative examples that include Burma, Malaysia and the Philippines – Duncan McCargo examines the various influences of the media as agents of stability, restraint and change. He also analyses pressures on the media from a range of state, non-state and market forces, and sets out to problematize simplistic readings of issues such as media freedom, ownership, partisanship, profitability, regulation and the public interest. The result is an in-depth and fascinating study of the interplay between the media and the political process.

Written in a clear and accessible style with numerous examples, this highly original book will be useful to academics, students, journalists, and general readers interested in Asian studies, media and politics.

Duncan McCargo is Professor of Southeast Asian Politics at the University of Leeds. His other books include *Politics and the Press in Thailand: Media Machinations* (Routledge: 2000), *Contemporary Japan* (Macmillan: 2000) and *Reforming Thai Politics* (edited, NIAS: 2002).

Politics in Asia series
Formerly edited by Michael Leifer
London School of Economics

ASEAN and the Security of South-East Asia
Michael Leifer

China's Policy towards Territorial Disputes
The Case of the South China Sea Islands
Chi-kin Lo

India and Southeast Asia
Indian Perceptions and Policies
Mohammed Ayoob

Gorbachev and Southeast Asia
Leszek Buszynski

Indonesian Politics under Suharto
Order, Development and Pressure for Change
Michael R. J. Vatikiotis

The State and Ethnic Politics in Southeast Asia
David Brown

The Politics of Nation Building and Citizenship in Singapore
Michael Hill and Lian Kwen Fee

Politics in Indonesia
Democracy, Islam and the Ideology of Tolerance
Douglas E. Ramage

Communitarian Ideology and Democracy in Singapore
Beng-Huat Chua

The Challenge of Democracy in Nepal
Louise Brown

Japan's Asia Policy
Wolf Mendl

The International Politics of the Asia-Pacific, 1945–1995
Michael Yahuda

Political Change in Southeast Asia
Trimming the Banyan Tree
Michael R. J. Vatikiotis

Hong Kong
China's Challenge
Michael Yahuda

Korea versus Korea
A Case of Contested Legitimacy
B. K. Gills

Taiwan and Chinese Nationalism
National Identity and Status in International Society
Christopher Hughes

Managing Political Change in Singapore
The Elected Presidency
Kevin Y. L. Tan and Lam Peng Er

Islam in Malaysian Foreign Policy
Shanti Nair

Political Change in Thailand
Democracy and Participation
Kevin Hewison

The Politics of NGOs in South-East Asia
Participation and Protest in the Philippines
Gerard Clarke

Malaysian Politics Under Mahathir
R. S. Milne and Diane K. Mauzy

Indonesia and China
The Politics of a Troubled Relationship
Rizal Sukma

Arming the Two Koreas
State, Capital and Military Power
Taik-young Hamm

Engaging China
The Management of an Emerging Power
Edited by Alastair Iain Johnston and Robert S. Ross

Singapore's Foreign Policy
Coping with Vulnerability
Michael Leifer

Philippine Politics and Society in the Twentieth Century
Colonial Legacies, Post-Colonial Trajectories
Eva-Lotta E. Hedman and John T. Sidel

Constructing a Security Community in Southeast Asia
ASEAN and the Problem of Regional Order
Amitav Acharya

Monarchy in South-East Asia
The Faces of Tradition in Transition
Roger Kershaw

Korea After the Crash
The Politics of Economic Recovery
Brian Bridges

The Future of North Korea
Edited by Tsuneo Akaha

The International Relations of Japan and South East Asia
Forging a New Regionalism
Sueo Sudo

Power and Change in Central Asia
Edited by Sally N. Cummings

The Politics of Human Rights in Southeast Asia
Philip Eldridge

Political Business in East Asia
Edited by Edmund Terence Gomez

Singapore Politics under the People's Action Party
Diane K. Mauzy and R. S. Milne

Media and Politics in Pacific Asia
Duncan McCargo

Media and Politics in Pacific Asia

Duncan McCargo

RoutledgeCurzon
Taylor & Francis Group
LONDON AND NEW YORK

302.23091823 M123m

McCargo, Duncan.

Media and politics in
 Pacific Asia

First published 2003
by RoutledgeCurzon
11 New Fetter Lane, London EC4P 4EE

Simultaneously published in the USA and Canada
by RoutledgeCurzon
29 West 35th Street, New York, NY 10001

RoutledgeCurzon is an imprint of the Taylor & Francis Group

© 2003 Duncan McCargo

Typeset in Times by Steven Gardiner Ltd, Cambridge
Printed and bound in Great Britain by
MPG Books Ltd, Bodmin

All rights reserved. No part of this book may be reprinted
or reproduced or utilized in any form or by any electronic,
mechanical, or other means, now known or hereafter
invented, including photocopying and recording, or in any
information storage or retrieval system, without permission
in writing from the publishers.

British Library Cataloguing in Publication Data
A catalogue record for this book is available from the
British Library

Library of Congress Cataloging in Publication Data
A catalog record for this book has been requested

ISBN 0-415-23374-7 (hbk)
ISBN 0-415-23375-5 (pbk)

Contents

	Acknowledgements	xi
1	Introduction: politics and media in Pacific Asia	1
2	Media in times of crisis: media and democratic transitions in Southeast Asia	19
3	Media in peacetime? Press and television in Japan	50
4	Media as an agent of stability? Suharto's Indonesia	77
5	Media in a time of transition: Hong Kong	100
6	International media and domestic politics: tales from Thailand	117
7	Conclusion	153
	Notes	159
	Select bibliography	165
	Index	177

Acknowledgements

This book arose from my ESRC project H52427002694, 'The politics of the media in Thailand and Pacific Asia'. It should ideally be read in conjunction with another output of that project, my monograph *Politics and the Press in Thailand: Media Machinations*, also published by Routledge (McCargo 2000b). The present work draws upon fieldwork carried out in Thailand (September 1992 and February 1995–February 1996) funded by the ESRC, the British Academy Committee for South-East Asian Studies and the Department of Politics, University of Leeds; in Tokyo (summer 1994), funded by the Japan Society for the Promotion of Science and the British Academy, and hosted by the International Christian University; in Jakarta (summer 1997), funded by the British Academy Committee for South-East Asian Studies and hosted by CSIS; and in Hong Kong (Easter 1999), funded by David C. Lam, and the Visitorship Programme of the Lam East–West Institute (LEWI) of Hong Kong Baptist University. The financial and institutional support of these bodies has been greatly appreciated.

Earlier versions of some of this material have been published in *Index on Censorship* (one section of Chapter 2, McCargo 1993); *Pacific Review* (much of Chapter 3, McCargo 1996); *The Harvard International Journal of Press Politics* (most of Chapter 4, McCargo 1999a), and *Modern Asian Studies* (much of Chapter 6, McCargo 1999b). They are reproduced here with acknowledgements and thanks.

I am also very grateful to the numerous people who have assisted me with my fieldwork, and in commenting on my draft materials. I should particularly like to thank the following:

Japan: Kyoko Altman, Koya Azumi, Roger Buckley, Paul Eckert, Hiroshi Hori, Kay Itoi, Ken Kondo, Hisahiro Kondoh, Yumiko Mikanagi, Jacob Schlesinger, Karen Shire, Robert Stern, Tatou Takahama, Hiroyuki Taniguchi, Mark Williams, Wayne Wilson, Karel van Wolferen, and Emi Yamazaki.

Thailand: Abhisit Vejjajiva, William A. Callahan, Chalinee Hirano, Shawn Crispin, Gordon Fairclough, Kevin Hewison, Jane Vejjajiva, Korakot Surakul, Glen Lewis, Nopporn Wong-Anan, Roj Ngamman, Sombat Chantornvong, Ubonrat Siriyuvasak, Walailak Priyisurawong, and Wilasinee Phiphitkul; and many others too numerous to list here.

Indonesia: Satrio Arismunandar, Endy Bayuni, Bambang Bujono, Harold Crouch, Daniel Dhakidae, Tatik Hafidz, Ariel Heryanto, Yuli Ismartono, Aleksius Jemadu, Clara Joewono, Aristides Katoppo, Herry Komar, Goenawan Mohamed, Rosfita Roesli, Hadi Soesastro, and Rizal Sukma.

Hong Kong: Chris Bale, Wendy Chan, Yuen Ying Chan, Judith Clarke, Michael DeGolyer, Kin-ming Liu, Kerry McGlynn, Joyce Nip, and Arnold Zeitlin.

At Leeds, I am very grateful to David Beetham and David S. Bell, two colleagues who strongly supported my research fellowship, and to Caroline Wise for her administrative wizardry. Thanks are also due to the late Michael Leifer, the 'Politics in Asia' series editor, and Craig Fowlie, my editor at Routledge.

Duncan McCargo
Leeds, April 2002

1 Introduction: politics and media in Pacific Asia

General issues

Radio Veritas was widely credited with helping to bring down the Marcos regime. The banning of *Tempo* and two other weeklies in 1994 marked the beginning of the end for Indonesia's New Order. Changing styles of television news led by TV Asahi contributed to a re-shaping of Japanese politics in the 1990s. The *de facto* sacking of a *South China Morning Post* China-watcher rekindled a long-running debate about self-censorship in Hong Kong. Thai prime minister Thaksin Shinawatra lost much of his international credibility following a wounding spat with the *Far Eastern Economic Review*. Unpacking the often inept interactions between media and politics is an essential task for all who seek to understand Pacific Asia.

This book begins with several (deliberately provocative) observations. Those who study politics generally have a limited understanding of media, and political scientists are mainly interested in 'political communication' issues such as election coverage and campaigning – what Cook (1998) calls 'the voter persuasion paradigm'. Those who study media generally have a weak understanding of politics, often espousing far-fetched and overly sympathetic interpretations of media. Most analyses of politics and media are based upon Western countries, and are of limited relevance to non-Western societies. The media specialist's over-riding preoccupation with outputs, typically studied through content analysis, often obscures the important processes that generate those outputs. Many arguments advanced about media and politics have limited value for developing countries, especially perhaps Asian ones (see Curran and Park 2000).

The result is that very little sensible and rigorous work has been done on the political role played by the media in Asian countries. Only a handful of academic authors have engaged in fieldwork-based research concerning political aspects of the Asian media. While there are three excellent recent book-length political studies in English of the Japanese media, drawing on extensive interviews and participant observation (Feldman 1993; Freeman 2000; Krauss 2000), similar Southeast Asian studies are limited to a book on Thailand (McCargo 2000b) and Australian doctoral theses on Indonesia and Vietnam (Hanazaki 1996; Heng 2000).

The study of the political role of media is a twilight zone, a shadowy territory that lurks on the border between two rather nebulous disciplines. This book works from two core assumptions:

1 The media are political actors and political institutions in their own right, and
2 As such, the media can play a variety of political roles, some of which support processes of democratic transition and consolidation, and some of which do just the opposite.

As Cook notes, the apparently obvious point that the media should be viewed as political institutions has long been overlooked in Western societies. Journalists have been very successful in discouraging people from viewing them as political actors, while political scientists have generally failed to recognize the media as political institutions. In a chapter entitled 'Why don't we call journalists political actors?' Cook argues that:

> First, journalists work hard to discourage people from thinking of them as political actors. Indeed, they may be so successful at this attempt that they have convinced even themselves. Second, the study of political communications developed amidst a tradition emphasizing 'media effects', and the disciplines most involved in the study of the politics of the news media have held back from the implications of their work. In particular, while political scientists have been quite comfortable referring to the media's political contribution, they have been less willing to see the news media as an institution.
>
> (Cook 1998: 4)

In other words, journalists have successfully persuaded academics that they are not political actors, and scholars working in both politics and media studies have missed the scoop. Even where scholars seem to grasp the nettle, the results are disappointing. While McNair does refer to the media as 'political actors', he proceeds immediately to an anecdotal discussion based entirely on British examples (McNair 1999: 73–89); Cook similarly confines himself to a detailed examination of the American media.

Alternative modes of agency

If we believe that the media are political actors, what kind of role do they play? In particular, what role do the media play in relation to processes of democratic transition and consolidation in the developing world? In developing countries such as Indonesia, the centrality of the media's political role has long been recognized. The state has often emphasized the importance of the press in the process of nation-building. As President Suharto himself declared in a speech on National Press Day in 1989:

> As an integral part of our developing society, nation and state, the press has an important role to assist in managing this nation in all its complexity through the dissemination of news, opinions, ideas, grievances and hopes to the masses. . . . It is in this respect that the press has a role to play in helping build and preserve our unity and cohesion as a nation.
>
> (Soeharto 1989: 131)

By performing this function, the media act as an *agent of stability*, charged with the task of helping preserve social and political order. This function is commonly associated with the term 'development journalism'.

A second function is that of day-to-day monitoring of the political order in the interests of more representative government, providing checks and balances. This monitoring could range from critical editorializing about government policies to full-scale investigative reporting about high-level corruption. In this second function, the media act as an *agent of restraint*.

A third function is a fire-fighting one: helping to shape political changes during times of crisis. Southeast Asian examples include the role of media in the ousting of the Marcos regime in the Philippines in 1986, or the support provided by the press during the May 1992 pro-democracy demonstrations in Bangkok (Serrano 1994: 62). In this third function, the media are an *agent of change*.

These three alternative modes of agency – of stability, restraint and change – are possible functions for the media as a political institution. They are broadly equivalent to three adjectival descriptions of the media's alternative roles: conservative, progressive and transformative. It is tempting to assume that the press performs a specific political role in a given society at a given juncture: an agent of stability in an authoritarian regime (such as Burma today); an agent of restraint in a liberal democracy (such as Japan in the 1970s); and an agent of change in a society in the throes of political transition (such as Thailand in 1992). But in practice, the media are multidimensional, and may adopt multiple modes of agency simultaneously. Different sections of the media may be cheering, reproving and denouncing power-holders on the same day. Indeed, a single publication may itself play diverse roles. Different columnists and editors may adopt different forms of political agency within the same issue of the same publication: a critical front page story indicates that the publication is seeking to restrain certain power-holders, while a bland editorial appears to offer them tacit support, and an aggressive columnist calls for their resignations. Evaluating the nature of the political roles performed by the press in any given situation requires close scrutiny of two factors: ownership and control of publications, and the relationships between owners, journalists, and power-holders. Received views about the media as a benign agent of change need to be problematized.

Alternative modes of regulation

Rather than focusing on the agency of the media themselves, it is also possible to see their roles through the alternative prism of modes of regulation. Kunda Dixit argues that three broad models of ownership and control can be seen in Southeast Asia; indeed, these models also obtain across Pacific Asia. The first is one of direct state control, as practised in Burma, Vietnam, Laos, and China, where media are monopolized by the state and serve as the propaganda arm of the ruling party, reflecting its concerns' (Dixit 1999: 55). The second is 'licensing control of private media', as practised in Singapore, Malaysia and until 1998, in Indonesia. The need to ensure licence renewal makes companies reluctant to 'ruffle official feathers for fear of losing their profitable media businesses'. At the same time, 'competing power centres have used the print media for exposés that have usually been quashed'. The third is the 'free-for-all press', as seen in Thailand, the Philippines and in Indonesia post-Suharto. While this model presents the appearance of a truly open information order:

> But there are also indications that profitable media ventures are averse to rocking the boat, and if they do critical exposés, it is usually of a rival business house.

The difficulty with this model-based approach is the need to enumerate exceptions. The information cartels created and controlled by Japanese media organizations are one example, transforming a 'free-for-all press' system into a kind of 'self-licensing' model. Another example is the self-censorship that most Hong Kong journalists believe pervades their profession. Regulation and control is not monopolized by the state, but takes on a variety of different modes in different settings. While models of control may provide a useful reference point, an emphasis on forms of agency is more likely to provide a clear explanation of diverse media phenomena across Pacific Asia.

Problematizing media

The first stage in unpacking simplistic assumptions about the media involves distinguishing between the various components of the term. There are four main categories: print media, broadcasting media, international media, and new media (mainly the Internet: see Atkins 2002). Naturally, some of these categories overlap: certain broadcasters cross national boundaries, while some websites are based mainly on the content of print publications. Each category needs to be unpacked in turn: in Japan, for example, there is a world of difference between a story that appears in a scurrilous weekly magazine and the same story in the top-selling *Yomiuri Shimbun*. Print media and electronic media each contain a variety of sub-sectors. Similarly, it is tempting to see the international media as 'Western', but many leading regional publications are produced in Hong Kong by editorial teams that include numerous Asians, while 'indigenous' Southeast Asian newspapers such as *The Nation* or *Straits Times* have gained a regional presence, especially through their online versions.

Within these sectors, some are more salient than others in political terms. Despite the greater reach of electronic media – and Japanese television news forms the main focus of Chapter 3 – much of the discussion in this book centres on print media: weekly magazines in Indonesia, and daily newspapers in Thailand and Hong Kong, for example. Print media remain the media of first choice for many political elites in Asia. Broadcast news is more immediate, yet print coverage is almost invariably much deeper and offers more scope for opinion and analysis. In times of crisis, broadcast media across the region have proved easier to muzzle; opposition voices and dissenting views have thrived in the print media, as well as most recently on the Internet. The media are large, but by no means monolithic. The main focus of this book is not on 'the media' in general, but on those parts of the media that are able to exercise the most salient forms of political agency at important junctures.

Problematizing Pacific Asia

By 'Pacific Asia' this book refers to the eleven countries of Southeast Asia (the ASEAN ten plus East Timor), as well as those parts of East Asia which adjoin the Pacific: China (including Hong Kong) Japan, the Koreas and Taiwan. The seventeen different geographical and political entities covered, embrace a wide variety of political systems and media regimes. A comprehensive study of the political role of the media in all seventeen territories would require a large volume or volumes, ideally compiled by a team of authors (see, for example, Williams and Rich 2000; Gunaratne 2000). The scope of the present volume is more limited. Since the main focus of the book is on the changing political roles of media, it emphasizes a number of territories where significant and discernible changes have occurred during and since the 1990s: Thailand, Indonesia, Hong Kong, and Japan. These four core cases range from a very small territory to one of the world's largest states, from an established democracy to a very new one, and from two countries involved in democratic transitions to another territory which may be experiencing a transition to authoritarianism. Other countries are addressed mainly in a comparative context.

Problematizing ownership

Who owns media? On the face of it, the answer seems simple. Media outlets may have traditional proprietors, such as the sole owners of newspapers; they may be public companies floated on the stock market; or they may be listed companies in which particular individuals or families hold a large or a majority share. In fact, however, these conventional cases do not do justice to the nature of media ownership.

In some Southeast Asian countries, power-holders may themselves have shares in media companies. Former Indonesian Information Minister Harmoko was at one point believed to have stakes in thirty-one media outlets. He did not buy these stakes; they were presented to him as a goodwill gesture, by owners who were anxious to ensure that their publications were not closed down by the government. In similar fashion, members of Class 5, the military faction behind the 1991 Thai coup, were widely believed to have been given shares in the leading political daily *Matichon*. Holdings of this kind are not transparent, and might not be evident from official company records; they could be assigned on the basis of informal understandings, and held in the names of formal owners or even third parties. In other words, there are two kinds of media shareholders: open shareholders and shadow shareholders. In some cases, the shadow shareholders may control most or all of the assets of a media organization.

Yet even the recognition that formal share listings might not reveal the real owners is only the beginning of an understanding of the ownership of many print media outlets in Asia. Where particular editors or columnists have become established figures within a newspaper, for example, they may have gained informal control over a certain page or a certain number of column inches in that newspaper. These column inches become a form of property held by given individuals, over which the formal owners of the newspaper have relinquished day-to-day control. As with other assets such as land-holdings or the right to receive commissions, jurisdiction over small territories within newspapers must be seen as a surrogate form of ownership. Editors and columnists may have considerable latitude to indulge in what some political economists call 'rent-seeking'; they have acquired unwritten lease to these territories and are entitled to sub-let them to the highest bidder. Some may choose to offer their services to politicians or other power-holders, effectively renting them space in a newspaper to push their ideas or opinions. Thus it is possible to find a newspaper column that is subject to four levels of ownership: the official ownership of the formal proprietor or shareholders; the unofficial ownership of shadow shareholders who provide the newspaper with cash or protection; the *de facto* ownership of the columnist who has become an 'institution' within the newspaper; and the paying tenancy of a politician who is funding the columnist to promote his own advancement. Even this could be an over-simplified model: the columnist may be working for more than one politician at the same time; the political editor may have brokered a deal between columnist and politician, and so be receiving his own 'rent' on the transaction; the formal owner may have a parallel relationship with one or more of the politicians; and so on. It might seem that media proprietors ought to be unhappy with the *de facto* leasing out of spaces within publications they formally own. Yet in the context of a highly factionalized political order characterized by multiple power-holders, this diffuse form of media ownership may serve useful purposes. In many countries, newspaper reporters receive cash and benefits from their sources: in a 1989 survey, 93 per cent of Korean journalists admitted receiving money from news sources (Kyu Ho Houm 1998: 187).

In Thailand, for example, such practices accord well with a prevailing culture based on ideas of benefit-sharing. They also conform effectively with prevailing political realities. Given that Thai governments since the mid-1970s have been complex and short-lived coalitions of political parties and factions – themselves tied to a range of bureaucratic and business interests – it becomes essential for newspapers to establish close connections with a broad range of actors. A fixed alliance with a single ruling party is not an appropriate model. By 'decentralizing' ownership through the informal subcontracting of space to a range of columnists linked to different political interests, a newspaper may adopt a chameleon-like identity. Whichever faction, party or interest group rises to the ascendant, the newspaper already has an inside connection to the new order. The top-selling newspaper *Thai Rath* – sometimes referred to as the country's 'second government' – demonstrated a mastery of these manoeuvres during the troubled 1990s, which saw eight governments come and go (McCargo 2000b: 44). Former *Tempo* editor Goenawan Mohamed described his magazine as 'polyvalent': speaking with multiple voices. While this fork-tongued discourse might seem evidence of trickery or unreliability, Goenawan sought to package polyvalence as a virtue, a linguistic facility required of those media practitioners who seek to thrive in an uncertain political order.

Problematizing partisanship

> Outside observers who look for examples of direct government censorship, monopolization of the distribution of newsprint and limitless government power to suppress or publicize news and commentary fail to grasp the nature of the relationship between the government and the media – a complex network of mutual benefits, commitments and favours, difficult to penetrate and even more difficult to reform.
>
> (Palacio 1997: 22)

Which Asian country is being described by Palacio? In general terms, what he writes applies to the majority of media-politics relationships in Pacific Asia – yet he is talking about Mexico. Outside a few over-studied Western states, common assumptions about censorship and partisanship that pervade most of the academic writing about politics and media hold little validity.

The term 'power-holders' is used deliberately in this book. Much of the literature on media in developing countries emphasizes the dominance or 'hegemony' of state power, the way in which media has been used as a tool of state propaganda. In the case of Thailand, for example, the focus is often upon the use of electronic media by the military and other state actors. Media are seen as pawns of state power, servants of the state. Similar arguments are made by Wolferen in his revisionist critique of the Japanese order (Wolferen 1989: 93–8). This emphasis upon censorship and government control, while appropriate to an understanding of how elements of the media do function at particular junctures, also tends to be unduly state-centric: it overlooks the plural and diverse character of media, and especially the inventiveness with which the print media has often covered political issues.

As the power of states declines across the world, preoccupations with state censorship are becoming increasingly dated. Attempts to influence the tone and content of news publications are not confined to states: opposition politicians, military officers, civil servants, lobbyists, companies, pressure groups, think tanks, and non-governmental organizations are all engaged in such activities. Given the frequent changes of government common in Thailand, the rapid turnover of Indonesian presidents after 1998, the constant rise and fall of different LDP factions and front-men in Japan, and the one-term limit for Philippine presidents, many media organizations in Pacific Asia have not enjoyed the luxury of enduring relationships with individual prime ministers or national leaders. In the absence of a stable party system organized along ideological lines, the idea of a newspaper that consistently supports a particular political party is not a valid one across the region.

Western media analysts generally tended view 'partisanship' as meaning formal and informal links between political parties and media (see, for example, Blumler and Gurevitch 1995: 64–5). In Pacific Asia, such a definition is often wholly inadequate; partisanship entails a whole raft of connections between practitioners in the parallel worlds of media and politics. In part this reflects the differing nature of political parties in many Asian countries, where factionalism and sectional interests loom much larger than party coherence. Yet it also reflects the extent to which parties themselves are not always key actors, or the extent to which politicians are obliged to share power with bureaucratic or business interests.

Lee and Chu argue that media power is a function of media ownership and the extent to which other power-holders are unified:

The press may attain power in three ways. One is to be owned by a powerful group which can counteract other power holders. Second is to be guaranteed a permanent share of power in a divided power structure, so that it can counteract other power holders by itself. The third way is to situate itself within a divided power structure and play up one interest group against another, or to exploit the power holders' differences

(Lee and Chu 1998: 74)

Across Pacific Asia in recent decades, examples of all three forms of media power may be identified. But in most cases, the best hope for media is the third alternative: media as broker between competing power-holders. The more major power-holders operate in a given political context, the more scope media have to exert influence and shape events. Broadly speaking, the smaller the size of the elite – and the fewer the number of parties and other political actors – the less likely media are to exercise effective forms of agency and intervention. As a rule, media thrive best in pluralistic settings.

Japan specialist Susan Pharr has suggested four competing concepts of the media: spectator, watchdog, servant, or trickster. She prefers the last of these (Pharr 1996: 24–36). The behaviour of media is indeed often inconsistent, hypocritical, and ambiguous – in other words, tricky. Though sometimes benevolent, this trickery may be dangerous and even destructive, especially where the trickster media – as is often the case in Pacific Asia – serve particularistic interests:

> Its trickiness derives not from its lack of loyalties, but from its multiple loyalties, the plurality of its obligations and the diversity of its stakeholders. It is precisely the multiplicity of stakeholders in the media that gives it both strength and weakness.
>
> (McCargo 2000b: 21)

Problematizing profitability

A tendency in much of the literature about media is to see media organizations as businesses driven by commercial interests. Thus editors and journalists are often faced with difficult choices between writing stories in the public interest and creating a 'product' that will attract investors and advertisers. While such choices may sometimes be very real, there is a serious danger of over-stating the degree to which media organizations in Pacific Asia really are genuine businesses as conventionally understood. It is quite clear that numerous newspapers and magazines in Thailand, the Philippines, Indonesia, and Hong Kong have existed for years or even decades with little possibility of ever making a profit. Why, for example, did Indonesian tycoon Abdul Latief launch the weekly newsmagazine *TIRAS*? In the context of his wider business interests, the venture was a trivial distraction from core activities. Yet the magazine gave him an outlet, directly or indirectly, to express his views during the crucial years of the late 1990s, which saw the unravelling of the Suharto regime.

The fact is that people want to own media outlets for many reasons that have little to do with straight profits. It is well known that a number of Thai financial publications made money during the boom years of the late 1980s and early 1990s by 'talking up' the value of stocks held by their owners or their business associates. Some engaged in the questionable practice of 'chain listing' (Handley 1997). Several of these publications folded immediately following the financial crisis of 1997; in the absence of a rising stock market, their *raison d'être* simply vanished overnight. Other publications received subsidies from owners seeking to advance their views or agendas, or from politicians who enjoyed the pleasure of owning or funding a vanity press. In other cases, publications might be clandestinely supported by the military (which in Thailand long controlled a large secret budget, for which it was not accountable to parliament), or by domestic or foreign security services. For a tycoon seeking to do business in China, owning a newspaper in Hong Kong might provide useful leverage for much larger contracts or projects; the expenses of the newspaper itself were simply a loss-leader.

Nor should it be assumed that the transformation of media organizations into successful and profitable companies necessarily entails the strengthening of their hands as more robust and stable institutions of civil society. Unlike publications run on a shoestring by a handful of dedicated journalists – such as the anti-Marcos 'mosquito press' of the early 1980s, which could bite the Philippine president with relative impunity – major companies with substantial assets, quoted on the stock market, were highly vulnerable to political pressures; potentially they had a great deal to lose from an antagonistic government. In some ways, small news outlets – even, sometimes, unprofitable ones bankrolled by individuals – could serve as more effective guardians of the public interest than larger organizations dependent upon a plurality of stakeholders.

In other words, the rise of the media as a business brought new threats as well as new opportunities. As Sheila Coronel puts it:

> In Southeast Asia's democracies, the problem is not so much the tyranny of the State but the more amorphous tyranny of the market, that brings with it such problems as irresponsible reporting, ethical lapses and the trivialization of the news.
>
> (Coronel 1999: 3)

Heryanto and Adi argue that by the mid-1990s, many Indonesian media practitioners had moved beyond the old rhetoric of passionate struggle, and chose their profession for economic reasons (Heryanto and Adi 2001). They argue that the emergence of a generation of journalists likely to give first priority to their own personal and financial security 'will have far-reaching implications for the dynamics of Indonesia's democratization'. McCargo has made the same argument about journalists at the Thai newspaper *Matichon*, many of whom quickly became relatively affluent after being given stock options in the late 1980s (McCargo 2000b: 82–5). In the case of China, Ma similarly argues that marketization does not lead inexorably towards democratization:

> in sharp contract to a romanticized view of a democratic market-place of ideas and values . . . . Mostly, the media are opening up spaces for a work-and-spend culture.
>
> (Ma 2000: 26–7)

For Ma, 'the media are empowering consumers, not citizens' (Ma 2000: 31), and it remains unclear whether this might eventually translate into demands for a more participatory polity. John Lent criticizes Asian media for undermining democratic trends by using 'mass communication formulas that trivialize or commercialize important issues, corrupt the electoral process, and generally dehumanize society as a whole' (Lent 1998: 168).

Problematizing the public interest

Given the difficulties involved in establishing the nature of formal and informal ownership and control of the media in much of Pacific Asia, and given the associated problems of mapping lines of partisan support for different power-holders within the press and among broadcasters, it is hard to make clear arguments about the extent to which the media may be regarded as guardians of the public interest. First and foremost, the media are the guardians of an aggregation of private interests, comprising those who hold stakes of various kinds in their operations. As Rupert Murdoch once rhetorically asked, 'What right have we speak in the public interest when too often we are motivated by personal gain?' (Schultz 1998: 235). Thus it is difficult to suggest that the media can be relied upon to serve as a 'watchdog' of the public interest, since the term immediately begs the obvious and troublesome question 'Who owns the dog?' (see McCargo 2000b: 18–21). At the same time, the rhetoric – if not always the practice – of watchdog journalism was adopted uncritically by journalists in many parts of the region, such as Taiwan (Lee 2000: 131). Nor would it be accurate to describe the media as a 'mirror' of society, passively reflecting the wider public sphere; in most Pacific Asian countries, the media function inevitably as a fairground distorting mirror, reflecting some parts of the social, political and economic reality more largely than others. The idea of the media as 'agenda-setter' may be more helpful, but the term implies a degree of neutrality and disinterest that is rather at odds with the actual role performed by the media in many societies. If 'agenda-setting' is done at least partly on behalf of partisan interests that own or influence the media, then it should not be regarded as an entirely benevolent and public-spirited activity. There is no inherent reason why agenda-setting should serve progressive, liberal or democratic ends; as Bogart argues:

> The existence of an advanced and diverse media system does not guarantee that it will serve democracy. Monolithic control over mass communications is no longer possible, but control need not

be total to be effective. Mass media can serve democracy only when those who manage them feel a passionate responsibility to create it and maintain it.

(Bogart 1998: 11)

Finally, there is the useful concept of the 'fourth estate', explored at length by Schultz. She argues that a modern version of the nineteenth-century ideal of the fourth estate does persist in Western countries such as Australia, in spite of commercial pressures. Schultz advocates an alliance between journalists and their audiences to create more space for investigative journalism:

> If journalists were able to build more meaningful, reflective alliances with their audiences they could be a more significant democratic force . . . . The ideal of the fourth estate remains ambiguous and subject to contest. It is also resilient and the key to defining the news media's democratic role, if it is to have one.
>
> (Schultz 1998: 238)

Schultz's call for an institutionalized democratic role of the media implies recognizing and legitimating the media's progressive and transformative modes of agency; it is the statement of an ideal, but by no means describes the current position of the media in Pacific Asia.

In other words, the political roles currently performed by elements of the media may or may not serve the public interest – and it would be deeply naïve to impute entirely altruistic motives to those who constitute important players in the political and economic life of a country. It is for this reason that this book approaches the role of the media in terms of a critical analysis of agency: what form of political agency is a given component of a given media outlet exercizing at a particular juncture? Only by building up an agency-based understanding of the multiple roles of media – conservative, progressive or transformative – can a more sophisticated analysis be developed.

Problematizing media freedom

The concept of media freedom is a central one in understanding the political role of the media in Pacific Asia. In many countries in the region, freedom of the media to cover events critically and in depth remains curtailed by legal limits, cultural norms and informal controls. Nevertheless, the study of and the struggle for media freedom is largely concerned with the limited terrain of state–media relations. All too often, media freedom is presented as a zero-sum game: the more the state rolls back its framework of rules and regulation, the more effectively media will be able to operate. Yet the examples in this book will illustrate that many media organizations do not take advantage of the full range of freedoms to which they have access. Arguments that press freedom is a Western concept opposed by 'Asian values' do not merit serious discussion here (for one such discussion, see Knight 2000); as Amando Doronila persuasively asserts: 'Press freedom is a language journalists know by instinct. It is not a Western construct' (Doronila 2000: xiv).

Drawing on a detailed study of the Vietnamese case, Heng makes a plea for a more nuanced framework of analysis than a simplistic 'press freedom' paradigm will allow. Citing three specific cases, he argues that in practice:

> The agents of the state and the media practitioners were locked in a negotiation process as two contending equals, each deploying its own professional resources to persuade the larger community of state and media organs of its version of the dispute.
>
> (Heng 2001: 227–8)

Beyond the specific context of Vietnam, there is considerable utility in Heng's depiction of state–media relations as characterized by a constant process of negotiation, in situations where ground rules are often unclear. Much the same applies to relations between the media and a variety of power-holders across Pacific Asia. Most Asian states are, like Vietnam's, 'a multi-segmented reality' (Heng 2001: 230).

Importantly, though, many of the unsatisfactory forms of agency practised by the media in Pacific Asia do not arise from limits or repression imposed from above. Rather, they reflect the deficiencies of the media themselves: their partisanship, their lack of professionalism, their willing collusion with the state or other power-holders, or their pursuit of sensationalism. Corruption among reporters and columnists is endemic in many countries. Media organizations are often reluctant to challenge the hierarchies that pervade the societies in which they operate. The Japanese media, for example, are themselves responsible for operating press clubs which function as formalized news cartels and limit public access to important information. Important though the discourse of media freedom may be, it also has the dangerous effect of diverting attention from many of the real shortcomings of media agency, which rest firmly within the control of owners and practitioners.

At the same time, it is not safe to assume that better training would cure many of these problems. The Thai newspaper group *Phujatkan* operated a wonderful training programme in the mid-1990s, teaching its reporters how to make use of investigative journalism techniques (McCargo 2000b: 55). Unfortunately, many of those reporters found that when they returned to their desks, they were given little scope to implement what they had learned. In the Asian context, media practitioners tend to blame the most junior staff – front-line reporters – for the deficiencies of their operations. Yet these reporters are usually directly following instructions from senior colleagues and editors, who have created the news-gathering structures within which they work. Some of those who advocate improved training for reporters are inherently partisan: they are themselves associated with training programmes that may attract substantial domestic or international funding. What media organizations in many countries actually need first is structural reform: abandoning information cartels, empowering reporters to pursue their own stories, getting the most experienced journalists out of the office, moving away from slavish repetition of the utterances of elite players, and paying far more attention to the interplay of political and economic interests, especially beyond their capital cities. In countries as diverse as Japan, Indonesia and Thailand, the media have been at the forefront of calls for political and administrative reform – yet have singularly failed to reform themselves.

Structure of the book

The arguments of this book are explored in five core chapters. Chapter 2 examines the role of Southeast Asian media in political transitions: successful transitions towards greater democracy in the Philippines (1986), Thailand (1992) and Indonesia (1998); and 'failed transitions' in Burma (1988) and Malaysia (1998). The chapter problematizes the idea of media as a benevolent agent of progressive change. Chapter 3 looks at the changing political role of the Japanese media, with special reference to new forms of television news coverage. While innovative programming led by private broadcasters has made political news more entertaining and accessible, critics charge that in recent years politics has become mere 'infotainment', as the media dwell on matters of image rather than policies and substance. Chapter 4 examines the 1994 bannings of three weeklies in Indonesia, bannings that revealed the extent to which President Suharto had grown unwilling to listen to constructive criticism. The bannings forced many Indonesian journalists to make difficult choices and significantly eroded the legitimacy of the New Order. Chapter 5 looks at the role of the media in Hong Kong following the hand-over to China in 1997. How far could a relatively open media order thrive under the ultimate oversight of Beijing? Chapter 6 scrutinizes the interactions between the international press and the Thai domestic media. When successive prime ministers fell out with foreign journalists, who was making use of whom? Finally, Chapter 7 offers a brief review of some of the book's key findings.

2 Media in times of crisis: media and democratic transitions in Southeast Asia

Political transitions in Southeast Asia

Since 1986, three unpopular Southeast Asian governments have been toppled by mass protest movements: those of the Philippines in 1986 (the 'People Power' movement, which ousted President Ferdinand Marcos), Thailand in 1992 (the 'May events', which forced out the government of General Suchinda Kraprayoon), and Indonesia in 1998 (the student-led protests and unrest that saw the downfall of President Suharto). A comparable but unsuccessful movement failed to oust the military regime in Burma in 1988, while a vigorous *reformasi* movement also failed to displace Dr Mahathir's administration in Malaysia in late 1998.[1] Though influenced by international developments, all of these movements were primarily shaped by specific domestic circumstances, particularly the strength of civil society forces and non-state actors. The media played an important role in every case.

A core assumption of much of the literature on democratization is that a more independent media with greater freedom would make a positive contribution to political change, supporting democratic transitions and the downfall of authoritarian regimes. In other words, the media can play an especially crucial role at the 'transition phase', where they may act as a decisive agent of change (Randall 1993). Neumann (1998a) argues that freedom is 'taking hold' in Southeast Asia, in a process of political liberalization inexplicably linked with the rise of a more open and critical press. Three relevant cases will be examined here: the Philippines, Thailand, and Indonesia.

The Philippines: radio station ousts Marcos?

Mass demonstrations in Manila in February 1986 culminated in the ousting of President Marcos from office. Marcos had ruled the Philippines for twenty years, initially as an elected president but later through martial law. Popular dissatisfaction with his rule increased after 1983, when opposition leader Ninoy Aquino was shot dead at Manila Airport under highly suspicious circumstances. Faced with growing international isolation and a disastrous economic position, Marcos called a 'snap election' in 1986, which he hoped would restore legitimacy to his rule. In the event, opposition forces rallied around Ninoy's widow Cory Aquino, who won a convincing electoral victory. Aquino assumed the presidency after Marcos fled to exile in Hawaii.

Accounts of the 1986 'people power' movement (sometimes known as the 'yellow revolution') often emphasize the contribution of the media, especially that of Radio Veritas, a radio station controlled by the Catholic Church. Hernandez describes the media as performing 'a role that in the final hours was crucial' (Hernandez 1986: 191). When General Fidel Ramos and Defence Minister Juan Ponce Enrile defected from Marcos on 22 February, they broadcast an appeal on Radio Veritas for people to rally around two army camps and protect them. This appeal triggered the EDSA demonstrations, and so indirectly led to the ouster of Marcos on 25 February. Nemenzo observes that: 'Without Radio Veritas, it would have been difficult, if not impossible, to mobilize millions of people in a matter of hours' (Nemenzo 1986: 46). According to one popular account of the events, 'Radio Veritas, in fact, was our umbilical cord to whatever else was going on' (Baron and Suazo 1986). On 24 February, however, the transmitters of Radio Veritas were destroyed by troops loyal to Marcos, an action that testified to the political significance of the station. Broadcasting continued from a series of safe houses.

Evaluating the political influence of the Philippine media as a whole, however, is a more difficult matter. Most Philippine newspapers are not published for profit and require subsidies from their owners. Despite the facade of a vigorous and critical press in the Philippines, much of the media-inspired political debate reflects the voices of powerful owners and interest groups closely tied to identifiable political and business interests. During the Marcos period, some of the subsidies were provided by cronies of the President, while publications hostile to Marcos faced harassment or closure. Writing before the events of February 1986, Doronila argued that the assassination of Ninoy Aquino in 1983 rekindled a critical press in the Philippines: small, independent newspapers mushroomed and the opposition initiated a somewhat successful boycott of controlled newspapers, so undermining the credibility of publications owned by Marcos cronies and supporters (Doronila 1985: 184). Nevertheless, he cautioned that this trend was a 'temporary tendency', and argued that even under a more liberal post-Marcos government, the dominance of big media companies would pose a threat to the free flow of information (Doronila 1985: 205–6). A decade later, Rivera noted that most Manila newspapers were still heavily subsidized by their owners, though he went on to claim that despite these subsidies, journalists exercised considerable autonomy (Rivera 1996: 7). While there are close to 30 national newspapers in circulation, circulation figures are impossible to obtain (Coronel 2000: 156); it seems safe to assume that many newspapers are not profitable in conventional business terms.

Accordingly, Smith claims that the role of the media in the events of February 1986 has been overblown. Quoting approvingly from a speech by Cory Aquino herself ('The media do not make or unmake governments, tanks do that, and more rarely but surely, people do'), Smith declares that:

> Some individual – usually minority – media outlets may reflect, 'mediate', and even facilitate change; they do not initiate it, either individually or collectively, whatever their own euphoric accounts at the time may tell us to the contrary. They also, rather, tend to reflect the class interests of their owners, advertisers and readers.
>
> (Smith 1996: 152)

While Coronel suggests it may be argued that the media 'tipped the scale' during the 'people power' events (Coronel 2000: 147–8), the ousting of Marcos was a more complex event than media-focused accounts suggest. The great bulk of the electronic and print media was supportive of Marcos almost throughout, whilst Radio Veritas was not a conventional media outlet but a voice of the highly partisan Catholic Church. As Smith writes:

> The perception of the media, alternative or otherwise, as 'heroes of EDSA', is likewise a distortion: 'people power' and the potential fire-power of military revolt were the factors which actively ousted Marcos. Radio Veritas did, it is true, prove a useful weapon in the logistical deployment of the Manila crowds who rallied around the rebel troops; the Manila press was at this point, however, simply reporting retrospectively a 'spontaneous' show of (largely urban middle-class) strength against a hated regime.
>
> (Smith 1996: 270)

Smith concludes that sections of the media could *help* challenge a regime if they received middle-class support, but that the media lack the capacity to initiate or lead the challenge to a regime. A recent study of corruption in the Philippine media emphasizes the hypocrisy of its high-minded stance:

> While fearless reporting helped inspire a revolution, segments of the press had also conspired to perpetuate a dictatorship. The media have relentlessly pursued investigations of wrong-doing, yet they have also shirked from confronting misbehaviour within their own ranks.
>
> (Florentino-Hofilena 1998: 3)

The study goes on to demonstrate that pervasive corruption in the Philippine media make them highly partisan and untrustworthy, long after the ouster of the Marcos dictatorship. Coronel notes that while crude use of state power to ban or muzzle the press is no longer possible, other issues such as bribery of journalists, tactical deployment of advertising and the diverse business interests of media owners provide alternative challenges to media freedom. President Estrada called publicly for an advertising boycott of the *Philippine Daily Inquirer* because of its critical coverage of his administration (Coronel 2000: 149; 163–6). Coronel describes such techniques as reflecting the 'privatization of media repression' by the state.

The Philippine case points to the dangers of generalizing about 'the media', especially based on minority news sources. Rather than assuming that the entire media adopted a pro-democratic or 'progressive' stance at a particular juncture, it is important to unpack the various components of the media and deal with them individually. Nor should it be assumed that progressive credentials 'earned' during a critical moment of transition will be translated into a sustained positive role in the subsequent period of consolidation. By the same token, media freedoms are inherently provisional and insecure, subject to new threats with each incoming administration or each emerging power-broker.

Thailand: vigorous print media bring down Suchinda?

Since 1932 the military has played a crucial role in the Thai political order, although the 1980s saw an apparent institutionalization of parliamentary politics. Contrary to most expectations, the Thai military staged a coup in February 1991, the first for almost fourteen years. There followed a period of intense confrontation between military and civilian political forces. In April and May 1992, mass protests took place on the streets of Bangkok against the unelected prime minister General Suchinda Kraprayoon (McCargo 1997a: 239-74).[2] Some analysts have seen the protests (which the military sought to repress by violent means) as a key moment in the development of a democratic order in Thailand. Many newspaper proprietors and journalists aligned themselves with the opposition movement, playing an important part in forcing Suchinda's resignation.[3] These same newspapers were also influential in creating the climate that led to the victory of 'anti-military' parties in the September 1992 general election.

The stance taken by the print media throughout the 1992 crisis was in contrast with the pro-government line taken by the state-controlled electronic media. There is a long-standing tradition of a critical and outspoken press in Thailand. In the early decades of the twentieth century, newspaper columns were used to articulate conflicts within the elite: columnists frequently hid behind pen-names, and included high-ranking officials and even the king himself. The press was a kind of parallel political universe, which permitted more open debate and contestation in an era of absolute monarchy. Influential individuals and groups (including the state) sought to present their views through owning or supporting newspapers (McCargo 2000b: 12–21). The absolute monarchy ended in 1932, but newspapers continued to be owned and controlled by those seeking to advance their power and influence. Historically, only a handful of daily newspapers in Thailand have ever been commercially viable. By the 1970s, when the country was riven with ideological conflicts between left and right, wider political debates were clearly reflected in the press: ownership and control broadened to include elements of the left. Repressive legislation made it possible for governments to close newspapers with relative impunity, and 1976 saw a major clampdown on press freedom as a short-lived 'democracy period' gave way to authoritarianism. But the vibrancy of the Thai press proved difficult to repress; by the 1980s it was once again the most open and critical in the region.

On 17 May, around two hundred thousand demonstrators gathered at the Sanam Luang, in the heart of historic Bangkok, to proclaim their opposition to the continuing premiership of General Suchinda Kraprayoon. The protests, which rapidly turned ugly following armed attacks on the crowd by government troops, were to last four days. As Army Commander-in-Chief, General Suchinda had led the February 1991 military coup, ousting the elected civilian government of General Chatchai Choonavan. From the outset, Suchinda and his fellow members of the 'National Peace-Keeping Council' junta claimed to have staged the coup solely in the public interest. Suchinda later gave an explicit televised promise that he would not accept the post of Prime Minister following the elections called for 22 March 1992. When he reneged on this pledge (*The Nation*, 9 April 1992), he precipitated a wave of popular opposition, opposition which was galvanized by the controversial decision of Phalang Dharma Party leader Chamlong Srimuang to stage an anti-Suchinda hunger strike during the first week of May (see McCargo 1997a: 239–74).

The Bangkok protestors were opposing more than the Suchinda government: they were challenging the hugely powerful role of the military and the bureaucracy in Thai politics. In the struggle between entrenched state power and the collective popular will, control of information was a crucial weapon. While the Thai press had historically enjoyed a relatively free rein, television and radio were subject to stringent state controls. Media coverage of the May events, in which scores of civilians were shot dead by the military, became an issue almost as large as the events themselves, as public anger at the manifest factual distortions of the electronic media reached fever pitch. Following Suchinda's resignation on 24 May, and the subsequent formation of a second interim civilian administration under respected former diplomat and businessman Anand Panyarachun (who had also served as prime minister during the NPKC period), an intense public debate began concerning the future of the media.

In 1992 there were more than a dozen Thai-language dailies, ranging from the mass-circulation *Thai Rath* and *Daily News*, to the established 'quality' papers *Siam Rath* and *Matichon*. In addition, there were six Chinese-language and two English-language dailies, not to mention ten or so weekly Thai-language magazines, which functioned as clearing-houses for political gossip. The Thai press had a long tradition of political outspokenness, partisanship and rabble-rousing. Many owners, editors and columnists had close personal ties to politicians, military officers and other influential figures. The press corps which confronted General Suchinda Kraprayoon when he 'reluctantly' accepted the premiership in the wake of the March 1992 election were a confident and assertive bunch, united by an active professional body in the form of the Reporters' Association of Thailand. Television was a different matter: all five television channels were controlled, directly or indirectly, by state agencies. As one anonymous Channel 3 reporter explained to a newspaper journalist during the May demonstrations: 'People normally have little trust in television news anyway. Even we think it is superficial.' Radio frequencies were owned by the military.

The first intimations that the Suchinda administration would prove to be a dark age for press freedom in Thailand came two days before Suchinda took office. On 5 April, a Thai employee of the press agnecy Visnews was accosted in front of a military building, and grilled for information in a dark corner (*Bangkok Post*, 11 April 1992). His four interrogators demanded the home address of Suthin Wannabovorn, a Reuters reporter who was known to have asked pointed questions of various leading pro-military politicians concerning the possibility that they might name an 'outsider' (that is, Suchinda) to the premiership. The men gave the distinct impression that they intended to harm Suthin. Subsequently, Banyat Tasaniyavej led an RAT delegation, calling upon the new prime minister to ensure that reporters were not intimidated, since this would have an adverse effect, not only upon personal liberty, but upon the country as a whole.

For Banyat, a *Bangkok Post* journalist and second-term President of the Reporters' Association of Thailand (RAT), the violence of 'Black May' marked a turning-point in public awareness regarding the relationship between politics and the media. She believed that the print media were widely seen to be taking the side of the people, and joining in their struggle for political freedom (McCargo 1993: 7). The Reporters' Association of Thailand, with over 700 members the largest of the country's three press associations, was at the forefront of this clash between free expression and crude state censorship. In all, 33 journalists received injuries during the clashes; many others were harassed, most commonly receiving threatening telephone calls. The Association subsequently put out an illustrated book about the May events in magazine format, a compilation of eyewitness accounts by its members (*Banthuk Yiaokhao* 1992).

The RAT warning, however, went unheeded; Suchinda persisted in adopting a heavy-handed approach to his dealings with the press, declining to answer their questions at public gatherings. On 16 April he hosted a dinner for government MPs at Bangkok's Central Plaza Hotel. Instead of the customary half-a-dozen bodyguards, he was surrounded by around twenty henchmen as he made his way into the dining room. His aides swore at waiting reporters, telling them to get out the way. One woman reporter had her arm cut by a sharp object, while another was elbowed in the stomach. All 68 reporters present signed a letter of protest, which was taken in to the Premier by a press representative, who told an astonished Suchinda: 'This is a civilian government, not a military regime' (*Bangkok Post*, 17 April 1992). The Prime Minister and his close political associates were jeered at by reporters when they left the function. Suchinda had made a serious miscalculation, turning much of the Thai press corps against him at a stroke. Again, the Reporters' Association stepped into the breach, sending a formal letter of complaint to the Prime Minister's office (*Bangkok Post*, 18 April 1992).

Although Suchinda pledged in his first parliamentary statement on government policy that he would promote press freedom, he told reporters on a visit to the provinces on 2 May that he wanted to see Thai newspapers practise self-censorship 'to ensure law and order and help the country's economy'. Suchinda claimed that 'most Thai people and the Press do not want disorder. I would like to ask the Press to help'. Far from helping, many Thai reporters did their utmost to undermine the Suchinda government, writing detailed blow-by-blow accounts of every development in the protest movement.

Before the large-scale protests against Suchinda's premiership began in early May 1992, censorship of television news had already intensified. Whereas prior to the March elections Channel 5 news had typically prepared around sixteen items for its main evening news broadcast, by May this had increased to twenty or more. The additional material, all of it supportive or uncritical of the Suchinda administration, was supplied by military journalists. The regular civilian reporters continued to produce clips on stories critical of the new Premier – but knew perfectly well that the programme's editors would use 'extra', Army-supplied footage in place of their own reports. On 21 April, an enterprising Channel 5 journalist managed to slip his piece on an anti-Suchinda demonstration into a pile of tapes for early morning transmission. His editor was subsequently summoned before the Army officer in charge of the station and given a coded reprimand. As of 23 April, all tapes for broadcasting required the signature of the station chief. Channel 5's example was closely followed by Channel 7. The remaining channels were believed to have received strongly-worded memos from the Public Relations Department, urging them not to rock the boat.

Radio was under similar official control. Although there were 496 radio stations in Thailand, none was privately-owned and many were run directly by the military. On 17 April, Suthichai Yoon – the outspoken publisher of the English-language newspaper *The Nation* – was abruptly cut off while discussing anti-Suchinda protests during his daily Radio Thailand programme *Direct Line from the Newsroom*. Suthichai had previously declined requests to submit the programme to censorship an hour before transmission, and to refrain from criticizing the government. Vandals subsequently entered his garden during the night, damaging Suthichai's car. This was one of many similar episodes of intimidation suffered by journalists who failed to toe the official line.

As the protests against Suchinda intensified, the gap between reporting and reality strained viewers' credulity beyond breaking-point. The pivotal decision of popular politician, party leader and former Bangkok governor Major-General Chamlong Srimuang to stage a hunger strike until Suchinda resigned was the main story in every Thai newspaper on 5 May 1992, but was ignored in television news bulletins (*The Nation*, 6 May 1992). During the next three weeks, television had no real credibility as a news source: people gained their information from the press and improvised communication networks based on mobile phones, computer bulletin boards and fax machines. People also began tuning into news broadcasts from abroad, notably the BBC World Service. On 7 May, in an attempt to curtail this news traffic, the Thai government moved to halt all satellite feeds used by foreign television organizations such as CNN, TV Asahi and Visnews (*Bangkok Post*, 9 May 1992); the following day, Deputy Army Chief Viroj Saengsnit held a meeting with the directors of all Thailand's television stations, at which he asked them to be 'careful' in covering current events.

Also on 8 May, Interior Minister Air Chief Marshal Anan Kalinta met editors and representatives of around twenty newspapers, telling them that the government had displayed tolerance thus far by refraining from taking action against the press, even when 'distorted' information – such as excessive estimates of protestor numbers – had appeared (*The Nation*, 9 May 1992). Although described by press participants as 'friendly', the meeting clearly represented a less than subtle attempt to cajole the newspapers into toning down their critical coverage. Demonstrators interviewed at the protest site were almost unanimous in denouncing the distorted portrayal of events by the broadcast media. Many explained that they had joined the protests as a direct result of their frustration with the television news coverage; far from curtailing dissent, government censorship had increased it. One protestor was quoted as saying:

> I think the news blackout makes more people want to see the demonstration. If they let the TV report the news, people would just sit and watch the event back home. Thai people are usually

lazy. But once they come, they become sort of addicted because of the excitement. And they bring along other people.

(*Bangkok Post*, 12 May 1992)

Beleaguered television crews, frustrated by their inability to report properly on the demonstration, became the objects of public derision. Following attacks on cars belonging to Channels 3 and 5, Channel 7 news teams removed identifying stickers from their vehicles. Ironically, when television news reported on 9 May that Chamlong Srimuang had abruptly halted his hunger strike, many Bangkokians simply refused to believe it, and thousands descended upon the Sanam Luang to check the story for themselves.

That night Jor Sor 100, a popular army-owned radio station well known for its traffic updates, suddenly began broadcasting a phone-in programme about the political crisis. Parts of the programme were hosted by the head of franchise-holder Pacific Intercommunications, Piya Malakul (*The Nation*, 11 May 1992). Listeners were outraged by Piya's obviously biased treatment of callers, as he consistently cut off those opposed to Suchinda's premiership, while encouraging Suchinda supporters to criticise the demonstrators. Worse still, Piya's fellow presenter was the one-time doyen of Thai newscasters, the highly-respected Dr Somkiat Onwimol. It later transpired that Piya and Somkiat had called on Suchinda that evening, to obtain his personal approval for the special phone-in. The highlight of Saturday's broadcast was a live link-up with opposition MP Thinnawat Marukapitak, speaking direct from the protest stage. Somkiat misrepresented Thinnawat's comments by claiming that the demonstrators were already dispersing; in point of fact, the Sanam Luang remained packed with protestors, who were awaiting some hard evidence to support government promises of a compromise with their demands. The episode seriously damaged Somkiat's journalistic reputation, apparently illustrating a distasteful complicity between politicians and newsmen (*The Nation*, 29 May 1992).

On Sunday 10 May, protest leaders resolved to give the government a week's grace to honour its pledges. The protestors were to reassemble on 17 May if the government had failed to act on its promises. A hastily-formed 'Centre to Promote Participation in Democracy' set up a 24-hour telephone hot-line to provide information: one of its main roles was to inform people that the renewed protest would definitely go ahead (*Bangkok Post*, 15 May 1992). Chulalongkorn University radio agreed to provide round-the-clock news coverage of the protest; a five-member working party on press freedom – which comprised RAT President Banyat Tasaniyavej, *Nation* publisher Suthichai Yoon, *Thai Rath* editor Manit Sooksomchit, plus two academics – was established following a panel discussion at Chulalongkorn University, and on 16 May the group petitioned the government to allow equal broadcast air-time for both pro- and anti-Suchinda views (*Bangkok Post*, 16 May 1992).

Unsurprisingly, this request was not met. When soldiers opened fire on unarmed demonstrators on the night of 17 May and stormed the Royal Hotel early the following morning, they unleashed a torrent of violence in which perhaps 85 or more civilians were killed.[4] These fatalities went unreported on the main broadcast media, which depicted the demonstrators as disruptive trouble-makers. Troops, on the other hand, were praised for their 'extreme discipline and restraint'.

Martial law was proclaimed late on Sunday evening, and newspapers were ordered not to publish any material that might inflame the unrest. By that time, however, most Thai-language papers were already going to press. But at the English-language *Bangkok Post*, editor Paisal Sricharatchanya decided to blank out several news stories, as well as his own editorial, to avoid the risk of closure. His staff was divided over the decision, some arguing that the *Post* should 'publish and be damned'. When its more liberal rival *The Nation* appeared the next morning, carrying full coverage of the previous day's events, the *Bangkok Post* was widely thought to have capitulated too readily to government pressure. Significantly, there were no white spaces in the *Post*'s 19 May edition.

By 18 May, Thailand's civil disturbances were the lead story in news broadcasts throughout the world. Expatriate Thais were phoning their friends and relatives at home, telling them of the shootings. The arrest of Chamlong and other pro-democracy leaders that afternoon conspicuously failed to quell the protests. In defiance of earlier orders to deny foreign television companies access to satellite links, staff at Channels 7 and 9 facilitated the transmission abroad of uncensored footage of the violent suppression of the demonstrations. Thais with access to cable and satellite television were able to see some of this coverage – especially that of BBC World Service TV, which the authorities never succeeded in blacking out. Atkins argues that while the precise impact of satellite broadcasting was difficult to isolate, discrepancies between terrestial and international television news probably further eroded Suchinda's legitimacy (Atkins 2002: 66). By the evening of 19 May, Channel 9 had begun screening, for domestic consumption, footage of the Army's attempts to put down the demonstrations. The following day, around 100 soldiers arrived at the television station, setting up 'protective' barricades around it; they did not, however, succeed in altering the new, anti-Suchinda editorial line taken by Channel 9. Clearly, the government was beginning to lose both its grip on events and its power to control even the usually tame electronic media.

On 21 May, the authorities made a desperate attempt to bring Thailand's newspapers to heel. Sawat Amornwiwat, the Director-General of Police, signed orders for the closure of three dailies, each for a period of three days, on the grounds that their reports were 'affecting national security and creating confusion among the public': *The Nation*, *Naeo Na*, and *Phujatkan* ('Manager'). The action, however, came too late. That evening, King Bhumitol appeared on television to deliver an extraordinary public admonishment to Generals Suchinda and Chamlong, telling them to 'desist from confrontation and to embrace conciliation'. From then on, Suchinda's resignation appeared inevitable. The beginning of the end of the crisis had been reached. Sawat revoked the newspaper closure orders within hours of having issued them.

The fall of the Suchinda government cleared the way for a renewed public debate about the future of broadcasting in Thailand. Adding fuel to the fire were the hot-selling pirate videotapes of the May events, which appeared on the streets almost at once. Most of the videos were based upon CNN and BBC footage of the demonstrations, though others were locally produced (Callahan 1998: 18–23). Millions of Thais were soon able to see for themselves the bloody scenes that had never appeared on domestic television news. Even during the crackdown, pro-democracy groups had been screening similar videos at rallies held at provincial universities across Thailand. The crudity of news censorship by the state was now plain for all to see. Disquiet over these developments led eventually to the launch of iTV, a new terrestrial television channel which emphasized 'independent' news coverage.

The picture was brighter so far as the print media was concerned. A number of new titles appeared following the events of May: *Siam Post*, a Thai-language *Nation* weekend news magazine and a weekly version of *Nao Na*, to name but three. The marketing of the media was also becoming increasing sophisticated; for example, forward-thinking media mogul Sondhi Limthongkul cut a deal with IBC cable television to supply his *Phujatkan* daily newspaper to all subscribers, free of charge. The continuing financial and professional vitality of its press appeared to be Thailand's best insurance policy against the return of May-style government attempts to restrict the freedom of information.

Some elements of the Thai print media emerged from the May upheavals with considerable credit, particularly a core group of reporters closely associated with the RAT, and the proprietors and editors of *The Nation*, *Naeo Na*, and *Phujatkan*. Yet while much of the press resisted the Suchinda regime, many owners, editors, columnists, and reporters were close to the NPKC and to the new government (Ubonrat 1994: 105). Intimate ties between politicians and journalists, some of them financial, played their part in ensuring favourable reporting of the Suchinda government almost until its downfall. While *The Nation* received an International Committee to Protect Journalists award for its 'courageous and straightforward' May coverage (*The Nation*, 23 October 1992), other newspapers dealt with the events in ways that were less than prize-worthy. Pajaree Tanasaomboonkit has shown in her impressive Chulalongkorn University master's thesis that the leading daily *Thai Rath* generally backed Suchinda until the opposition momentum was clearly winning the day (Pajaree 1995). In other words, the stance of the press during the May events was largely a function of the personal alliances of key columnists, editors and owners. The press was far from monolithic. While the print media was infinitely more oppositional than the captive electronic media, the quality of critical coverage in the press varied significantly from one publication to another.

The Thai press emerges from the events of May 1992 as an extremely partisan political actor, pursuing agendas of its own based largely on personal ties and connections. When the weight of those connections (coupled with wider political trends) favoured a positive outcome (from the perspective of democratization), the net contribution of the press might support positive developments (such as the ouster of Suchinda in 1992). However, when the weight of those connections and wider political trends supported a negative or retrograde outcome, then the press could actually exert a malign influence.[5] The role of the press in Thailand is highly situational: sometimes progressive, sometimes just the opposite. Even in a society as open as Thailand's, the media can be bought off or toned down by a variety of state or non-state actors. In short, the press is not a trustworthy political actor that can be relied upon to support political liberalization or democratic transition. The May 1992 events trained the Thai press in how to help bring down governments, a trick that the press successfully repeated in 1995, 1996 and then 1997. The more difficult long-term task of supporting democratic consolidation has largely eluded the Thai media. As Randall observes concerning the role of the national media in democratic transitions:

> Generally they have responded eagerly to the new democratic openings and opportunities, but have been better at knocking down the old regime than in positively shaping the new.
> (Randall 1993: 644)

Nowhere is this observation more apposite than in the case of Thailand. Following the end of Democrat rule in 1995, the governments of Banharn Silpa-archa (1995–96) and Chavalit Yongchaiyudh (1996–97) proved themselves willing to silence critical voices in the electronic media. Chavalit even set up a much-ridiculed Media Monitoring Centre to curtail criticism of his administration (Kavi 2000: 227).

When Thailand ran into serious economic trouble in July 1997 – and had to be bailed out by the IMF – the media business suffered a severe recession. About a dozen publications and several radio stations closed down, 3500 staff were laid off, media ownership was narrowed, and the range of views expressed in the media was greatly curtailed. This trend was exacerbated following the rise to the premiership of telecommunications magnate Thaksin Shinawatra in

2001. Thaksin used his vast wealth and considerable power to buy, bully, co-opt, and control the media in a variety of ways. These included purchasing a controlling interest in iTV and allegedly even ordering assets investigations of critical journalists. The record of the Thaksin government abundantly demonstrated that the 'gains' apparently obtained by the media in May 1992 were by no means secure.

Indonesia: information age destroys Suharto?

Retired general Suharto presided over Indonesia from 1966 to 1998. His 'New Order' regime was based on a successful blend of anti-communism, secular nationalism, economic development, military influence, highly centralized power structures, and strict limits on popular political participation. For three decades it proved a winning formula. The New Order state curtailed much of the public sphere – including strict curbs on press freedom – as part of the 'bargain' of developmental authoritarianism. Yet by the 1990s a substantial groundswell of resistance was beginning to emerge against Suharto. Key developments such as the banning of three weekly news publications in 1994 (see McCargo 1999a) and the ouster of Megawati Sukarnoputri from the leadership of the Indonesian Democratic Party (PDI) in 1996 illustrated Suharto's growing ruthlessness in the face of dissent. Suharto ensured that the press was limited in its criticisms of the New Order by using a variety of methods: formal and informal censorship, bannings (both temporary and permanent) of publications that overstepped the mark, a strict licensing regime for all news publications, and monitoring and control of journalists through a state-sponsored journalists' association, the Persatuan Wartawan Indonesia (PWI) (for details, see Hill 1994 and Hanazaki 1996). Suharto's problems intensified with the collapse of the rupiah in late 1997, part of the Asian financial crisis. Although re-elected as president early in 1998, he was ousted by mass protests a few weeks later. The media played a variety of roles in these developments.

In early 1998, there were systematic efforts to blame the ethnic Chinese for Indonesia's economic woes. Suharto's son-in-law Prabowo distributed copies of Sterling Seagrave's 1996 book *Lords of the Rim* (which offered a sensationalized account of the activities of the Chinese in Southeast Asia) while the press was urged by senior military officers to write stories criticizing wealthy Chinese businessmen (Eklof 1999: 135–7). A militant Islamic magazine called *Media Dakwah* responded with a nineteen-page cover story entitled 'Exposing the national traitors', discussing the prominent think-tank Center for Strategic and International Studies (CSIS) and its backer Sofyan Wanandi (*Media Dakwah*, February 1998). The anti-CSIS campaign by the military, certain Islamic groups and sections of the media had all the hallmarks of an attempt to divert attention from the economic mismanagement of the regime, suppressing dissent at a crucial juncture before the re-appointment of Suharto.

As student protests and demands for reform became more widespread, the media was initially cautious in reporting the core demands of the protestors. From the start, students called for Suharto's resignation, but most media reports played down this issue, concentrating instead on their demands for lower prices, *reformasi*, and an end to collusion, corruption and nepotism (Eklof 1999: 159). Later, however, the demand for Suharto to resign was reported, as were the suspicious disappearances of student activists and human rights activists, disappearances which were attributed to the military (Eklof 1999: 165–70). These revelations helped to firm up opposition to the regime, and undermined attempts by the military to broker some sort of deal with the opposition. Media coverage of the fatal shootings of four students at Trisakti University on 12 May 1998 marked an important turning point in the 'long fall' of Suharto (Eklof 1999: 182–3).

Radio played a role in reinforcing a sense of opposition during Suharto's final days. One Jakarta radio station kept playing the John Lennon song 'Imagine' following the 12 May shootings, while a Bandung station asked those who favoured Suharto's resignation to wear a white ribbon. Despite a notional ban on offering their own news reports, many stations provided detailed coverage of unfolding events during April and May 1998, reporters often calling in live on their mobile phones. Some stations also provided various forms of support for the demonstrators (Sen and Hill 2000: 100–1). While the military made a last-ditch threat on 16 May 1998 to close private television stations if they failed to toe the official line, and private stations were directed not to send unescorted camera crews to cover riots and demonstrations, this edict proved impossible to enforce (Sen and Hill 2000: 130–1). For those caught up in the events unfolding in Jakarta, it was difficult making sense of the situation in May 1998. Geoff Forrester's diary reports that on 19 May one afternoon paper carried the headline 'Suharto not retiring' and another 'Elections ASAP' (Forrester 1999a: 37).

There was an 'explosion of free political expression' in the days that followed, as old taboos were broken: newspapers began reporting critical comments made about the president, for example (Forrester 1999a: 64–5). Atkins argues that this 'breakdown in the culture of compliance' at various Indonesian news organizations was accompanied by a 'sharp focusing of attention' on Indonesia by international organizations (Atkins 2002: 198). Existing restrictions – such as a ban on foreign television crews freely transmitting footage back to their organizations – became unenforceable. Harsono notes that:

> On the part of the Soeharto regime, the dramatic events of May 1998 illustrated a failure to understand the international and local media, and the impact the media, and information technology, could have on politics in the late 1990s. The controls in place – such as visa restrictions for foreign journalists and threats to suspend licences of local publications – relied on a bureaucracy which believed in the power of its political leaders.
> (Harsono 2000: 86)

When Suharto undertook an ill-advised trip to Egypt early in May 'an ambiguity emerged among those charged with controlling the media about what was allowed' (Atkins 2002: 199). This new element of ambiguity proved fatal for the President, whose grip on the reins of power had long been entirely unambiguous. Despite a brief six-day clampdown on the output of domestic television, Suharto never regained control.

In part, the demise of Suharto was brought about by the globalization of the media, which provided inspiration to opposition activists inside Indonesia. The Finance Minister's reluctance to communicate with the international press prior to the new cabinet of March 1998 was a significant issue (Hill 1999: 98). Globalization was more than just Americans interfering (Sen and Hill 2000: 15).

Sen and Hill note the importance of the Internet in disseminating news and information in the final years of the New Order. In particular, the *apakabar* e-mail discussion list moderated by John MacDougall in Maryland, USA, helped Indonesians learn about and debate important developments such as the ousting of Megawati supporters from the PDI headquarters in July 1996 (Sen and Hill 2000: 200–1). Yet they stress that:

> Our argument is not that the Internet and its ability to transgress the national boundaries were a cause of the decline in Suharto's power, but that those transgressive capabilities were harnessed with great effect by opposition forces generated by the long repressive reign.
> (Sen and Hill 2000: 211)

They argue that the Internet was only available to a limited proportion of Indonesians, who chose to make use of it as a political medium in the distinctive circumstances of the New Order. David Marcus observed that the Internet played a crucial role in the downfall of Suharto: where other forms of communication were censored or controlled, the Internet played a vital role in keeping lines of communication open across the vast Indonesian archipelago (Marcus 1998). He cited Tufts University academic W. Scott Thompson, who described Suharto's fall as 'the first revolution using the Internet'. The impact of the Internet could be felt even by those with no direct access to it: materials could be downloaded, photocopied, and distributed as conventional flyers, leaflets and posters. Kawamoto notes that e-mail communication was crucial in mobilizing student protests across the country, while newsgroups and bulletin boards were also 'a place to proclaim fear and frustration' as violence erupted (Kawamoto 1998). Yet even Atkins, with his emphasis on the salience of new media, acknowledges that:

> During the crisis itself, the most significant media players would have appeared to be the local press, radio and television organizations who by all accounts were well ahead of the international television networks in both accuracy and immediacy.
> (Atkins 2002: 203)

Globalisation of communications was a factor in Suharto's downfall, but its principal impact was that a more competitive international media environment had strengthened the quality of Indonesian news output.

One of the leaders of the anti-Suharto movement, Amien Rais, was a regular columnist for the Indonesian Muslim Intellectual's Association (ICMI)-backed newspaper *Republika*, which ironically afforded opportunities to disseminate the views of some who later came out against the New Order (Schwarz 1999: 329). Hefner notes how, contrary to expectations, a Suharto crony with close ties to Harmoko was placed as editor of *Republika* (Hefner 1999: 52); yet even so, the newspaper did articulate some criticisms of the regime. The ICMI-linked magazine *Ummat* was an outspoken advocate of reform, calling for Suharto's resignation as early as late 1997. Criticisms by *Ummat* rankled with Suharto, and may have contributed to his virtual exclusion of ICMI members from his ill-fated March 1998 cabinet (Hefner 1999: 60). Lane noted that the urban poor were able to read about protest actions by students and peasant farmers, through a range of popular newspapers (Lane 1999: 247). Familiar with the idea of sending protest delegations to parliament or the National Human Rights Commission: 'They imitate these actions, sing leaflets, placards, press releases and even giving interviews to the media' (magazine interview with political organizer, quoted in Lane 1999: 247). Aspinall notes that:

> Despite the climate of political uncertainty and repression, journalists, too, became increasingly bold in reporting the political crisis, with a rapid (although not complete) breakdown of government control over the media after the Trisakti killings (on the following day, even the official TVRI news broadcast incorporated a statement of condolence from station staff).
>
> (Aspinall 1999: 144)

Ultimately, Suharto was brought down by a cumulative wave of onslaughts:

> Each crisis placed new pressure on the walls the state had built around the information culture. Each new assault weakened the

walls until parts began to crack: loss of faith by the military elite in Suharto; an emboldened local media; saturation attention by international news organizations aided by mobile satellite technology; and finally the overwhelming power of frustration by impoverished urban dwellers that turned to violence.

(Atkins 2002: 203)

Harold Crouch has argued that intellectuals within the Indonesian armed forces had recognized by the late 1990s the rise of the middle class and the 'globalization of communications which made it impossible to hide developments in Indonesia – including human-rights abuses – from the outside world'. Thus he credits media with a central role in changing the Indonesian military mind-set – though it should be noted that the crucial seminar he refers to took place in September 1998, after the fall of Suharto (Crouch 1999: 138). The military were shocked by the degree of criticism they received in the press after Suharto fell, including numerous demands for investigations of human rights abuses and calls for the end of 'dual function' doctrine which had long legitimized military dabbling in politics (Crouch 1999: 127).

Bourchier notes that the remarkable degree of media freedom after May 1998 meant that 'A host of new (and resurrected) magazines pumped up by a spirit of *reformasi*, competed to sell the stories they had not been allowed to tell before' – including questioning the official version of the 1965 coup (Bourchier 1999: 152). Perhaps in a deliberate attempt to distance himself from his predecessor, new President B. J. Habibie gave more interviews to foreign journalists in his first six weeks than Suharto had given in 32 years. Robison sketched the outlines of a 'descent into chaos' for post-Suharto Indonesia, a scenario which saw continuing economic and political turmoil, leading ultimately to the reimposition of controls on the media (Robison 1999: 229). Evidence of this began to emerge when the Habibie government started to claw back media freedoms by pressurizing media owners who were in debt to state banks (Forrester 1999b: 16).

In the wake of Suharto's downfall, the Indonesian media faced new challenges. A symbolic moment in the long demise of the New Order came in October 1999, when new President Abdurrahman Wahid closed down the Department of Information. Sen and Hill, however, argue that the legitimacy of the Department's censorship and propaganda functions had been gradually eroding during the final decade of Suharto's presidency (Sen and Hill 2000: 8). Habibie had already recognized the legitimacy of the Aliansi Jurnalis Independen (AJI), and abolished the permit-revocation provisions that had permitted the banning of *Tempo*. Around two dozen new press associations were created in the year following Suharto's downfall. Five hundred new publishing permits were issued in the six months following 5 June 1998, including permits for *DeTak* (a revamped *DeTik*) and a new incarnation of *Tempo*, which was launched in October 1998 (Sen and Hill 2000: 70). Many of the new ventures were unfortunately short-lived, partly because the country's continuing economic woes made newsprint expensive and profits elusive. Television stations were cutting broadcasting hours because of the economic situation. Local radio stations such as Jakarta's Safari FM sought to create a new, outspoken '*reformasi* radio' genre, with programming hosted by critics of the Suharto and Habibie administrations; yet these stations struggled to find enough advertising revenues to survive (Neumann 1998b). While the content of news programmes in the electronic media became relatively open, formal ownership of the stations often remained in the hands of Suharto cronies (CPJ 1999).

Much of the new press was startlingly aggressive, such as publications called *Opposisi* (Opposition) and *Gugati* (Accuse); their mottoes were 'Critical and on the side of Truth' and 'Trial by the press' respectively (CPJ 1999; Olle 2000). Another important publication was the cut-priced tabloid *Bangkit*, owned by the very reputable *Kompas* group but dedicated to the lowest forms of sensationalism. Olle listed around twenty other tabloids, mainly of them regionally focused and often mixing the critical with the merely sleazy: one known as *SkandaL* used the slogan 'sex, money, power' (Olle 2000). Others, such as *Adil* and *Tekad*, had a more 'Islamic' tinge. For these tabloids, the main struggle in Post-Suharto's Indonesia was not that between '*reformasi*' and the status quo, but one centring around different understandings of the terms '*reformasi*', 'sekular', and 'Islam'. Olle argues that a further debate was emerging over the definition of 'openness' in an era of reformasi: did 'opening up' mean that even 'pornography' was now acceptable?

It would be misleading to see this as simply a battle between Islam and a 'western-style' reformasi. When the tabloid press depicts the extremes of discourse it is not only chasing sales but is engaged in a process of defining the limits of a post-Suharto field of politics and culture.

(Olle 2000)

Real control was now in the hands of media proprietors rather than the New Order state. Indonesia was now looking like other democratic countries, but the durability of democratic discourses remained in some doubt.

Habibie's Information Minister Yunus Yosfiah (despite his troubling past as a former military commander in East Timor) won praise for his efforts to reform Indonesian press laws, on which he consulted UNESCO and the international anti-censorship NGO Article 19. Yet he still retained the right to suspend publishing permits for publications deemed to have violated the terms of their licences, and journalists were still required to join a recognized organization (such as PWI or AJI). These continuing restrictions failed to satisfy those who demanded 'total reform' of the regulatory climate for media, since there was still scope for clampdowns on critical journalists and publications (Astraatmadja 1998). A fear of disorder and chaos remained an important part of Indonesian popular discourse, and even reform-minded activists voiced fears about press 'irresponsibility' which reflected decades of New Order thinking (CPJ 1999).

In July 1998, Habibie proposed a widely-criticized plan to license all journalists; in August, Home Affairs Minister Syarwan Hamid filed lawsuits against three newspapers that had accused him of involvement in July 1996 raids on the PDI headquarters;[6] and in September, the military threatened to sue the weekly *Tajuk* for publishing damaging allegations. New mechanisms for press control continued to emerge, but Sen and Hill have argued that the bitter repression of the media in the late Suharto era produced a lasting determination to ensure real press freedom in post-Suharto Indonesia (Sen and Hill 2000: 71). *Tempo* editor-in-chief Bambang Harymurti advocated a voluntary press council system to mediate disputes, which he viewed as a means of avoiding costly litigation. He noted that it was now possible for those dissatisfied with press coverage either to buy courts or rent mobs (Sandeen 2000). Mobs were now regularly appearing at newspaper offices or radio stations, often triggered by stories related to religion. As in the Philippines, repression of the media had literally been privatized.

When Habibie as president was replaced by the Muslim leader and intellectual Abdurrahman Wahid (popularly known as Gus Dur) in October 1999, there was an immediate improvement in the media freedom. The much-loathed Ministry of Information was simply abolished at a stroke. Gus Dur argued that the ministry was simply the propaganda arm of the Suharto regime (Sng 2001). Independent media watch groups were established around the country, and once-rival journalists' associations AJI and the PWI began working together under the auspices of the Indonesian Press and Broadcasting Society to campaign for the abolition of repressive media legislation, and amendment of the constitution to guarantee press freedom (Harsono 2000: 90–1). Yet Harsono also noted the irony that former press stooges of the New Order were 'reinventing themselves as champions of media freedom'. Many leading figures in the world of Indonesian media had a track record of pragmatic accommodation to the prevailing order; they could not be relied upon to fight for media freedoms. Gus Dur lasted less than two years in the presidency, complaining bitterly that the press had engaged in a concerted campaign against him (Sng 2001); certainly, control of many media outlets remained in the hands of his political opponents

Megawati Sukarnoputri, who replaced Gus Dur as President in August 2001, appeared less committed to openness. She quickly pledged to establish a new ministry of communications and information, which she insisted did not amount to re-opening the old information ministry (*Jakarta Post*, 2 and 14 August). In a vast and troubled country that had been led by four different presidents in just over three years, the pace of change was bewildering. Under such conditions, the role and rights of the media were subject to constant renegotiation. Heryanto and Adi argue that:

> In the dramatic disappearance of long-term and well-defined common enemies, namely, the military and the State Department of Information, journalists and publishers have begun to

be exposed to a host of internal contradictions within their own ranks and institutions. Many of these problems are greater and more complex than most journalists have been prepared to confront, or even admit.

(Heryanto and Adi 2001)

Despite Megawati's claims that Indonesia's media were 'the freest in Asia', there were many gaps between rhetoric and reality (Greenlees 2001; Nurbaiti 2002). In March 2002, the New York-based Committee to Protect Journalists issued a statement of concern about indications of declining press freedom in Indonesia, including the denial of a visa extension for a critical Australian journalist and large numbers of attacks and threats to local reporters (*Straits Times*, 27 March 2002).

During the last weeks of the Suharto regime in April and May 1998, critical reporting (for example, by the English-language daily *Jakarta Post* and the outspoken weekly *Detektif & Romantika*), the Internet, and alliances between domestic and international media served as agents of change. These agents helped to undermine the ailing New Order. This is not to suggest that an increasingly vocal Indonesian media directly brought down the government in 1998. Indeed, the media itself was always polyvalent, reflecting the cracks and fissures that existed within the New Order regime. Suharto was ultimately forced out by a combination of international and domestic, political and economic forces. At various junctures during the final years of the Suharto regime, the Indonesian press performed each of the three alternative modes of agency: stability, restraint and change. Yet much of the time, much of the Indonesian press was engaged in the kind of essentially uncritical 'development journalism' favoured by the authorities, serving primarily as an agent of stability.

When Suharto's demise came, much of the impetus was external. The economic pressures that brought about the collapse in the value of the rupiah, and the subsequent restructuring forced upon Suharto by the IMF, undermined the rhetoric of successful economic development that had been crucial in legitimating the New Order. Suharto was not simply toppled by a vocal civil society, but by a domestic 'sub-establishment' opposition. Such an opposition existed, but it gained the confidence to mobilize only when the regime had already been badly wounded during earlier rounds of combat with international investors and with the IMF and the World Bank. Domestic opposition to Suharto took heart from critical coverage in the Western media, from the solidarity expressed by Indonesians living and studying abroad, and from other sources that might be described as an 'international civil society'. Yet such an international civil society had long existed, a global community of Indonesia-watchers expressing critical views on issues such as the New Order's human rights record and the regime's handling of East Timor. The existence of such a community contributed to the demise of the Suharto regime, but international civil society was powerless without a strong combination of international and domestic economic pressures, working in conjunction with domestic political protest. During April and May 1998, a barrage of critical reporting in the international press, coupled with pockets of critical reporting in the domestic press and with information posted on the Internet, were all factors that contributed to the demise of Suharto. At the same time, the media were not prime movers in the downfall of the New Order. Without a powerful combination of pressures – especially the collapse of the rupiah and a crisis of confidence in the banking system – the media could have done little.

The Indonesian case support's Smith's argument that the media may help promote a political transition but are unlikely to initiate one without strong allies. From 1994 to 1998, progressive elements in the Indonesian media waited for their opportunity to help topple Suharto: yet without student demonstrations, the economic crisis and a rising groundswell of resentment against the New Order, their role would have been tightly constrained. Even during the final weeks of Suharto's rule, by no means all media outlets were quick to exploit his weakness and support his ouster. Indeed, the great majority of Indonesian newspapers and magazines were owned or part-owned by prominent New Order supporters and collaborators. While post-Suharto developments such as Gus Dur's abolition of the Information Ministry appeared encouraging, the greater political space open to the media lacked a firm legislative or institutional basis. In other words, 'The Indonesian media is now unfettered. But it is also unprotected' (Heryanto and Adi 2001).

Non-transitions in Burma and Malaysia

By concentrating on the media's role in successful political transitions in the Philippines, Thailand and Indonesia, there is a danger of over-stating the success of such transitions, and the role of the media in promoting them. For the same period saw two major failed transitions in Southeast Asia, transitions in which the media also played a part. These will now be briefly reviewed.

Partly inspired by the Philippine 'people power' movement, a mass movement to oust the military regime of the ruling Burma Socialist Programme Party emerged in March 1988 (see Smith 1991: 1–26). The immediate catalyst for the movement was the revelation that Burma had been granted 'least developed country' status by the UN, an indicator of the depths of the woes besetting this resource-rich but chronically mismanaged economy. Following the retirement of authoritarian ruler Ne Win that July, huge student-led anti-government demonstrations had culminated in a short-lived 'democracy summer'. For much of August, protestors 'liberated' public buildings and established peoples' committees to take over the functions of local government. But after promising to hold elections and recognize opposition parties, the new State Law and Order Restoration Committee (SLORC) junta imposed a violent crackdown on protestors, killing perhaps 10,000. Although elections were held in May 1990 – and 81 per cent of parliamentary seats were won by the opposition – the junta refused to implement the results.

The local electronic media were kept under strict control throughout, but international broadcasters – especially the BBC World Service Burmese-language radio programme, and to a lesser extent *Voice of America* – played a crucial role in the dissemination of information that made the 'democracy summer' possible. Smith describes huge audiences across the country for these radio broadcasts: gongs were used in many towns to announce the start of the transmissions. Opposition leader Aung San Suu Kyi and former Prime Minister U Nu were able to use telephone interviews with international broadcasters to communicate directly with people inside Burma: their messages were effectively exported, and then promptly re-imported. Later, the SLORC leadership even claimed that the chaos produced by false BBC reports had forced them to seize power (Smith 1991: 18).

The democracy summer also saw an extraordinary flowering of new print media. An estimated 40-plus new newspapers or mimeographed news-sheets in Mandalay and 50-plus in Rangoon – testify to the resilience of free press traditions (Article 19 1991: 28; Allot 1990). Many of these lively publications were the mouthpieces of new political organizations. Influenced by this new climate, even the state-run papers started to offer more accurate news coverage, featuring pages of photographs of the demonstrators, and bold political pieces (Lintner 1990: 117). But following the crackdown after 18 September 1988, all these new publications were closed down and many journalists were obliged to flee to insurgent-controlled areas. In the years that followed, clandestine media – especially independent Burmese-language magazines – have continued to circulate despite severe penalties for those caught engaging in their production and distribution (Khin Maung Win 1999: 63).

The Burmese case demonstrates the extent to which media pressure and 'people power' alone are not always sufficient conditions to ensure transition. Even when a regime has completely lost its legitimacy (as shown by the 1990 Burmese election results), an internationally isolated military junta can nevertheless perpetuate itself in power, so long as it remains internally united, is in control of strategic resources and is willing to employ brutally repressive measures (Diamond 1999: 237). Neither international media attention nor the emergence of progressive domestic media can be of much effect under such circumstances.

Following on closely from the May 1998 ouster of Suharto, the Malaysian *reformasi* movement at one point seemed poised to precipitate the departure of long-standing Prime Minister Mahathir Mohamed. The movement was partly a response to the economic crisis but was triggered primarily by Mahathir's abrupt dismissal of Deputy Premier and Finance Minister Anwar Ibrahim, who was subsequently arrested on charges of corruption and sodomy, tried, convicted and jailed. Despite large street demonstrations and the emergence of new political groupings to challenge the ruling coalition led by Mahathir's UMNO party, the government survived.

Domestic media played an ambivalent role during Mahathir's crisis of legitimacy. Mainstream publications such as the *New Straits Times* continued to support the government vigorously, one senior newspaper figure having argued that: 'The government may not be too perfect, but it is not too bad either' (Wong 2000: 133). Frustrated by what they saw as bland or biased reporting, audiences began turning to other sources of information, especially to the Internet. Sites carrying anti-Mahathir stories and presenting a pro-*reformasi* stance mushroomed in popularity (at least thirty appeared within three months of Mahathir's arrest) while newspaper sales slumped.[7] Given Mahathir's enthusiastic promotion of the Internet as part of his Multimedia Super Corridor project, this was an ironic twist (Alford 2000). The government had pledged in writing to project investors that the Internet would not be censored. As in Indonesia, the Internet had a reach far beyond the 500,000 estimated Malaysian users; materials could be readily downloaded and circulated in more conventional forms (Atkins 2002: 209–10).

At the same time, *Harakah* – the newspaper of the Islamist party PAS – saw sales of its biweekly rise to a peak of 270,000; ironically, many of these new readers were not even Muslims, let alone party members (Wong 2000: 135–6). The newspaper was soon in trouble for selling to non-party members: predictably, the editor was charged with sedition, and the newspaper was forced to scale down to bimonthly instead of twice-weekly publication. Local commentator Zaharom Nain insisted that it was inappropriate to speak of developments such as the 'resignations' of two leading Malay-language newspaper editors in July 1998 as part of a 'crackdown on the media', arguing that: 'Such assertions merely reinforce the myth of an independent Malaysian media' (Wong 2000: 134).

Local electronic media made little attempt to provide balanced coverage of the protests: Information Minister Khalil Yaacob declared in 1998 that state-run RTM television would not be covering opposition voices in the news, an announcement heavily criticized by democracy advocates (Wong 2000: 128). The international media carried extensive coverage of the *reformasi* movement: publications such as *Asiaweek* and the *Far Eastern Economic Review* were widely circulated and many Malaysians watched international television broadcasts from CNN, CNBC and the BBC, as well as listening to BBC World Service radio. In 1999, reports about Malaysia on CNN and CNBC feeds were censored by satellite provider Astro, whose owner is close to Mahathir (Wong 2000: 129). But intense pressure on the international media has forced foreign correspondents to tread carefully in Malaysia; Murray Hiebert, former bureau chief of the *Far Eastern Economic Review*, was actually jailed for contempt of court in 1999.

The Malaysian case illustrates the potential effectiveness of using formal and informal pressures to maintain state control of most media outlets. The Mahathir government has never hesitated to use various items of legislation to curtail the press, but to a large extent relies on a well-established culture of journalistic self-censorship. Despite very considerable support for *reformasi* and for Anwar, opposition forces were never able to mainstream their views through the media – although they fared better at deploying the Internet on their behalf. The example of Malaysia also illustrates the limitations of new media technologies as a tool of political struggle.

Conclusion

Media come into their own during times of crisis. Some scholars have argued that most crises are essentially constructed by the media: that the manufacture, management and coverage of crises are among the main functions of media (see, for example, Bruck 1992: 108). It has been argued here that in Southeast Asian countries on the verge of political transition, crises really do occur. But the media do more than simply describe and interpret unfolding crises; elements of the media become political players in their own right. Performing various roles as agents of stability, restraint and change, the media become actively involved in shaping political outcomes. As Raboy and Dagenais argue, 'it is in times of crisis that the media reveal themselves, their workings and their motivations' (1992: 13), with all their associated inconsistencies and contradictions.

This survey of the role of media in Southeast Asian political transitions has suggested the following general conclusions:

- Many studies over-emphasize conflicts between state power and media freedom, as though these were some kind of zero-sum game.
- In practice, many threats to media freedom come from outside the state, or even from within the media itself.
- State repression of media may be 'privatized', effectively subcontracted to agencies or political forces outside the state.

- Many elements of the media may be inherently partisan, playing a direct role as political actors. There may be close financial or personal ties between sections of the media and other parts of the political establishment.
- Thus it would be wrong to assign a blanket description to the media as 'progressive' in their political orientation.
- The media need to be unpacked into component parts; individual publications, journalists or broadcasters may play very different roles in times of transition.
- Media may play a crucial supporting role at times of political transition, though there is little evidence for media-initiated transitions.
- International media and new media technologies can offer sources of support for transition, but may be of limited impact unless tied to strong domestic forces and linked to progressive elements within conventional domestic media.
- Where a unified regime retains control of major state resources and is determined to face down opposition, media and other non-state actors may be unable to force a political transition.
- In the aftermath of transitions, media face different tasks and challenges. Even where they have supported a democratic transition, they may fail to offer consistent support for a consolidation process. Alliances may fracture; ownerships and orientations may change.
- New regimes, leaders or power-brokers may view the media differently and may seek to roll back the political space within which media operate. Media may be more free, but less protected.
- Political transitions may present fresh problems for media practitioners, as they face new and diverse enemies (such as employers, rival publications and politicians) rather than the old and predictable forces of state repression.

3 Media in peacetime? Press and television in Japan

From 1955 to 1993, Japanese politics was characterized by one-party dominance: the Liberal Democratic Party (LDP) enjoyed an extraordinary thirty-eight year period of unbroken rule. This spell was broken (briefly, as it turned out) when a rival coalition came to power in July 1993. Understanding the significance of this change involved a new assessment of the quality of Japanese democracy. Japan's critics had long argued that liberal democracy and one-party dominance were incompletely compatible, while the demise of LDP rule offered a boost to those who asserted that Japan was genuinely democratic.

It is generally argued that a mature liberal democracy possesses strong institutions of civil society that counterbalance the power of the state.[1] Such institutions typically include trade unions, interest groups, non-governmental organizations, and the mass media. Mainstream scholars who see Japan as a liberal democracy emphasize the role of the Japanese media as a 'watchdog', monitoring and criticizing the actions of government; revisionist scholars, by contrast, have argued that Japan is not a liberal democracy in the Western sense.[2] The role of the media in the 1993 end of LDP rule was therefore an important test. The Japanese mass media are portrayed by 'revisionists' such as Karel van Wolferen as the servants of the political establishment (Wolferen, 1989: 93–100). Following the demise of LDP rule in 1993, even a booklet published by the very mainstream Foreign Press Center (an important source of official and semi-official public relations materials) argued that 'some people' felt Japanese newspapers had long been so intent on following the manoeuvring among the various factions that they took LDP rule for granted and failed to perform their primary function of providing the full information that the people need to play a meaningful role in participatory democracy.

(Foreign Press Center 1994: 30)

A revised version of this booklet published in 1997 was even more explicit – 'some people's' criticisms were now voiced directly by the author: 'Having grown comfortable with the established 1955 structure, the media ended up sustaining that order and being part of it' (Foreign Press Center 1997: 35).

The Japanese case is an important one in the context of wider debates about the growing political role of the mass media in the Pacific Asia region. In Taiwan, for example, political liberalization since the end of martial law in 1987 has gone hand-in-hand with the emergence of a 'rejuvenated', 'watchdog' press (Rampal 1994: 647–8). Given Japan's high level of economic development and the sophistication of its mass media, the relationship between media and politics in Japan may be of considerable comparative relevance for its fast-growing Pacific Asian neighbours. If the highly developed mass media of Japan fail effectively to monitor government behaviour and to check the power of the Japanese state, how realistic is it to expect the media in other Asian countries to perform this important role? How far was the Japanese media truly an agent of restraint, and how far was it simply an agent of stability, serving the needs of the state and other power-holders?

Structure of the Japanese media

A small number of organizations are responsible for most of the national-level news output in Japan.[3] NHK is a semi-governmental broadcasting agency modelled on the BBC (see Krauss 2000), while each major newspaper group has close commercial links with a private television station. The *Yomiuri Shimbun* (circulation 14.46 million) runs NTV, the *Asahi Shimbun* (12.64 million) operates TV Asahi, the *Mainichi Shimbun* (5.88 million) is involved with TBS, the specialist financial paper *Nihon Keizai Shimbun* (Nikkei for short) (4.53 million) with TV Tokyo, and the *Sankei Shimbun* (2.88 million) with Fuji TV.[4] The big newspaper groups also operate a flotilla of other ventures, ranging from weekly and monthly magazines to amusement parks and even their own professional baseball teams. Whereas in the 1960s the three major newspapers followed a similar 'oppositional' editorial line, led by the *Asahi*, during the 1970s the *Yomiuri* won out in the circulation war and adopted a more conservative, pro-LDP stance. The *Asahi*, however, has continued to espouse left-wing editorial positions on key issues such as Japan's 'peace constitution'. The *Mainichi* has suffered from financial and circulation problems, and so has somewhat lost its way over the past twenty years. Both the *Nikkei* and the *Sankei* are conservative-oriented business newspapers, most comparable with the *Wall Street Journal* and *Financial Times*.

Each of the major newspaper groups adopted new business strategies in the 1990s. While *Yomiuri* continued to maximize circulation, *Asahi* sought to become an integrated information company through use of new media, and the smaller groups sought to pursue alternative strategies of their own (Westney 1996: 69). The stress on 'lean management' and cost-cutting in post-bubble Japan could have particular dangers for the newspaper industry, since resource constraints may lead to less diversity and 'a concentration on established beats and less slack for developing in-depth coverage and new sources of information' (Westney 1996: 81).

Constraints on freedom of information

On the face of it, Japan has free mass media. Freedom of speech is guaranteed under Article 21 of the Japanese constitution (though this does not apply to radio and television), state control of the press is negligible, libel laws generally favour media organizations, and a Freedom of Information Bill was passed in 1999 (Hamilton 2000: 107–10). Yet in practice several threats exist to that freedom. The most conspicuous of these is the threat of co-optation. Successive LDP administrations gave special privileges to the large media groups, allowing them (for example) to purchase prime office sites in central Tokyo at prices well below market value. In return, the media have often worked in close tandem with the political establishment: for example, participating in illegal stocks-for-favours and loans-for-favours deals, censoring footage of American President George

Bush throwing up at an official banquet in January 1992, and embargoing news about the Crown Prince's wooing of Owada Masako (Freeman 2000: 4–5). The culture of media 'restraint' on sensitive issues can produce a climate of selective self-censorship.

Particularly controversial is the system of *kisha* (reporters) clubs that operates in Japanese government circles and also in the private sector (for a detailed discussion, see Freeman 2000, and Feldman 1993: 63–79). Freeman has identified 121 major *kisha* clubs in Tokyo alone; the total number of clubs in Japan is not known, but informed estimates suggest that there may be between six and seven hundred (Freeman 2000: 68–69). The most important clubs are those close to the main seats of power. Around seventeen major news groups have privileged access to press clubs at the Prime Minister's office, at party offices and the offices of party factions. These news groups generally include the five national newspapers, four large regional newspapers, two news agencies and six broadcast companies. This does not mean that a club has only seventeen members; major news organizations may send up to ten journalists to a given club, so that some important clubs may have over a hundred members (Freeman 2000: 91). Club members are provided with extensive facilities at the expense of the relevant government agency, party, or faction: these may include meals and sleeping quarters, as well as free telephone and fax lines. More than half of the *kisha* clubs covered in one 1993 survey were permanently staffed by employees of the host organization (Freeman 2000: 82). The system has the effect of turning the reporters concerned into 'insiders', in contrast to other journalists who are excluded from the special access to information available to club members. Those working for local newspapers, weekly or monthly publications, and foreign correspondents are generally excluded from clubs. Journalists on the inside are not limited to contacting politicians at their offices: *kisha* club members conduct regular 'night attacks' on the homes of the figures to whom they are assigned, sometimes playing *mah jong* with them into the small hours. 'Night attacks' are followed up by morning visits: leading Japanese politicians such as the Cabinet Secretary can fully expect to be tailed by reporters throughout their waking hours.

Understandably, such intense relationships between politicians and the small team of reporters assigned to cover them may lead to a falling off of journalistic objectivity and standards. In each of the major scandals that have beset LDP politicians over the past thirty years, reporters were well aware of what was going on long before the stories broke. There was, in effect, systematic collusion between press and politicians to conceal shady goings-on. *Kisha* clubs maintained an internal discipline that prevented members from obtaining 'scoops': a common line was agreed upon by reporters, and anyone going it alone faced being ostracized by the club. Politicians expected club members to produce favourable coverage of their activities, while club members jealously defended their news sources from the prying eyes of rivals outside the charmed circle.

When scandals did break, it was generally because outsiders had managed to expose sleaze concealed by the clubs. Prime Minister Tanaka Kakuei, for example, fell from grace in the 1970s following exposure of his corrupt practices in a weekly magazine, followed up by pressure from foreign correspondents and later an investigation by the US Senate. The Recruit Cosmos scandal was exposed by *Asahi Shimbun* reporters – but reporters in the Yokohama bureau, not those on the Tokyo parliamentary beats (see Farley 1996: 148–9).

In other words, the *kisha* club system itself merely reflects the internal structures of Japanese news organizations: the clubs are not the actual root of the problem, but cartels set up by rigidly hierarchical media groups that do not regard the critical quest for information as a fundamental institutional goal. While there are limited parallels between the *kisha* clubs and structures such as the British Westminster 'lobby system', the interface between political and civil society appears singularly blurred in the case of the *kisha* clubs. The most distasteful feature of *kisha* clubs is that journalists themselves use the club system to exclude other journalists and so preserve information cartels: this is media censorship and control exercised not by the state, or even by media owners, but by reporters on the ground (Hall 1998: 46–7).

It has long been argued that *kisha* clubs presented a particular barrier to foreign correspondents, and even that Japanese government officials gave deliberately misleading briefings on sensitive issues to the international press (Mayes and Rowling 1997: 122–4). Adverse coverage in the international media and pressure from news organizations such as Bloomberg has led some *kisha* clubs to allow limited access to foreign journalists. By 1996, the major international wire services eventually gained a kind of associate membership of clubs at the Tokyo Stock Exchange and other key sources of financial information (Hall 1998: 69–71). Ivan Hall holds that despite these and other limited concessions, foreign correspondents remain 'segregated scribes' in Japan (Hall 1998: 45–79). He argues persuasively that the clubs' survival reflects the continuation of a pre-war mentality in Japan: news organizations see themselves as working primarily in the national interest, and only secondarily as the guardians of the public interest or the democratic process (Hall 1998: 73–4).

Freeman identifies four main outcomes of the information cartels created by the kisha club system (Freeman 2000: 164–70). The first is the emphasis on what she terms 'credentialing' information: the higher placed (and closer to power) the source of information, the more credence is given to that information. In other words, the value assigned to news information is bound up with the status and hierarchy of news sources, a process that disempowers those lower down the pecking order. A second outcome is a 'weakening of the political auditing function'; proximity to key actors and issues, plus a preoccupation with minutiae, makes it difficult for journalists to present the larger picture. Journalists become more comfortable with routine reporting than with the pursuit of scoops. The third outcome is a limiting of the agenda-setting process – in Japan, newspapers tend to follow public announcements rather than pre-empt the government and drive the news agenda, as often happens elsewhere. At the same time, the Japanese media are adept at ensuring that certain critical issues rarely obtain much publicity, which counts as a kind of 'negative' agenda-setting. A fourth outcome is the marginalization of alternative media, those media outlets that reside outside the charmed circles of *kisha* club access are unable to present credentialized information, and so lack popular trust and respect. Freeman's final outcome is the extent to which news and opinion is homogenized in Japan; press clubs and patterns of media ownership conspire to produce a standardized coverage of important issues. Taken together, these outcomes constitute a comprehensive indictment of the performance of the Japanese media in general, and the press in particular. Freeman concludes that the media limits, rather than sets, the information agenda in Japan (Freeman 2000: 179).

The growing political clout of television

Given the high level of newspaper penetration in Japan, coupled with literacy levels above 99 per cent and a traditional reverence for the written word, newspapers have generally enjoyed a privileged status in the Japanese order. Japanese print media journalists habitually look down on their counterparts in broadcasting. Although a partial exception is made for NHK staff, in view of their high standards of training and their reputation for impartiality, those working in the electronic media are often seen by their newspaper colleagues not as 'real' journalists, but as dabblers, amateurs preoccupied with superficial concerns and incapable of analysing issues in any depth. This view was shared by 'most senior politicians, who had little respect for television and chose to rely for the most part on the print media' (Altman 1996: 174). In a society where age and seniority were of enormous importance, a generational gap existed between print and broadcasting journalists. One effect of this gap was to prevent intellectuals from recognizing the growing importance of television news programmes in shaping public perceptions of the political order. Since the mid-1980s, the main initiative for change in the Japanese media has come neither from the dinosaur-like flagship newspapers nor from worthy-but-dull NHK, but from private television stations seeking to steal a march on their competitors.

Until quite recently, the conventional interviewing style of Japanese television journalists was extremely non-confrontational. They addressed politicians in polite, respectful language, following a predictable line of questioning – indeed, politicians were often supplied with the questions in advance. Old-style LDP politicians were not, for the most part, very telegenic: they built up their power through the assiduous cultivation of local personal networks of supporters in their constituencies, coupled with close ties to major business enterprises. Many made little attempt to communicate with the public, peppering their utterances with 'abtruse expressions and vague or even incomprehensible phrases', such as 'Well, it is just as you know' (Feldman 1996: 22). According to some observers, about a third of LDP Diet members were little more than stooges for Japan's enormously lucrative construction industry (on elections and voting in Japan, see McCargo 2000a: 98–126).

During the mid-1980s, commercial television stations began to produce a different style of news programme that featured more critical presentation of political stories. The prime mover behind these changes was TV Asahi. Two programmes led the way: *News Station*, screened every weeknight at 10 p.m. for over an hour, and *Sunday Project*, which included a weekly interview slot. *News Station* was hosted by Kume Hiroshi, who had previously presented a pop music show and had no journalistic experience. Kume employed an avuncular style, and was well known for his use of gestures and his facetious comments about news items. His critics saw him as a comedian who mocked the government; Kume described himself as an 'MC' (master of ceremonies). Kume's primary objective was to make the news comprehensible to ordinary viewers, using plain language, charts and even toy dolls rather than the more arcane vocabulary favoured by NHK (Altman 1996: 170–2). On *News Station*, a woman newscaster shared the actual news reading with Kume, while a commentator from *Asahi Shimbun* discussed the latest developments from a more serious perspective. Anyone used to the racy presentational style of American or European television news programmes would find *News Station* slow and rather dull viewing: some items last about fifteen minutes. Yet Japanese media analysts raved about Kume's masterful tempo, his sense of just when and how to slip in a sardonic quip. Kume made no pretence at being neutral: he was overtly emotional, often frowning with obvious disapproval or bursting into laughter. NHK presenters, by contrast, absolutely never laughed, while presenters on commercial stations such as TBS could only do so now and again.[5] Print journalists were scathing about the programme, arguing that it was characterized by trivial comments and a lack of proper analysis;[6] yet *News Station* had audience figures of around 20 million and advertisers were queuing up to sponsor the programme.

TV Asahi and the downfall of the LDP

Observers (especially foreign correspondents) have given Kume a great deal of the credit for the downfall of former LDP kingmaker

Kanemaru Shin in 1992. *News Station* ran a nightly feature on a corruption scandal centred on Kanemaru, who had been let off by the public prosecutor's office with a token fine of around $2000.[7] A popular outcry over this favourable treatment forced the authorities to re-open the case, and drove Kanemaru out of his position as Japan's leading power-broker. It was the demise of Kanemaru that paved the way for the 1993 split in the LDP, when Kanemaru's old protégé Ozawa Ichiro launched the breakaway Japan Renewal Party (JRP). The JRP exploited popular discontentment with the level of political corruption, a discontentment that had been fostered by television programmes such as *News Station*.

Yet Ellis Krauss has stressed that for all its anti-establishment posturing, *News Station* was a programme sponsored by Japanese business interests, notably the giant advertising agency Dentsu:

> Nor does *News Station* provide either a marked alternative viewpoint or true investigative journalism. Rather, this newfound diversity in television news may merely be contributing to the trend toward a new form of conservative polity rather than to true oppositional politics.
>
> (Krauss 2000: 238)

Hamilton similarly argues that possibly: 'On reflection . . . Kume was more a product of the times than a free agent of change' (2000: 103). Programmes such as *News Station* saw the demise of the old Cold War stand-off between left and right that had characterized the 1955 system. Their existence would make it difficult for the LDP to regain its former hegemonic standing, since they promoted greater pluralism and a more critical scrutiny of the actions and utterances of political actors. Yet such programmes were ultimately 'a contributor to and reflection of the much diminished former political cleavages in Japan', in which opposition amounted to little more than 'a form of cynical alienation combined with vague conservative populism' (Krauss 2000: 239). *News Station* was dedicated to deconstructing political realities rather than constructing alternative ones.

If *News Station* helped create the conditions for an LDP split, *Sunday Project* was sometimes credited with having dealt the *coup de grace* to the *ancien regime*. On 31 May 1993, premier Miyazawa

Kiichi agreed to be interviewed by *Sunday Project*'s Tahara Soichiro. This was the first time a serving prime minister had been interviewed by Tahara. Tahara was well known for his controversial tendency to press politicians well beyond the bounds of conventional politeness, a tendency that had earned him criticism for being 'un-Japanese'. Some old-style Japanese broadcasters regarded him with a certain high-minded disdain, arguing that he adopted an aggressive 'American' style of interviewing, with the sole aim of boosting audience ratings for the resultant spectacle. Western observers, however, tended to see Tahara as a force for democratic change in Japan, bringing politicians face-to-face with public criticisms and forcing them to account for their actions. *Sunday Project* included a morning political talk show that frequently made headlines in the Monday editions of leading newspapers, often serving as a forum for reform-minded politicians critical of the established order (Altman 1996: 172).

Prior to 1993, LDP leaders had believed they were under no obligation to address the public directly and frankly. A variety of factors made this stance no longer tenable. One view is that the end of the Cold War undermined the continuing legitimacy of conservative government; another argument holds that criticism from 'revisionist' foreign scholars such as Karel van Wolferen and Chalmers Johnson had placed Japan's leadership on the defensive. Whatever the reason for Miyazawa's having agreed to grant an unprecedented interview to *Sunday Project*, Tahara's questioning played a significant role in ending both LDP rule and Miyazawa's prime ministerial career. During the fateful May interview, Tahara raised the question of 'political reform' – the need for fundamental change in the electoral system and party funding arrangements that had promoted decades of what Chalmers Johnson famously termed 'structural corruption' (Johnson 1995: 183–211). Although Miyazawa had told Tahara prior to the interview that he did not wish to discuss the reform question, Tahara warned him that he intended to ask about it anyway. He insisted that if Miyazawa failed to talk about the subject uppermost in the minds of the electorate, the public would regard him as a 'faceless man'. Confronted with the issue, Miyazawa agreed to discuss it, and pledged again and again during the course of the subsequent interview to implement a political reform package to avert a 'crisis of democracy' (Tahara

1993).[8] TV Asahi showed this clip repeatedly; when it became evident that opposition from within the LDP was preventing Miyazawa from fulfilling his pledge, public opinion created the necessary conditions for a no-confidence vote and the splitting of the LDP, thereby precipitating a snap general election.

When the July 1993 general election saw the demise of LDP rule, a slew of articles appeared in the domestic and international press crediting television with a crucial role in the party's fall from grace (for examples, see Sanger 1993, McKillop and Itoi 1993, Dieter 1993). It was argued that television had raised popular political consciousness, thereby sowing crucial seeds of voter discontent. The thesis was an engaging one for those eager to see evidence of democratization in the Japanese order; the fact that private television stations played the main role was particularly gratifying to the free marketeers who assumed a direct causal connection between economic and political liberalization. Despite some elements of truth in these analyses, the 1993 general election results simply did not point to a decisive rejection of the LDP by the voters. If the voters were not the primary agent of change in the political order, then it is difficult to argue that the mass media (and certain television news programmes in particular) were in any position to initiate such electoral change through their agenda-setting function.

In fact, the LDP was not significantly weakened by the July 1993 poll itself. The party lost its edge primarily because of defections to new conservative parties, rather than by the outcome of the election. Since LDP MPs have their own private constituency organizations or *koenkai*, the defectors were able to take the great bulk of their support with them when they joined new parties (on *koenkai*, see Er 1994). The old Japan Socialist Party, by contrast, lost heavily in the elections, dropping from 134 seats to 70. It seemed that many voters who wished to express their dissatisfaction with the LDP were very happy to do by switching their allegiance to new conservative parties. The fact that these new parties were stuffed with seasoned LDP hacks actually made it easier for voters to shift their support, secure in the knowledge that they were choosing people with extensive experience in government who could continue to run the country in the time-honoured post-war fashion.

Stephen Johnson has pointed out that the popular view of the elections – the LDP losing power as a result of a wave of voter discontentment – simply did not square with the facts. He insists that the LDP would have held onto power 'had the Hata/Ozawa group not defected from its ranks before the election' (Johnson 1994: 9). In other words, the demise of the LDP was a direct result of manoeuvring at the elite level, rather than the outcome of popular electoral politics. Christensen argues that the scandals of the late 1980s and early 1990s were not a convincing explanation for the political upheavals of 1993–94, since similar scandals had taken place 'with frightening regularity in the postwar period' (Christensen 2000: 19). Another important factor was the record low voting turnout of just over 67 per cent, lower in urban areas, and only around 51 per cent in Tokyo. The LDP lost power, not with a bang, but with a whimper. Television undoubtedly helped create the conditions for the 1993 election, yet its influence over the final outcome was highly debatable. The Japan New Party, for example, led by former journalist Hosokawa Morihiro, benefited from favourable treatment at the hands of the media – but despite the fact that Hosokawa assumed the premiership in the 'reformist' coalition administration assembled in July 1993, the JNP was essentially a bit player in the unfolding drama of Japanese politics.

Politicians strike back: the Tsubaki case

Whether or not the Japanese media did play a crucial role in ousting the LDP, there is little doubt that many political journalists were eager to see the ruling party fall. This was especially true of television journalists working for commercial stations, who had long been treated as second-class citizens by the press-club system. For such journalists, the downfall of the LDP offered an opportunity to reform the traditional relationship between reporters and politicians, breaking the intimate ties between the two that had all too often prevented critical coverage. These feelings were boldly expressed by TV Asahi's news division chief, Tsubaki Sadayoshi, at a meeting of the National Association of Commercial Broadcasters on 21 September 1993. Tsubaki declared:

> In discussion with editors and other news staff at the end of June, I encouraged them, but not instructed them, to conduct

our news reporting with a view to assisting the non-LDP forces
in establishing a coalition government

(*Asahi Evening News*, 23 October 1993)

This entailed, for example, going easy on allegations that JRP co-leader Ozawa was implicated in the Sagawa Kyubin scandal. Tsubaki considered Ozawa's possible misdeeds to be of secondary importance: the main target was the LDP itself. He went on to explain:

I believed that such thinking was in tune with political winds that were blowing. This is how TV Asahi reported news . . . . Of course, I did not say these things to the programming director because it was a major deviation from fairness in broadcasting . . . . It may not be fair to report news with a view to breaking the (LDP-dominated) 1955 regime. But we handled our news program based on my judgement that the news division seemed to be moving in that direction.

(*Asahi Evening News*, 23 October 1993)

Although Tsubaki made his comments in what was supposedly a private meeting, they were leaked a couple of weeks later by the *Sankei Shimbun*. It appears likely that executives from Fuji TV, the conservative arch-rival of TV Asahi, passed on the information to their newspaper colleagues in an attempt to embarrass Tsubaki and his company. The story immediately made headline news; Tsubaki was removed from his post by TV Asahi, and resigned shortly afterwards. This was not the end of the matter, however.

Japan's commercial television stations receive operating licences from parliament, and by an unfortunate coincidence of timing, TV Asahi's licence was due for renewal at the beginning of November. This placed considerable pressure upon the company's management. Under the terms of the 1950 Broadcast Act, Japanese broadcasters have a legal obligation to be politically impartial (Saito 2000: 573). The Diet's Communications Committee summoned Tsubaki and TV Asahi President Ito Kunio to give testimony concerning the station's coverage of the election on 25 and 27 October respectively. This was an opportunity for LDP parliamentarians to have their revenge by lording it over upstart journalists. Some politicians felt bitterly that they had been 'defeated by television', a view echoed by pundits who had nicknamed the Hosokawa administration 'the Kume–Tahara Coalition Government' (Altman 1996: 165). The LDP had long sought to use allegations of bias to cow the media, especially commercial broadcasters (Sugiyama 2000: 195). The media community was deeply divided over the decision to send Tsubaki to testify; many within TV Asahi felt uneasy about the way the company was using Tsubaki as a fall guy, and many outside the company argued that TV Asahi was setting an extremely bad precedent by complying with the Diet's summons. Although TV Asahi had its licence renewed, parliament attached conditions, including a requirement that the company conduct an internal investigation into the charge of biased election coverage. The internal investigation released its report on 29 August 1994, more than a year after the election: unsurprisingly, it concluded that there was no evidence of bias during the election period. The delay in producing this report was criticized by commentators who felt that a prompt investigation would have helped spark a more serious debate about the issues of media freedom involved in the case.

The Tsubaki case exposed a number of fault-lines that help explain the limited effectiveness of the Japanese media as a political watchdog. The first was the rivalry between print and broadcasting journalists. With the exception of Asahi-owned publications, the print media largely failed to support TV Asahi, instead seizing the opportunity to bash television journalists for their supposedly inferior professional standards. This was particularly clear in the case of the *Yomiuri* group.[9] The second was that journalists working in the electronic media failed to demonstrate any solidarity with their colleagues in other companies, but leaked the details of a private meeting in a deliberate attempt to harm their competitors. A third fault-line was the spinelessness of TV Asahi in ordering Tsubaki to attend a committee of the Diet. A fourth was the vulnerability of private television stations to political pressures linked directly to the licence renewal question, and the willingness of politicians to exploit their parliamentary privilege as overseers of the broadcasting media for their own ends. In each case, it was clear that those working in the media were dedicated to the commercial interests of their own organizations: there was no body able to transcend those factional concerns and act as a pressure group on behalf of the media as a whole.

Despite the apparent increase in the political influence of the Japanese media as manifested in its critical coverage of the events leading up to the 1993 general election, the Tsubaki case seemed to point to underlying weaknesses in the media as an effective institution of civil society. Tsubaki's alleged crime was his contention that television could help create the 'wind' of political change, rather than simply depicting this wind to the viewing public. Yet Tsubaki firmly believed that TV Asahi had been subject to various forms of LDP control for many years (Hamilton 2000: 111): pro-LDP bias was fine, but expressing other sympathies was not. It must also be noted that Tsubaki's blustering manner was one factor that brought about his downfall – even commentators sympathetic to Tsubaki privately described his behaviour and demeanour throughout the episode as foolhardy.

Media and politics after the LDP's fall

The Tsubaki case also illustrated the way two distinct issues appeared conflated in the minds of many Japanese media practitioners and analysts. All too often, using television as a medium for the critical analysis of political issues was confused with using television to express personal opinions. To present a critical discussion was regarded as tantamount to making a personal criticism. Japanese television newscasters were divided between those who did directly express their personal views, and those who did not (Yamazaki 1994: 59–60). Some television journalists seem to feel that by inserting their private opinions into a news programme, they are raising its quality. In fact, however, their often indirect and heavily-coded comments may do little to improve a weak-kneed programme that lacks critical bite, and in some cases serve primarily to appease the consciences of newscasters who find themselves presenting inanities.

According to one Japanese television journalist: 'The defeat of the LDP in 1993 was an opportunity for the media to change our traditional role. We failed.'[10] He compared political journalists in Japan with people studying a huge elephant: some watching the tail, some monitoring the ears, other keeping an eye on the legs, but no one attempting to analyse the big picture. This was a problem rooted in the system of specialized reporting favoured by the main news organizations, a system which produced all kinds of detailed factual information but no overview, no commentary and no investigative insight. In this respect, there were similarities with the paucity of analysis to be found in the Thai print media, where front page political stories were packed with baffling details (see McCargo 2000b). The collapse of the LDP's monolithic power provided an opportunity for the media groups to revamp their own structures, but this had not been done. In March 1994, veteran Nikkei journalist Tase Yasuhiro published a book in Japanese entitled *Crime and Punishment of Political Journalism*, which highlighted the low ethical standards of reporters (Tase 1994). Although the book attracted considerable interest and attention, its impact was very limited.

Nor did commercial television stations sustain their critical fire with the same vigour in the period following the Tsubaki case. Audience figures for programmes such as *News Station* began to fall off, and Hiroshi Kume went out of his way to stress that he did not support any particular political party. He was obliged to make a public apology after a false pollution scare on his programme resulted in a libel suit (Hamilton 2000: 103), and took a lengthy 'sabbatical' at the end of 1999 after saying that he was exhausted (Krauss 2000: 239–40; *Mainichi Daily News*, 7 and 8 October 1999). More disturbingly, politicians became less enthusiastic about appearing on interview programmes, especially with Tahara. There were persistent rumours of a growing climate of self-censorship within the news departments of the various stations.

The role of NHK

At the public NHK, morale was also low (see Brull 1994). Traditionally, NHK had enjoyed a privileged position in the Japanese broadcasting order, with high ratings, immense prestige and formidable news-gathering resources. At the same time, the sheer size of the organization and its bureaucratic character limited its ability to compete effectively with the private sector, especially since NHK's strict code of political neutrality impeded it from pursuing the more aggressive style of news presentation favoured by its competitors. NHK was almost totally dependent upon government-imposed user fees for its funding, and its budget is subject to parliamentary approval. As one former insider put it:

'When a political story is edited at NHK, the editing booth is always crowded by the ghosts of bureaucrats, ministers, and ruling and opposition party politicians who may be offended' (Sherman 1994: 35). Since the beginning of the 1990s, NHK had seen its audience share plunge: its morning news programme was watched by only around 10 per cent of viewers, for example. Internal political problems have plagued the corporation: in July 1991 President Shima Keiji was forced to step down following a sexual scandal. Shima – who was President for only two years, but had been the prime mover in NHK during the time of his predecessor – had a background as a political reporter and a former foreign correspondent in the United States. An unusually forceful man who made enemies on account of his allegedly dictatorial management style, Shima attempted to impose his own vision upon the organization. Krauss describes Shima as:

> A man with vision who sensed that the balance between state and society had been shifting and knew that NHK had to respond, but who ultimately was too much the product of the very institutional networks that needed changing.
>
> (Krauss 2000: 268)

Shima's vision included two key elements: at a domestic level, he sought to spice up NHK news programmes and make them more like their American counterparts; at an international level, he sought to give NHK global reach, producing satellite programmes that could be marketed abroad.

For this latter project, Shima pioneered English-language programming over which foreigners (mainly Americans) would have editorial control, rather than the traditional NHK approach of using native speakers of English simply as the mouthpieces of Japanese staff. From the outset, these projects led to considerable conflict. Some of the foreign staff argued that unless the material shown was incisive and sometimes controversial, the programmes would have no appeal to non-Japanese audiences. In particular, *Japan Business Today* was plagued with problems, non-Japanese staff insisting that it was not acceptable simply to depict positive aspects of Japan.[11] Even more problematic was the 'friendship programme' *China Now*, which screened material supplied by

Chinese government television; staff were forbidden to mention Tiananmen Square, Taiwanese independence, or unrest in Tibet (Cunningham 1993).[12] Such policies reflected Japanese desires to avoid offending Asian neighbours, especially those who had previously suffered at the hands of the Japanese military. In view of this ultra-cautious stance, the idea that NHK could seriously compete with CNN or BBC World Service Television was difficult to credit. Following the precipitate departure of Shima, there were moves by the incoming President to rid NHK of his legacy. In September 1994, *Japan Business Today* was taken off the air, while most of the English-language staff of another programme, *Asia Now*, were laid off. NHK reacted indignantly to the charge that it was carrying out 'ethnic cleansing' of its news staff, arguing that the changes reflected differences in editorial approach.[13] The new programming regime at NHK was essentially a function of policy changes and organizational politics, rather than a concerted attempt to suppress dissenting foreign voices: Shima loyalists were gradually moved out of key positions, and Shima projects quietly wound down.

The climate of the post-Shima era at NHK, however, was one of caution and conservatism. NHK did not try to capitalize on the end of the '1955 system' of LDP dominance in order to establish a more critical stance on the reporting of political news. If there was an 'opening up' of the Japanese political order around the time of the July 1993 general election, then NHK was neither willing nor able to come out and play in the new democratic space. Krauss argues that NHK ultimately 'serves the LDP-dominated state far better than Kume's deconstruction of it' (2000: 271), and was likely to enjoy political protection from the Japanese establishment even as the public broadcaster's once-huge influence waned. Whereas in many other countries conservative ruling parties took a hostile view of public broadcasters, in Japan the LDP felt more threatened by commercial networks. This sympathetic understanding between NHK and the LDP was clearly a mixed blessing for NHK, reducing pressures to liven up its coverage.

Beyond political realignments

Given the inertia that seemed now to beset NHK and many other Japanese news organizations, the way forward for political journalism in Japan remained unclear. A serious problem was the lack of an independent sector. There were relatively few freelance journalists and they were hard-pressed to make a living, given that the big media groups filled their publications almost entirely with material generated in-house. One exception was the weekly and monthly magazine sector, which did use freelance material and also published critical, often scurrilous and almost invariably anonymous, articles by moonlighting 'mainstream' journalists. This allowed an outlet for frustrated reporters to express their real views – but since sensationalism is more or less obligatory in these magazines, the impact of stories appearing in them is strictly limited. Although the flourishing (if somewhat disreputable) magazine sector could be seen as evidence that press freedom was alive and well in contemporary Japan, critics viewed it as a typical social-defence mechanism that helped perpetuate the prevailing order.

With the benefit of hindsight, the optimism of foreign correspondents that the Japanese media had made major political breakthroughs at the time of the 1993 election soon looked distinctly premature. Whilst the relationship between the media and politicians certainly altered – and press clubs were somewhat side-stepped during the Hosokawa and Hata administrations (Cooper-Chen 1997: 43–4) – there was no decisive break with the old convivialities of the *kisha* club system. The electronic media was somewhat chastened by the experience of the Tsubaki case. Japanese journalists shared with other citizens a sense of perplexity about political developments since the 1993 election, including the rise to power in June 1994 of a once unthinkable hybrid LDP–Social Democratic Party coalition, and the eventual reconciliation of Ozawa and the LDP at the end of 1998. The Japanese media, like the Japanese public, had somewhat lost their political bearings, unable any longer to distinguish between government and opposition, progressives and conservatives, pro-reformers and anti-reformers, left and right, right and wrong. Subsequent political developments brought little clarification. For the time being at least, the capacity of the Japanese media to function as an effective institution of civil society remained in serious doubt. Discussing the related question of Japan's much trumpeted 'political reform', Chalmers Johnson warned commentators to see Japan 'as it is, rather than as theorists or propagandists wish it to be' (Johnson 1995: 231). The dangers of over-estimating the forces of reform or political change in a society such as Japan's were very real.

Nevertheless, Japan's leading newspaper groups sought to present themselves as opinion-leaders and focal points for important political debates, a trend epitomized by the decision of the *Yomiuri* group to publish its own proposals for revision of the Japanese constitution in 1994 (Sugiyama 2000: 199–200). The *Yomiuri* group had established its own research institute, with the explicit aim of studying important political and social issues.[14] The *Yomiuri* proposal was met by counter-proposals for a 'Basic Peace Law' from the pacifist magazine *Sekai*, and for an 'International Cooperation Law' advocated by the *Asahi* newspaper.[15] Hook and McCormack observed that the constitutional debate was monopolized by 'elite political intellectual and media groups' and did not deeply engage wider Japanese society (Hook and McCormack 2001: 42). It was as though, stung by criticism of its unhealthy preoccupation with the minutiae of LDP factional politics, the media sought the moral and political high ground after 1993.

Despite this high-minded posturing, major media groups emerged with little credit from their coverage of important news stories during the 1990s.[16] A particularly shameful episode was their appalling coverage of events relating to the Aum Shinrikyo sarin attacks. The media initially colluded with the inept police investigation of the 1994 Matsumoto attack, blaming an innocent salaryman and failing to finger the obvious culprits (Hamilton 2000: 93–4). Japanese media coverage of the 1995 Kobe earthquake was similarly problematic; in particular, the fact that many earthquake victims were members of minority groups – ethnic Koreans and 'untouchable' *burakumin* – was systematically ignored in news reports. With a few exceptions, such as a television crew working on the NTV infotainment programme *Sunday*, the media stuck to official views of the earthquake, and ignored criticisms of the Japanese relief efforts that appeared in the international media (MacLachlan 2001: 122–5).

Koizumi, Tanaka and the politics of the 'wide show'

The rise to the premiership of Koizumi Junichiro reflected significant changes in the nature of Japanese politics. Koizumi was expressly selected as LDP leader, not because of his strong support among party factions, but because of his potential appeal to voters and his outstanding media credentials. Despite the fact that only party members were eligible to vote in the internal LDP elections, Koizumi and three other rivals campaigned on the streets, and appeared on more than twenty talk shows. One independent Diet member argued that 'television programmes were created to make Mr Koizumi a leader' (Nomura 2001). Koizumi's role was to act as an attractive front man for a tarnished and weary party, exploiting his personal popularity for political advantage. Given his weak standing within the LDP itself – his image was that of a loner and maverick, nicknamed 'the eccentric person' – Koizumi was obliged to engage in political grandstanding in order to promote his agenda. His relationship with the media thus became a central part of his *modus operandi*; like Western politicians such as Bill Clinton or Tony Blair, he placed enormous emphasis on media management, working closely with 'spin doctors' who sought to present his actions and policies in a positive light. Media coverage of Koizumi focused on such unlikely details as the kind of blue hair gel he used to maintain his lion-like permed mane (Magnier 2001a), as well as his private life as a divorced single parent with a fondness for kickboxing, heavy metal and wrestling, who often travelled on ordinary trains. Opinion polls within weeks of Koizumi's inauguration as Prime Minister in April 2001 gave him approval ratings of nearly 90 per cent, while his parliamentary speeches proved popular even with viewers of daytime television. More than half a million people signed up to receive the Prime Minister's weekly e-mail 'magazine', believed to be a world record (*Japan Times*, 14 June 2001). The first magazine opened with a message from Koizumi, stating:

> Many people know me as an eccentric with leonine hair. I want you to learn more about the real face of the Koizumi cabinet from this magazine. My cabinet is pushing for reform. Successful reform calls for dialogue with each and every one of you.
> (Quoted in NHK Broadcasting Culture and Research Institute News, no. 17, Summer 2001.)

Koizumi clearly preferred direct language to the elliptical utterances favoured by many of his colleagues; he sought explicitly to appeal directly to voters, over the heads of established political institutions and practices.

The upper house elections of July 2001 were preceded by an extraordinary hour-long NTV television programme entitled '100 women vs. Koizumi', in which Koizumi took questions from a studio audience of women. The programme drew criticism from other broadcasters and opposition parties, who accused NTV of pro-Koizumi bias (Nomura 2001). Because his enthusiasm for appearing on so-called 'wide shows', (down-market television programmes typically featuring celebrity gossip and sensational crimes) was shared by other associates, such as Foreign Minister Tanaka Makiko, Koizumi's team was popularly labelled the 'wide-show cabinet' (*Asahi Shimbun*, 20 July 2001). Koizumi's chief spin-doctor was his so-called 'general producer' Iijima Isao, who had served as his secretary for thirty years. Iijima decided to allow the television cameras into the Prime Minister's official residence for the first time, and encouraged Koizumi to address the public directly through television, rather than following normal practice and leaving the Chief Cabinet Secretary to handle the media via scripted, bureaucratic speeches. Tahara Soichiro, the interviewer who had mercilessly pressed Miyazawa on political reform in 1993, admired Koizumi's mastery of the medium of television, arguing that television interviews clearly revealed the trustworthiness of a politician: 'if Koizumi starts to split hairs, viewers will soon drop him'. Miyazawa himself declared 'In all my 50 years of Japanese politics, this is the first time I've felt such a free atmosphere. I hope he can do what he's outlined' (Magnier 2001a). Others were more critical. Karel van Wolferen argued that Koizumi and Tanaka had become a daily media soap opera, diverting attention from substantive discussion about reform. He described the media as 'the biggest obstacle to political reform' in Japan (Nomura 2001). Ellis Krauss observed that prime ministerial popularity was a double-edged sword; while Koizumi could wield his popularity to good effect so long as it endured, any tarnishing of his public image could rebound on him with disastrous consequences.

The new marketing of politics by television was illustrated by a new Nippon TV weekly drama serial *Let's Go Nagatacho*, which provided a thinly fictionalized account of Japanese politics under Koizumi (Brasor 2001). In this series, the fictitious prime minister's extraordinary good looks had women reporters swooning at press briefings. Meanwhile, the real Koizumi was celebrated in a wide range of marketing spin-offs, including photo books, mobile phone straps and other consumer items. Yet, as *Time* argued, 'Koizumi the maverick is very much a product of the establishment' (Larimer 2001), shaped by his early political experiences as the secretary of former Prime Minister Fukuda. Among his best slogans was 'Change the LDP, change Japan'; but Koizumi's beloved 'structural reform with no sacred cows' was arguably more about destroying certain LDP factions than transforming Japan's governance. As a result, his enemies within the party were watching him, waiting for mistakes that could prove his undoing: his Thatcherite plans for privatizations and spending cuts would have undermined the traditional patronage basis of Japan's politics. Larimer argued that Hosokawa had been a 'proto-Koizumi' whose media-based premiership quickly unravelled following a minor scandal; Koizumi could all too easily suffer a similar fall from grace. In an interview, Hosokawa suggested that Koizumi was trying to reform from the inside what he had tried to reform from the outside, but warned against underestimating the deep and strong roots of the Japanese system (Larimer 2001).

Ironically, one of the secrets of Koizumi's success, his alliance with the highly popular Foreign Minister Tanaka Makiko, proved a window of vulnerability. Daughter of legendary former Prime Minister and kingmaker Tanaka Kakuei, who was himself ousted from power following a series of corruption scandals in the 1970s, Tanaka was well-known for her barbed criticisms of leading figures in the LDP – and was quickly at loggerheads both with fellow politicians and with bureaucrats at the Foreign Ministry (Kwan Weng Kin 2001). Despite her apparently strong credentials for the post, including an excellent command of English, Tanaka soon became infamous for her public gaffes, and by late 2001 she had been largely bypassed: foreign policy was being made in practice by the Chief Cabinet Secretary and the Prime Minister's Office (Magnier 2001b). Tanaka was systematically undercut by her own bureaucrats in what was termed a 'death-by-1000 leaks strategy', turning the normally sleepy Foreign Ministry into a media circus. While Koizumi apparently planned to send her on more overseas trips and 'lean on her to tone down the trash talk' (Larimer 2001)

Foreign Ministry officials sought instead to marginalize her by not letting her move, not letting her speak and depriving her of information about what was going on. The discrepancy between her terrible professional reputation and her extraordinary public support grew ever more vast, reflecting popular distrust of politicians and bureaucrats, and Tanaka's capacity to present herself as ranged against the entrenched sources of power Koizumi termed 'resisting forces' (*teiko seiryoku*) (Ishikawa 2001). When the row over Tanaka's performance reached fever pitch in February 2002, Koizumi responded by firing her – thereby dramatically undercutting the popularity on which his administration so heavily relied (*Japan Times*, 6 February 2002). By the end of March, his government's approval rating had fallen to around 45 per cent, while Tanaka had begun a campaign to rebuild her career by wooing the domestic and international media with stories of Koizumi's perfidy (Green 2002).

The antics of Koizumi and Tanaka, while extremely entertaining and generating greatly increased public interest in national issues, testified to the emergence of a new form of media engagement with Japanese politics. Politics was increasingly becoming itself a 'wide show', a sensationalized spectator sport in which substantive polices were subordinated to sound-bites. Despite public fascination with Koizumi, he had no effective control over his own party, let alone his government; despite the popularity of Tanaka, she was a pariah inside her own ministry.

The triumph of presentation over substance epitomized by the rise of politicians such as Koizumi and Tanaka was now a key feature of Japanese politics.[17] These figures sought to bolster their popularity and image as 'reformers' – a singularly ill-defined concept in the Japanese context – by making extensive use of media opportunities for self-promotion. In the absence of substantive policy debates, media profiling and hype surrounding individual politicians became an alternative way of engaging the public with the political order. The elevation of certain politicians to 'stardom' by the press and by television had become an alternative form of political agency by the Japanese media, a form of agency with potentially unhealthy consequences for the democratic process.

'Wide-show' politics was a phenomenon fraught with dangers. Since 'wide-show' programmes were often based on groundless rumours and poorly substantiated news – sensational so-called 'report floods' (*houdou kouzui*) – politicians could use them to build up a flimsy form of popularity, lacking in substance and largely unrelated to actual policy positions. By contrast, important policy debates that could not be marketed through this medium would not be properly aired, and thus could not win public interest and support. Koizumi's inability to implement a programme of reforms partly reflected the vagueness of many of his proposals, but was also inextricable from the media's fixation with short-term and superficial questions of image. Tanaka remained popular as Foreign Minister despite displaying troubling views on the US–Japan partnership (the cornerstone of Japanese foreign policy), an excessively pro-China stance and a willingness to leak military secrets. Her policies would not withstand critical scrutiny, but wide-show politics did not require this kind of attention to inconvenient details.

If the Japanese media prior to 1993 was overly dull and excessively deferential towards dinosaur LDP politicians who were profoundly inept communicators, the situation had been transformed a decade later. Now, politicians rose and fell on the basis of their ability to manipulate the media. During the 1990s, the great bastions of Japanese success so lauded in Ezra Vogel's classic *Japan as Number One* (Vogel 1979) were demolished one at a time by an increasingly iconoclastic media: the bureaucracy, medical services, the police, and big companies fell like skittles in quick succession. Yet the media singularly failed to engage in any substantive self-criticism, often preferring to trivialize rather than to offer more constructive and serious analyses. Koizumi was a creature of this new 'wide-show' politics, living and dying at the whim of daytime television audiences.

Conclusion

Prior to 1993, the Japanese media frequently treated politicians with fawning obsequiousness. Relations between the media and politics under the 1955 system were characterized by:

- The dominance of print media over electronic media.
- The primacy of the 'big five' daily newspapers and NHK over all other news sources.

- A cosy and collusive *kisha* club system that excluded 'outsiders' and favoured the creation of close ties between key reporters and prominent politicians.
- Difficulty in breaking controversial news stories, especially scandals or issues likely to cause embarrassment to the ruling LDP.
- Preoccupations with the minutiae of factional politics at the expense of the bigger picture.

The temporary downfall of the LDP in 1993 reflected (but was by no means entirely caused by) new trends in media coverage of politics:

- The rise of commercial broadcasters, notably TV Asahi, and a tendency for certain news programmes to present politics in a more accessible style.
- Tougher treatment of LDP politicians in interviews, and more critical and satirical presentations of political developments in news programmes.
- The rise of more telegenic politicians with better communication skills.

In the wake of the 1993 Tsubaki case, however, the internally divided nature of the Japanese media became apparent; critical broadcasters seemed to lose some of their nerve, and for a time the press and television lost its political bearings. In the mid 1990s, the media were still presenting important stories such as the Aum gas attacks and the Kobe earthquake in a distorted and uncritical fashion, illustrating a failure to reform their working practices. At the same time, they developed an appetite for muck-raking, highlighting a series of scandals in many of Japan's most respected institutions.

The late 1990s saw the emergence of a new form of media-focused politics:

- Politicians such as Koizumi and Tanaka became adept at using 'wide-show' television programmes to promote themselves.
- Television became a means of reaching out directly to voters, so bypassing formal party and political structures.

- Yet this form of politicking was highly superficial, and arguably diverted attention from more substantive policy questions about the real nature of much-needed reforms.
- Media had become a more important actor than before.

It might be argued that 'wide-show' politics promoted greater public engagement with politics, and thus saw media acting as more effective agents of restraint, checking and balancing the power of politicians. Yet it could also be suggested that electronic media were now simply doing the bidding of power-holders, in a different and perhaps more dangerous way from the old model of sycophantic *kisha* clubs. Given that the wide-show mode of media engagement with politics is relatively new, the verdict on both of these readings must remain for the moment the Scottish one of 'not proven'.

The Japanese case raises important comparative questions relevant to an understanding of the politics of Pacific Asia more generally. Evidence for political liberalization needs to be closely scrutinized. In Japan, as in many other Asian countries, media practitioners and media organizations have ambiguous relationships with holders of political power. Apparent signs of incipient media-induced or media-backed democratic change need to be treated with considerable caution, given the limitations of the mass media as an institution for effecting and sustaining political transformations. Greater empowerment of the media vis-à-vis politicians may or may not prove a positive step for programmes of political change and reform.

4 Media as an agent of stability? Suharto's Indonesia

Introduction

On 21 June 1994, three leading weekly publications in Indonesia were permanently banned by the government. These bannings raise important questions about the political role and functions of the press, which will be explored here.

A core assumption of this book is that the press should be regarded as a political institution in its own right. Broadly speaking, students of politics have underestimated the extent to which media serve as political institutions, while journalists have successfully discouraged observers from recognizing their role as political actors (Cook 1998: 4). Yet in developing countries such as Indonesia, the centrality of the media's political role has long been recognized; as discussed in Chapter 1, President Suharto saw the media as agents of stability that would serve to legitimate his authoritarian, developmentalist rule. He was therefore resistant to more critical forms of media agency, which could involve the media in acting to restrain or even to change the activities or policies of the state.

Much of the Indonesian press was engaged in the kind of essentially uncritical 'development journalism' favoured by the authorities, serving primarily as an agent of stability. But during the last weeks of the regime in April and May 1998, critical reporting (for example, by the English-language daily *Jakarta Post* and the outspoken weekly *Detektif & Romantika*) served as an agent of change, helping to undermine the ailing New Order.[1] This chapter deals with the regime's attempts to prevent the Indonesian press from institutionalizing an intermediate role as an agent of restraint.

The Indonesian press

Indonesia[2] has a long tradition of an outspoken press (Hill 1994, Hanazaki 1996). During the revolutionary period (1945–9) and the early years of independence from the Dutch, the Indonesian press was an agent of change, a 'fighting press' dedicated to the cause of popular freedom. When President Sukarno replaced the constitutional democracy of the early independence period with his populist authoritarian 'guided democracy', the domestication of the press began in earnest. The New Order – a semi-authoritarian political system led by President Suharto from 1966 until his dramatic resignation in May 1998 – gradually refined mechanisms for state control of the press.[3] Only licensed publications could be sold, and publication licences could be revoked either on technical grounds or because their editorial content displeased the government (see Hanazaki 1996: 89). Newspapers and other publications were banned regularly during the New Order. All Indonesian publications were subject to close monitoring and control by the Department of Information, which was headed by a Cabinet minister. Formally, all journalists were required to be members of the PWI, a journalists' association, which was thoroughly penetrated by the government, effectively serving as an instrument of state policy. Only approved PWI members were entitled to serve as chief editors and publishers.

Various means of formal and informal control were used to limit press freedom. Editors commonly received telephone calls from Department of Information officials or military officers warning them that a particular story had over-stepped the mark, a practice joking referred to as the 'telephone culture' (Hanazaki 1996: 84). There were carrots as well as sticks: reporters covering ministerial or other official activities commonly received envelopes containing money, referred to as the 'envelope culture' (Hanazaki 1996: 127–30). From the 1980s onwards, it became common for individuals close to the government to acquire shares in media enterprises. Former Information Minister Harmoko himself was reliably reported to have shares in thirty-one different media concerns (Hanazaki 1996:

137–8, 150–1). Essentially, this ministerial 'share ownership' was little more than a protection racket intended to shield the publication from problems with the government. Practices such as these encouraged a climate of self-censorship. While some commentators claimed that the Indonesian press was very free if you knew how to 'read between the lines' – parodied by former editor Aristides Katoppo as 'reading between the lies' (Hill 1994: 46) – various sensitive matters were permanently off-limits, especially any stories that might inflame racial, ethnic or religious tensions. Other stories frowned upon by the government included those which revealed conflicts or tensions within the ruling elite, such as disagreements between military leaders and civilian ministers.

By the 1990s, the Indonesian press was big business. Leading quality daily *Kompas* sold over 500,000 copies, downmarket *Pos Kota* sold only slightly fewer than *Kompas* and ten other newspapers had circulations above 100,000, including regional dailies in major Javanese cities outside Jakarta. There were also thriving weekly and monthly sectors (Hill 1994: 165–9). Television was perhaps an even more important medium for communicating information, but broadcasters were permanently caught in a tension between the state's demands for 'development television' and other pressures for more openness (Kitley 2000: 334). In 1989 and 1990, President Suharto gave some public hints that he would tolerate a greater degree of political openness than before, and the press became more daring than hitherto (Hanazaki 1996: 156–63). As a result, there was extremely bold reporting of issues such as the 1991 Dili massacre and other military abuses, reporting which would have been unthinkable in the 1980s.[4] By 1994, the weekly tabloid *DeTik* was leading the way by printing what were, by Indonesian standards, breath-takingly provocative articles, usually in the form of interviews with various dissidents, including outspoken military officers. The weekly news magazines *Editor*, and (rather more cautiously) *Tempo* followed suit. In many ways, *DeTik*'s coverage was the most significant development, since this brash new publication appealed to a wider audience than the largely well-educated readership of traditional weeklies. This apparent loosening of restrictions on press freedom came to an abrupt end on 21 June 1994, when three leading weekly news publications, *Tempo*, *Editor* and *DeTik*, were unexpectedly banned.

What was *Tempo*?

The attack on press freedom represented by the June 1994 banning of *Tempo*, *Editor* and *DeTik*, was greeted with outrage by observers both inside and outside the country. *Tempo* had been banned for two months in 1982, on account of its incisive coverage of the general election campaign. This new and permanent ban was far more draconian, coinciding as it did with the two other closures. The Information Department called in the editors of four publications (*Jakarta Post*, *Sinar Pagi*, *Media Indonesia*, and *Forum Keadilan*) to complain about their coverage of the bans. There were street demonstrations protesting about the closures, and on 27 June riot police and soldiers attacked two separate groups of around 150 demonstrators with rattan canes, resulting in ten injuries and twenty arrests (McBeth 1994). The intense and unprecedented public reaction to the bannings illustrated the strength of feeling the clampdown aroused, a popular sense that expectations of greater openness had proved groundless.

Asked about his reaction to the banning of *Tempo*, media analyst Daniel Dhakidae explained:

> *Tempo* is part of the New Order thing . . . it is a part and parcel of the New Order . . . so why should they ban *Tempo* which is part of their personality, part of the development of Indonesia? . . . How could they do it, it's impossible, it's like killing one's own self.[5]

For Dhakidae, the act of killing *Tempo* signified a form of suicide by the Suharto regime. Aristides Katoppo made a similar point, arguing that *Tempo* was 'really the product of the Establishment. You cannot say that *Tempo* was the opposition.'[6] *Tempo* chief editor Goenawan Mohamad himself acknowledged that *Tempo* could best be seen as a 'mainstream' publication.[7] He argued for a more nuanced understanding of the magazine, rejecting both establishment and anti-establishment labels: 'it's very hard to say that *Tempo* is radical and it's even harder to say that it's progovernment'. Instead, *Tempo* was a 'polyvalent' publication, 'many voices, many colours, inside one publication', changing over time depending on a variety of factors, including the demands of its readers. He explained *Tempo*'s relations with the government, especially during the magazine's early years, as follows:

> Our strategy was not to be close to the government, but not to be distant from it – for the sake of power, access to information, we had to be close. And the government itself was not a monolithic one, never was. So you have to keep some distance from certain elements of the government, and keep some proximity to some elements . . . we always had a problem with the security branch of government, not because we were radicals, no, because we wanted more stories.

Early *Tempo* was broadly aligned with the technocratic policies of the original New Order and its 'Berkeley mafia', which emphasized the rational management of economic issues.[8] The New Order was in no sense monolithic: rather, it was semi-porous, and *Tempo* sought out leaks and openings wherever possible. As journalists, *Tempo* staff found themselves in conflict with the military and intelligence services when they experienced difficulty in getting stories.

Herry Komar, a former *Tempo* journalist who became chief editor of the new magazine *Gatra*, argued that *Tempo* always supported the government.[9] It contained 'critical content' on certain issues and there were divergences of political views among the editorial team, but much of the focus of reporting was the coverage of government activities. *Tempo*'s mission was to communicate political developments to the people. Another ex-*Tempo* staffer spoke of the excitement of the early period of the New Order, the sense of being involved in a new beginning for Indonesia after the mismanagement and chaos of the late Sukarno years.[10] The contradiction inherent in the bannings was highlighted by a *Tempo* journalist interviewed in 1994:

> I consider myself a nationalist . . . . Before, I made excuses for what the government did to others. Now I can't. When are we going to grow up?
>
> (McBeth 1994)

By 1994, the New Order was not so new any more – but almost thirty years old. *Tempo* had become more questioning and more critical, as the Suharto regime (itself, of course, like *Tempo*, always containing many voices) was becoming less rational, and more centred on the President personally. As Goenawan put it:

> Why has the President increasingly become less tolerant of other voices? He could have stepped down as one of the greatest leaders in the history of Indonesia. But the latter part of his government consists of less and less rational bureaucratization of the way Indonesia should be ruled. It has become more and more personalized.
>
> (AJI 1997: xv)

Senior staff at *Tempo*, led by Goenawan, were becoming less happy with the actions of the government and increasingly wanted to be more outspoken in their reporting and commentary. In feeling this way, they believed they were simply reflecting the views of their readers. Goenawan acknowledged there was a 'slight change' in the tone of the magazine in its final years,[11] though he also argued that examples of more critical reporting could also be seen in early *Tempo*, notably the disclosure of the magnitude of state oil company Pertamina's debts in 1975. *Tempo* did run features on certain stories that were embarrassing to the government and often adopted an extremely cynical writing style which must have made senior government figures very uncomfortable.[12] Yet if *Tempo* is seen partly as of the regime as well as against the regime, then the banning of *Tempo* signifies not simply the closure of a magazine by a government but the onset of the disintegration of the New Order as hitherto understood. The closure of *Tempo* was the beginning of the end for the Suharto government. *Tempo* was as much an agent of stability as an agent of restraint. So why was *Tempo*, so close to some elements of the regime since the beginning, the victim of a summary execution?

The bannings as a reflection of wider political developments

The New Order covered and sometimes criticized by *Tempo* was originally represented as an attempt to replace ideology, fervour and fanaticism with bureaucratic rationality. Nationalism was not swept aside, but was largely displaced for most practical purposes by a preoccupation with economic development. For the New Order, the pursuit of economic development became a kind of substitute ideology. Policy decisions were supposed to be made on rational grounds by economists with American PhDs, rather than by charismatic demagogues who relished symbolic action. By 1971, the year of *Tempo*'s founding, the Cabinet contained ten professors and several other members with impressive academic credentials; it included six leading economists, among them the Ministers of Trade and Finance (Crouch 1988: 321–6). The military assumed a dual function, dominating civilian politics as well as security matters. The considerable autonomy the military possessed enabled many Army officers to use their positions for economic gain.

Despite its rhetoric of technocracy and developmentalism, the New Order was afflicted from the outset by a grave discrepancy between appearance and reality. Whole sectors of the economy were effectively outside the control of the relevant ministers. Technocrats continued to play an important role in the New Order, but in a March 1993 reshuffle several key figures were dropped from the Cabinet (Schwarz 1999: 73). The technocrats had become fall guys for economic problems, some of which were the result of structural corruption outside their control. The New Order appeared to be renewing itself, shifting in a different direction. Arief Budiman argued that Suharto was changing his strategic alliances, shifting from Chinese business to Muslim business, from Christian brain to Muslim brain, and from the military to Islam (Budiman 1994).

This new direction was symbolized by the rise of B. J. Habibie, whom Suharto had known since Habibie's boyhood. Habibie had trained as an aeronautical engineer and spent his early adult life in Germany before being invited by Suharto to return to Indonesia to help develop the country. As one foreign correspondent noted when looking to explain the 1994 press bannings: 'Everything leads back to Mr Habibie's vision for Indonesia and the enemies he has made while pursuing it' (Williams 1994). Habibie argued that there was a convergence between power and technology: really powerful countries had always been at the cutting edge of high technology. If Indonesia was to move beyond a subordinate position vis-à-vis the West (and, for that matter, Japan and the newly industrializing economies) it could only do so by pioneering its own high-tech industries. In other words, instead of the incremental economic development and industrialization advocated by the technocrats (echoing the advice of the American-dominated World Bank and IMF), Indonesia ought to make a quantum leap to a high-tech economy. This had to be accomplished by substantial government investment of money and resources to kick-start new industrial projects. The showpiece for this new policy was to be an Indonesian aircraft industry. Habibie and his supporters were generally described as 'technologists' or 'technologues'. At the same time they were also nationalists, basing their arguments upon a vision of Indonesian greatness rather than a purely technical and scientific rationale. In addition, they emphasized their Muslim identity; Habibie was the first head of the Islamic intellectual association ICMI, established in December 1990 (Ramage 1995: 75–121). William Liddle observed that the ICMI was 'an organization with an Islamic name but with minimal Islamic content', a 'state corporatist' organization controlled by the President himself (Liddle 1996b: 615).

Distrust of Habibie's ideas was widespread. The cabinet was divided over projects such as the aircraft plan, which promised to consume considerable government funding with no certainty of success. Habibie's control over ten 'strategic industries' brought him into conflict with some elements of the military: 'the military lost lucrative commissions, and the ability to decide for itself what needed to be purchased' (Williams 1994).

During the period from 1990 to 1994, there were numerous indications that Habibie was positioning himself politically, setting up a number of projects to support his challenge to technocratic arguments. In 1993, Habibie set up the Indonesian-language newspaper *Republika*, partly as a Muslim counterweight to the best-selling quality newspaper *Kompas*, which had strong Christian connections (Hanazaki 1996: 178–83). *Republika* rapidly established itself as a major newspaper, with an August 1993 estimated circulation of 125,000. He subsequently bought an English-language newspaper, *The Indonesia Times*, with which he sought to challenge the relatively small-circulation (but high-quality and very influential) *Jakarta Post*. Habibie also established a think-tank known as the Center for Information and Development Studies (CIDES), to counter the influence of the technocratic Center for Strategic and International Studies (CSIS).

While economists at the World Bank – supported by sections of the media, including *Tempo* – were calling for deregulation of the Indonesian economy and the breakup of monopolies and cartels, Habibie argued for selective protectionism of key industries. Suharto himself was becoming increasingly irritated by technocratic voices that were often critical of the business privileges obtained by his children. Habibie's ideas, with their promise of a future Indonesia not reliant upon Western technology or aid – and therefore not obliged to listen to moralizing voices from either inside or outside the country – struck the right chord. Problems in the Indonesian economy could be blamed, not on distortions created by nepotism and structural corruption, but on the shortcomings of Western-educated technocrats who had advocated a form of dependent development. Habibie argued that whereas the pursuit of 'comparative advantage' brought short-term gains, in the long term this approach would fail, as international investors moved capital to other economies with lower labour costs. Only through gaining technological competitive advantage could Indonesia ensure that 'national economic development will no longer be determined by the international division of labour' (Schwarz 1999: 86).

Habibie faced strong opponents on two fronts: the military, and the secular and Christian media and intelligentsia. He had encroached into the spheres of influence of both groups. *Tempo* – whose deputy chief editor Fikri Jufri was a close associate of CSIS patron Benny Murdani (Crouch 1994a) – was not a natural supporter of Habibienomics. Both *Tempo* and CSIS belonged to the old New Order, and had grown more critical of the Suharto regime during the 1980s and early 1990s. This is not to suggest that CSIS and *Tempo* were always close. Rather, by the 1990s Murdani had found in Fikri Jufri an agreeable companion, and a useful media ally. By 1994, Fikri had taken over day-to-day management of *Tempo* from Goenawan. Just as CSIS was losing much of its influence, so *Tempo*'s circulation was starting to decline, having fallen from a peak of 200,000 during the Gulf War, to around 160,000. As the New Order sought to renew itself with a technologist, nationalist and Islamicist hue, the climate was changing. When it emerged that Finance Minister Mar'ie Muhammad had initially refused to authorize the purchase of thirty nine ex-East German warships, claiming that their refurbishment was overpriced, *Tempo* and other publications covered the story with some relish. At the centre of the row was Habibie, who had engineered the purchase of the second-hand ships (Crouch 1994c: 123–5). Here was a futurologist, an expert in high technology, advocating the purchase of obsolete warships from a country that had already ceased to exist. Worse still, the ships would be too expensive. When one of the warships actually sank on the way to Indonesia, the story was irresistible.

The story of the 39 warships, written up in detail by many publications including *Tempo* and *DeTik*, did not result from investigative reporting by the media. This was not a news agenda emanating from a critical press hostile to Habibie, a vocal civil society criticizing the policies of the state. On the contrary.

There were two main sources for the story: the Finance Minister himself, and the military. The critical reporting that led to the closure of the three publications in June 1994 was reporting licensed and incited by elements of Indonesia's political elite. In 1993, *DeTik* had carried an interview with senior army officer Major General Sembiring Meliala in which he expressed open antipathy to Habibie. Crouch noted that:

> Although the military in the past had not been especially dedicated to the principle of a free press, some senior officers appreciated the opportunities that the presence of independent magazines offered to undermine Habibie. They were therefore reluctant to endorse Soeharto's closure of the three weeklies.
> (Crouch 1994b)

In other words, an independent media could operate successfully where its independence served the purposes of elements in the ruling elite. The weeklies were performing an important function as agents of restraint, sending crucial signals to the President concerning the limits of his lieutenants' tolerance. However, when Suharto came to feel that critical media coverage was serving the interests of the military at the expense of Habibie, opening up fissures and conflicts in the elite that he preferred to conceal and to suppress, he took the decision to close down the three publications. What appeared on one level to be an increasingly pluralist order characterized by greater openness and more political and press freedom, was also an elite-dominated order in which the media served as an outlet for high-level infighting.

Explaining the 1994 bannings

Hanazaki has suggested three 'theories' to account for the 1994 bannings: the 'Habibie–*Tempo* antagonism theory', the 'political intrigue paranoia theory', and the 'intimidation theory' (Hanazaki 1996: 206–12). The first theory argues that the publication were banned because it antagonized Habibie, who sought retribution. The second theory argues that the publications were in league with other anti-Habibie elements, led by Benny Murdani, in trying to topple Habibie; the bannings were a punishment for their plotting. The third theory argues that the bannings were Suharto's way of reasserting control, warning critical voices in Indonesian society not to overstep the mark. Hanazaki himself dismissed the Habibie–*Tempo* antagonism theory in less than a page (Hanazaki 1996: 207). Arguing that Suharto would not have accepted the political costs of the bannings simply to please Habibie, Hanazaki supported a combination of the second and third theories. Some commentators have gone further, arguing that Habibie himself opposed the bannings as counter-productive and would have preferred to take the publications to court.[13]

An alternative way of understanding the bannings is to see them primarily in terms of a response to a perceived elite conflict that posed a challenge to Suharto's revised New Order. This interpretation borrows elements from all three theories referred to by Hanazaki; it perhaps owes most to his 'political intrigue paranoia theory'. Yet hostility towards Habibie in various quarters did not necessarily lead to any real intrigue, let alone a full-blown conspiracy. Nor, given the political conditions in Indonesia, was paranoia necessarily confined to the second-order players: the President himself could suffer from a degree of paranoia.

It is not necessary to believe that Benny Murdani actually served as the direct information source for the East German warships story, though Hanazaki suggests that he may have done (Hanazaki 1996: 41). Even if Murdani or another military-connected source did provide such information, as was entirely probable, this did not amount to a conspiracy. The story was a genuine news story of legitimate public interest, and whatever the source, a magazine such as *Tempo* had every right and reason to publish it. Nevertheless, Suharto saw the criticism of Habibie and the warships deal as a disguised challenge to his own authority. As Hanazaki observed, 'those who wanted change but were not yet brave enough to point at Suharto himself, directed criticism at Habibie' (Hanazaki 1996: 208–9).

This was the real strength of the Habibie–*Tempo* antagonism theory; for 'Habibie', read 'Suharto'. The warships' coverage may not have been inspired by a conspiracy, but it certainly revealed the extent to which a range of hostile voices were now speaking out against the New Order, and especially against the regime's bid to revise and revive itself with a new Islamic, nationalist, technologist agenda. Conspiracy or no conspiracy, to a somewhat paranoid President in an intensely paranoid political order, it looked like hostile intrigue. The degree of actual intrigue was irrelevant: the three publications were banned because Suharto believed (rightly or wrongly) that they were part of a movement against him, a challenge to his authority, and a threat to his attempts to renew the New Order.

The order to close the magazines must have come from Suharto himself. Former Information Minister Harmoko confirmed this years later in an interview with an ex-*Editor* journalist: Suharto always paid close personal attention to the press, had been disturbed by the warships story coverage, and simply instructed Harmoko to ban the three publications.[14] Yet despite Suharto's ultimate responsibility for the bans, Habibie never expressed any regrets concerning them. Hefner quotes Lukman Harun, a Muhammadiyah leader, as saying:

> *Tempo, DeTik, Editor* – why should we do anything for these magazines? What have they ever done for us? They are not Muslim publications. We Muslims have to be realistic about who our friends are and what we should support.
>
> (Hefner 2000: 165)

The bannings confirmed the growing importance of what Hefner terms 'regimist Islam' for the Suharto administration.[15]

The outcome of the bannings

The bannings of *Tempo, Editor* and *DeTik* in June 1994 were a drastic action, which provoked demonstrations across Java and inevitably aroused protests from the international community. They had the effect of backfiring. The closures implied that there really was a skeleton in the closet, something suspicious about the warship purchase that the Indonesian government did not want discussed. The robustness of the bannings indicated a hesitancy about the New Order's attempts to redirect itself in a 'technologistic' as opposed to a 'technocratic' direction. Aristides Katoppo argued that the bannings (like the government's attempts to oust Megawati from the PDI in 1996) were a big mistake: 'these things don't add to the stability of the system: they may have won the battle, but not the war'.[16] The fact that the state took such drastic action smacked of desperation, showing that it could not hold the line.

Faced with the loss of their publishing permits in June 1994, *Tempo, DeTik* and *Editor* pursued a variety of different strategies that reflected a range of alternative responses. Broadly speaking, there were two main strategies available to the publications. The first was compromise with the authorities, seeking a way to obtain a new licence and so to begin publishing again under a new title. The second was resistance, campaigning against the bannings as an injustice and seeking either to start a new publication to continue the work of the old one, or to engage in alternative politics instead of conventional journalism. *DeTik* chose resistance; *Editor* chose compromise; *Tempo* was torn in two.

Immediately after the bannings, there were a number of public protests, including meetings addressed by representatives of the banned publications. *DeTik*'s Eros Djarot was one of the main speakers at these events, along with *Tempo*'s Goenawan Mohamad. Prominent journalists from the banned publications who took part in the events were later 'blacklisted' by the PWI, making it impossible for them legally to work as editors again. Goenawan explained that he made a decision early on that he would play no part in any attempt to secure a new publishing permit. By contrast, Eros Djarot, who had taken over the weekly tabloid *DeTik* in 1993, was in no mood to quit the fray. *DeTik*, with an extremely popular formula of hard-hitting political stories that pulled few punches, had achieved a circulation of over 200,000 in the space of only a year (Hill 1994: 41).

DeTik's resistance took two forms: open participation in protests against the banning, and attempts to subvert it through legal machinations. The weekly had been formally banned on technical grounds: for violating the terms of its permit. *DeTik*'s original permit had been granted for a publication focusing on crime stories, and by turning the weekly into a political publication without official permission, the new owners had left themselves vulnerable to closure. However, *DeTik* sought to exploit legal loopholes to reinvent itself. The company bought the permit of another existing weekly, *Simponi*, and after a grand launch at the beginning of October 1994, began republishing *DeTik* under this new name. The new publication was largely staffed by ex-*DeTik* reporters and its logo was extremely similar to that of *DeTik*. This time the PWI was instrumental in halting publication: the journalists' organization withdrew its recommendation for *Simponi*'s editor the day after the first issue appeared. Perhaps unwisely, Djarot told the *Jakarta Post* that he had been reliably informed the problems experienced by *Simponi* were actually a 'personal attack' on himself. *Simponi* never appeared again.

Editor adopted the opposite course, seeking to avoid confrontation with the government, quietly accepting the banning order and concentrating on behind-the-scenes negotiations to obtain a new licence. Indeed, journalists from *Tempo* and *DeTik* were unimpressed by *Editor*'s failure to participate officially in any of the anti-banning protest activities. *Editor*'s Eddy Herwanto argued that he was in a weaker position than Goenawan or Eros, since he was not officially the editor in chief of *Editor*[17] – an argument criticized as legalistic and self-serving by journalists from other banned publications. Herwanto preferred to compromise with the regime. He sought a new publishing licence, which he eventually obtained for the new *TIRAS* magazine in January 1995 (*Republika*, 10 January 1995). In a hearing at the House of Representatives the previous month, Information Minister Harmoko had praised the former staff of *Editor* for accepting the government's decision to revoke the licence (*Jakarta Post*, 13 December 1994). The main shareholder in the new magazine was the Minister of Manpower, Abdul Latief.

Tempo faced a more difficult situation than the other two publications, since its editorial team was divided over the best course of action. On the very day of the bannings, Hashim Djojohadikusumo, brother of the special forces commander and a relative by marriage of the President, declared he could revive *Tempo* under the same name if *Tempo* would give him the power to appoint editors.[18] The offer was refused, but only ten days later (Hidayat 1999: 189) a company was formed that would subsequently publish a new magazine called *Gatra*, first appearing in November 1994. The majority shareholder in *Gatra* was Bob Hasan, an immensely wealthy timber magnate and Suharto crony. Although a large number of ex-*Tempo* secretarial and support staff joined *Gatra*, only about 35 journalists did so. The majority of *Tempo* journalists followed the lead of Goenawan Mohamad in dissociating themselves from the new magazine. While Goenawan declared he would not seek a new publishing licence, a team of ex-*Tempo* journalists made efforts to obtain another licence. The government, however, declared it would issue only one new licence to replace each of the three licences which had been revoked: in effect, *Gatra* had 'taken over' *Tempo*'s licence and no other group of ex-*Tempo* staff could hope to be granted one.

Nevertheless, Heryanto and Adi contend that those who decided to join *Gatra* have been the subject of unfair criticism, and suggest that they should not be judged simply on moral grounds. They also note that:

> The heroic-sounding struggle for justice and democracy among *Tempo* supporters did not operate purely on moral or political grounds. It also had its own economic basis and material interests at stake to an extent greater than was usually admitted by these activists or noted by observers.
>
> (Heryanto and Adi 2001)

The political economy of the bannings[19]

The closure of *Tempo* had laid the foundations for a business takeover of the magazine, creating a gap in the market that could be filled only by a well-connected investor. As with *Editor*, *Tempo* was replaced by a magazine owned by an individual very close to the government, who could be relied upon to 'police' its political coverage. The business transactions involved in the takeover of *Editor* and the 'replacement' of *Tempo* were clearly politically motivated; for men such as Bob Hasan, the quest for profit was secondary to the desire to buy more power and influence. *TIRAS* boss Eddy Herwanto argued that for A. Latief Corporation, the owner of his magazine, the economic returns of the business were 'peanuts': Latief's motive for buying the magazine might have been political.[20] The willingness of Suharto trusties to take over the magazine businesses reflected the political imperative to bring these unruly voices into line. Although chief editor Herry Komar insisted that Hasan had not interfered in *Gatra*'s editorial content,[21] when the magazine was established, Hasan had declared that if any article was published attacking the government 'I myself will intervene and handle the editorial board' (*Jakarta Post*, 16 September 1994).

AJI: alternative media and alternative politics

A few weeks after the bannings, a new journalists' organization was formed in Indonesia known as AJI, the Alliance of Independent Journalists. AJI's formation partly reflected the mood of anger in the wake of the bannings and frustration with the failure of the PWI to act in support of the three publications (Stanley 1994; *Jakarta Post*, 5 August 1994). With around sixty formal members (including many top-notch journalists) and two to three hundred supporters, AJI quickly established itself as a force to be reckoned with (Article 19 1994: 12–13). Formal members of AJI were expelled from the PWI and effectively banned from working for mainstream publications (*Jakarta Post*, 23 March 1995). While the government was clearly uncomfortable with AJI and sought to harass the organization in various ways, AJI was not itself an illegal body. However, a publication produced by AJI, *Independen*, which ran critical articles on political issues, quickly fell foul of the law for operating without a permit. In two separate incidents in 1995 and 1996, four people associated with AJI publications were arrested, tried and jailed.

According to AJI secretary-general Satrio Arismunandar, the organization had two broad 'tendencies', one emphasizing the role of AJI as a professional organization aiming to improve the conditions of Indonesian journalists, and a second which emphasized the political dimensions of AJI's campaigns for press freedom, seeing AJI as part of a broader prodemocracy movement.[22] Some of AJI's publications – such as *Jakarta Crackdown*, a book on the protests surrounding Megawati's ouster from the leadership of the PDI in July 1996 – were extremely 'activist' in tone. Faced with legal problems in distributing *Suara Independen* (successor of *Independen*), AJI began publishing the magazine on the Internet (Santoso 1997). Students and political activists in various parts of the country were downloading the text, printing it out, photocopying it, and selling the publication. AJI was forging links and building networks with NGOs and other elements of the prodemocracy movement, a form of politics which Aristides described as 'subestablishment' rather than antiestablishment.[23] Goenawan argued that AJI had helped create a climate of resistance: 'I think what AJI did is inspire more courage, so you have pockets of resistance in almost every publication, kind of guerrilla warfare, which can shoot any time, even in the government newspapers'.[24]

Media analyst Ashadi Siregar urged the public to launch their own underground media – such as leaflet, bulletins, and cassettes – and not to rely on conventional media, which was subject to censorship (*Jakarta Post*, 18 November 1994). He argued that the mainstream press had surrendered to the will of the authorities, so preoccupied with the need to survive that it was unable to fight for the good of society (*Suara Pembuaran*, 12 February 1996). The newsweekly *Detektif & Romantika*, which was revamped in mid-1996 (when it hired some staff from the publications banned in 1994), became an important source of independent, critical, political journalism, occupying a special location poised between the alternative and conventional press. Several of those working for the magazine were 'journalists without names', members of AJI; if their names appeared in the magazine, problems with the authorities were bound to follow. Unbeknown to the government, an 80 per cent stake in the magazine was now owned by Grafiti Pers, the holding company of *Tempo*.[25]

Growth in the use of new technology such as the Internet was laying the basis for alternative forms of media. *Tempo* itself continued to be published on the Internet, in the form of *Tempo Interaktif*. This widely read website,[26] inaugurated in March 1996, was maintained by a team of ex-*Tempo* journalists, who were paid using residual capital by *Tempo*'s holding company Grafiti Pers. In 1995, the Indonesian military set up its own Internet database, known as Hankamnet, to counter 'negative information' about Indonesia circulating on the network (Harsono 1995). The authorities also announced plans to crackdown on other alternative media, such as *samizdat* leaflets. But the reality was that access to information was already becoming impossible for the government to regulate (see Hill and Sen 1997); one limiting factor was the lack of widespread Internet access (an estimated 100,000 Indonesian users in 1997, Santoso 1997: 58), but the potential for downloading Internet material and photocopying it for wider distribution meant that this obstacle could readily be surmounted.

At the same time, pockets of resistance in the mainstream press and open resistance in the alternative media were not in themselves sufficient. As Goenawan put it: 'You have alternative publications but you don't have alternative political forces. So you now have to develop an alternative political force, and people are trying to do that now.'[27] Here was the paradox of the Indonesian press: the New Order had grown so monolithic that there were no political alternatives left. Before it could begin advocating a different kind of politics, the media had first to create such an alternative. Hence the conflicts within AJI; what began as a journalists' association inevitably found itself intimately involved in the pro-democracy movement. There was no political space within Indonesian society for non-state-aligned groups to operate; they were forced out of the mainstream. What William Liddle called a 'de facto anti-Suharto coalition' still lacked coherence and leadership (Liddle 1996a: 71).

Yet as Suharto grew older (the death of his wife Tien in 1996 brought home Suharto's mortality to many Indonesians) and uncertainty about the succession remained, Indonesia became increasingly, to use Schwarz's title phrase, 'a nation in waiting'. The examples of the former Soviet bloc (or, closer to home, the Philippines under Marcos) showed how quickly a regime could disintegrate, how the legitimacy of a once-mighty government could vanish literally overnight. It was precisely because so much was up for grabs, both politically and economically, that the media attracted so much attention. On the one hand, those allied with the 'subestablishment' believed that alternative media could provide a key to inaugurating a more progressive political order, post-Suharto. At the same time, the 'players', big-business people and military officers who had flourished during the New Order, had every incentive to seek to shore up their influence over the media, in order to use ownership and control as mechanisms for defending their interests when the crunch came.

If the three press bannings were the most important political event of 1994, the central political event of 1996 was the government's blatant attempts to intervene in the internal affairs of the Parti Demokrasi Indonesia (Heryanto 1996: 109–16). The party had been enjoying increased public support since the election of Megawati Sukarnoputri (daughter of former President Sukarno) to its leadership in 1993. Seeing the PDI as a growing challenge to Golkar as the 1997 general election approached, the government engineered a so-called 'PDI Congress' in Medan, North Sumatra, in July 1996. This Congress elected a new PDI leader, government stooge Surjadi. Hundreds of men claiming to be Surjadi supporters stormed the PDI headquarters on 27 July, resulting in riots that left five people dead. In many respects, the government's actions against the PDI followed the same pattern as the 1994 press bannings: a crude, rather paranoid response to a perceived movement against Suharto, which had the effect of hardening elements of public dissatisfaction with the New Order.

The fall of Suharto

Although the New Order regime appeared deeply entrenched in power, by the mid-1990s the regime's internal coherence was much weaker than many observers believed. When Indonesia ran into serious economic difficulties following the devaluation of the rupiah in late 1997, the extent to which Suharto's rule was based on cronyism and bad debt quickly became obvious. Indonesia was obliged to seek support from the IMF. In January 1998, Suharto signed a crucial agreement while IMF boss Michel Camdessus stood watchfully behind him, arms folded, in the manner of a headmaster checking whether a naughty pupil was doing his homework. This media image shocked the Indonesian public, bringing home the weakness and vulnerability of their President, his subordination to the forces of international capital.

Suharto never recovered his authority. Although there was scarcely a whisper of dissent when he was reappointed President by a hand-picked, one-thousand member assembly in March 1998 (with Habibie as his new Vice-President), Suharto was able to serve out only two months of his new five-year term. A combination of popular unrest and rioting fueled by unemployment and rising prices, along with nationwide political protests by students and other pro-democracy groups, generated an irresistible tide of opposition. Ultimately, even those in Suharto's own inner circle began calling for his resignation, which he finally announced on 21 May. Habibie assumed the presidency, later announcing that he planned to step down in 1999 after fresh elections had been held.

Suharto was brought down by his closest supporters, by the very same group of men who had been intimately involved in the 1994 bannings. After his 're-election' as President, Suharto had made *Gatra* owner Bob Hasan Minister of Trade, a foolhardy appointment which immediately undermined Suharto's domestic and international credibility. Abdul Latief, owner of *TIRAS*, was the first rat to leave Suharto's sinking ship, announcing his resignation from the Cabinet a few days before Suharto went down. The death of the New Order was effectively announced on 18 May by parliament speaker Harmoko – who had signed the three banning orders in his previous post as Information Minister – when he declared that parliament intended to seek Suharto's resignation. And it was Vice-President B. J. Habibie, a central figure in the events leading up to the bannings, who helped persuade Suharto to step down gracefully in his favour. Directly and indirectly, Suharto was eased out by the questionable associates who had served him so ill over the 1994 press bannings.

Conclusion

In many respects, the banning of three weekly publications in 1994 reflected and symbolized all the tensions of the late Suharto era. One view is that Suharto hoped that he could revive the flagging New Order by shifting from an exclusive focus on developmentalism to a more potent mixture of economic development, high technology, Islam, and nationalism. Another view is that Suharto was simply tactically juggling competing elements of the elite to perpetuate his own position. Whichever view is more accurate, the generals and the technologists jostled for power, irritating Suharto. *Tempo* and other weeklies ran the story, and Suharto closed three publications in an attempt to suppress what he saw as resistance to his authority. Denied the option of a middle way between promoting stability and promoting change, the Indonesian press saw a parting of ways after the 1994 bannings. *Tempo* and the two other publications were torn apart, as some of their staff accepted new terms as stooges for Suharto cronies Hasan and Latief, while others went underground: forming AJI, entering the subestablishment, or creating pockets of resistance within mainstream media publications. Superficially, the bannings were successful. Three outspoken voices were silenced, replaced by two new, milder voices. Rogue journalists and editors were brought into line, and reliable owners were put in place. In the long term, however, the bannings were an ill-conceived failure. The limitations of Suharto's balancing tactics became abundantly clear following the onset of Indonesia's financial crisis in 1997. Playing off opposing forces against one another did not address structural economic or political problems. Such tactics could not ensure long-term stability; indeed, in some respects they were destabilizing.

- This is not to suggest that an increasingly vocal Indonesian media directly brought down the government in 1998.
- Indeed, the media itself was always polyvalent, reflecting the cracks and fissures that existed within the New Order regime.
- When Suharto could not bear to hear the sounds of dissent and discord inside his own camp, he punished the messengers who brought him the news.
- The permanent closure of three publications in 1994 showed that Suharto was beginning to lose his grip on power.
- An intolerable proportion of the polyvalent voices were now critical ones.
- The suicidal press bannings of 1994 were the clearest indicator of the impending demise of Suharto and the New Order.

The demise of the Suharto regime provoked considerable soul-searching. How had the New Order successfully curtailed freedom of expression for so long, in such a huge country as Indonesia? Adam Schwarz cited former *Tempo* editor in chief Goenawan Mohamed as an example of a 'moderate, inside-the-establishment' Suharto critic who was radicalized by the closure of *Tempo*, and who later reproached himself with having been 'a participant, however unwittingly, in a conspiracy of repression'. He explained in an interview:

> We didn't work hard enough to get around the government's efforts to silence us. We were silent too long about so many things, about East Timor, about the treatment of [novelist] Pramoedya [Ananta Toer], about the rebellion in Aceh and Irian Jaya, about how Soeharto came to power.
> (Schwarz 1999: 320)

Overall, the Suharto period was not one from which the Indonesian media – even those publications actually banned by the regime – emerged with great credit.

The end of the Suharto regime illustrated the extent to which the New Order's understanding of the media was captive to outdated ideas of national sovereignty. John Keane has argued that: 'Our globe is beginning to resemble the *form* of the medieval world, in which the political powers of the monarch or prince were forced to share authority with a variety of subordinate and higher powers' (Keane 1992: 30). Central to Suharto's demise was his preoccupation with the maintenance of absolute sovereign authority, his unwillingness and inability to co-exist either with higher powers (such as the IMF) or with subordinate powers (such as a more outspoken press) reflecting divisions in his regime and in Indonesian society. By refusing to allow the Indonesian press to evolve from serving as an agent of stability to functioning as an agent of restraint, Suharto may actually have destabilized the New Order. The kind of restraining influence practised by *Tempo*, *Editor* and *DeTik* – alerting both rulers and readers to important tensions within the elite – actually served valuable purposes for the regime. As Borsuk notes:

> The Indonesian media, under difficult conditions, were trying to play such a [critical] role in those final years when the ageing,

stubborn President could not see – or refused to see – that he was perilously putting family interests ahead of national ones.

(Borsuk 1999: 136)

But Suharto refused to read the message, choosing instead to kill the messenger. By viewing the press merely as a threat to be neutralized, Suharto failed to heed the weeklies' warnings of his own declining legitimacy and impending downfall.

5 Media in a time of transition: Hong Kong

The handover of Hong Kong to China in 1997 was widely billed as one of the greatest threats to press freedom in modern times. It was the theme of numerous media articles and of a special issue of *Index on Censorship*. Crudely summarized, the argument went like this. Under British rule, Hong Kong enjoyed 'Western' standards of media openness; post-Tiananmen China was not to be trusted to maintain such outspoken critical traditions, and the handover was bound to be accompanied by a clampdown on freedom of expression (see, for example, Schidlovsky 1996). As one analysis argued:

> Theoretically, even though mass media may reflect a plurality of perspectives, they depend primarily on the dominant power structure as a legitimate point of reference.
> (Chan, Lee and Lee 1994: 239)

Some of the direst warnings were clearly overstated: the most striking feature of the handover was just how little it appeared to change the relationship between government and media. While the Patten period may have looked like a period of relative democracy, it could also be argued that John Major's decision to send a prominent politician to serve as Hong Kong's governor reflected Britain's attempts to salve its conscience over its failure to democratize Hong Kong decades earlier.

The realities were considerably more complex than any simple narrative of a transition from openness to censorship could convey. Rather than a process that began in July 1997, the shift in control over Hong Kong media began several years before the handover. By mid-1997 there were China-friendly owners everywhere in Hong Kong, following a remarkable re-ordering of press ownership in the Territory (for details, see Hutcheon 1998: 6–11). The press was already well prepared to meet its new masters (Lee and Chu 1998: 76). The once-powerful *Ming Pao* ('Indisputably the premier intellectual newspaper in Hong Kong', Lee and Chan 1990: 151) had seen its reputation dissipated following its sale to Malaysian tycoon Robert Kuok, who also acquired the *South China Morning Post*. *Ming Pao* had a long tradition of reporting critically on China, but Kuok changed all this. Sally Aw had lost control of the once-mighty *Sing Tao* group to an investment bank, Lazard Asia, in April 1999 (for background, see Berfield 1999). No major owner remained who was prepared seriously to challenge China. Given this sort of climate, there was no need for crude forms of censorship. The Chinese adopted a hands-off approach, tolerating critical editorials within the context of an essentially manageable press stance. Zhu Ronghi was widely believed to see the media in Hong Kong as a barometer for public opinion critical of China.[1]

As late as 1990, no indigenous political parties were permitted in Hong Kong, and hence newspapers were classified primarily in terms of their stance towards Taiwan. 'Ultra-leftist' newspapers were those that adopted a pro-Beijing, anti-Taiwan line; 'centrist' newspapers were market-oriented and had a neutral stance on Taiwan; 'rightist' newspapers tilted somewhat towards Taipei; and the one 'ultra-rightist' newspaper was owned by the KMT (Lee and Chan 1990: 142–3). The Sino–British Joint Declaration of 1984 (which marked the beginning of the transition to Chinese rule) ushered in a paradigm shift in the Hong Kong media, changing the emphasis from pro- and anti-KMT stances to a new emphasis on coverage of Britain and China, and attitudes towards political change. This shift was made clear following the Tiananmen Square massacre of 4 June 1989, which forced 'centrist' newspapers to clarify their positions. It proved a day of reckoning for figures such as *Ming Pao* publisher Louis Cha, who eventually abandoned his long-standing support for Deng Xiaoping (Lee and Chan 1990: 151–4), declaring that the Chinese Communist Party had 'gone mad'. *Sing Pao* was even more explicit in its criticisms. Within a decade, both of these newspapers had changed hands, and both had also lost much of their former influence. The creation of political parties in Hong Kong after 1990 was accompanied by a new set of media alignments.

Most Hong Kong newspapers evince no hesitation in running critical coverage of the Hong Kong government. Yet the barometer for press freedom in Hong Kong is not coverage of Hong Kong itself; a much more important indicator is the way in which Hong Kong media covers China, especially at the level of Beijing politics. Chinese newspapers in Hong Kong no longer carry translations of articles by *The Times* correspondent Jonathan Mirsky, a bitter critic of Beijing who is not permitted to enter China. Nor did Hong Kong newspapers carry much incisive coverage of Chinese issues, especially matters relating to politics. Frank Lu Siqing – a former student movement leader and the son of a PLA officer – founded in 1996 a one-man agency rather grandiosely known as the 'Information Centre for Human Rights and Democratic Movement in China', drawing on a network of dissident informants across the country. To the surprise of many, this vocal critic of Beijing was granted permanent residence by the Hong Kong authorities in 2000. Lu was routinely quoted by Hong Kong newspapers as a source of interesting snippets about Beijing politics. However, those same newspapers rarely used their own resources to explore these or similar stories, though some clandestinely employed stringers of their own on the mainland (Chan 1999: 85–6).

Challenging *SCMP*: the rise of the Chinese-language press

Most outsiders based their assessment of the Hong Kong media on the English language press, notably the *South China Morning Post* (*SCMP*). For the Hong Kong government and for Beijing, the existence of a professional and credible looking English-language daily was extremely valuable, suggesting a free and vibrant Hong Kong media. Yet the *SCMP* was not representative of the Hong Kong press more generally, nor was it terribly outspoken, particularly on the sensitive subject of Beijing politics. Compared with, say, the authoritative and highly influential *Jakarta Post* (which had formed a key part of the critical alliance that had helped undermine Suharto) the *SCMP* never pushed a critical line likely to embarrass Beijing. Some observers argued that the *SCMP* had toned down its critical coverage in the years prior to the handover, so that since 1997 there might even have been a slight strengthening of its independence. Yet because it was considered a foreign publication, *SCMP* was the only Hong Kong newspaper permitted to maintain bureaux in China (Chan 1999: 85).

SCMP faced a new challenge from the tabloid *Hong Kong iMail*, launched in May 2000 to replace the troubled *Hong Kong Standard*. Yet in September 2001 the *iMail* suddenly laid off 100 of its 140 editorial staff, announcing a shift in emphasis towards business and financial news. This was a disturbing trend, given the *iMail*'s reputation for independent and critical coverage of topical issues. Columnist Nury Vittachi linked the changes to criticism of the paper's line by high-level figures in the Hong Kong government and the acquisition of the newspaper by a pro-Beijing businessman (Zeitlin 2001b).

SCMP generated controversy when it hired Feng Xiliang, former editor of the Beijing *China Daily*, as a consultant in 1997. While there were persistent whispers that Feng's appointment was a ploy to curry favour with Beijing, or even a subtle way of creating a climate of self-censorship at the paper, this was denied both by Feng himself and by then-editor Jonathan Fenby in interviews with Alan Knight (Knight and Nakano 1999: 168–9; 177–80).[2] Two visiting journalism fellows wrote that Feng 'occupies a bare, anteroom-sized office, and appears to be a man with little to do', while Fenby told them that he would resign at once if Feng even spoke to one of his journalists (Shirk and Woo 1998: 7). In principle, Feng's appointment was by no means unusual: mainland Chinese journalists were hired by many Hong Kong publications. While the specialist knowledge and connections of these reporters served to improve some aspects of China coverage, there were also concerns that 'their Chinese background lends a partisan Chinese perspective to reporting' (Lee and Chu 1998: 69).

Yet concerns about the newspaper's China coverage were underlined when longstanding and highly respected China editor Willy Wo-Lap Lam quit *SCMP* in November 2000. The *de facto* dismissal of Lam came a few months after one of his articles had been criticized by the former chairman and majority shareholder of the newspaper, Robert Kuok Hock Nien, in a vitriolic letter to the newspaper. In the article in question, Lam had suggested that Kuok and other Hong Kong tycoons were 'such idiots and morons that their only way of business survival is to become running dogs of the Chinese central government'. Lam claimed that he had been intimidated and frequently asked to tone down his work (Marshall 2000). Former editor Jonathan Fenby wrote an article in *The Times* recalling that when he arrived in Hong Kong in 1995 to take over the helm of the *SCMP*, he was told that the owners wanted Lam sacked. Fenby refused, but pressure to oust Lam remained. One of the newspaper's directors told him in 1997 'We'll never get anywhere in China so long as we employ Willy Lam' (Fenby 2000). Fenby noted that 'Robert Kuok is used to being obeyed' and that the two regularly clashed over his frequent instructions for journalists to be fired or editorial policy to be changed. He expressed concern that Lam's departure might mean that 'journalists at some papers may think twice before sticking their necks out'. In an unusual move, Lam's departure was criticized by the Hong Kong Foreign Correspondents' Club, who wrote that 'the possibility that Mr Lam might have been removed from his post for political reasons is too serious to disregard' (letters, *SCMP*, 9 November 2000).

Concerns about editorial policy at the *SCMP* were further exacerbated when Jasper Becker, another of the paper's China correspondents, was abruptly fired on 29 April 2002. Becker claimed that he was dismissed as part of the *Post*'s tendency to curtail stories critical of the Beijing government, while editor Thomas Abraham insisted that he had simply dismissed Becker for 'insubordination'. The *Far Eastern Economic Review* argued that the sacking left a serious hole in the *SCMP*'s China coverage, since Becker was 'probably the *Post*'s only internationally acclaimed journalist' (Lague 2002: 16). In another *Times* article, Fenby wrote that – despite the plausible explanations offered by the *Post* for the departures of three controversial journalists in two years (Willy Lam, Becker, and comment section editor Danny Gittings) – 'isn't part of the challenge for a self-confident newspaper to keep valuable individuals on side, even if they do not fit in comfortably?' (Fenby 2002).

At the same time, the *SCMP* was becoming less important in the wake of the handover. Given that Hong Kong was now run by a Chinese Chief Executive rather than a British Governor, and that the territory's ultimate masters resided in Beijing rather than London, the Chinese-language press was of far greater importance. In circulation terms, Chinese-language publications accounted for the overwhelming majority of Hong Kong newspaper sales. Much more significant now were *Apple Daily*, *Oriental Daily News*, *Hong Kong Economic Journal*, *Hong Kong Economic Times*, *Ming Pao*, and *Sing Pao*. Whereas previously exclusive coverage of policy changes, government reshuffles and behind-the scenes business dealings had been largely the preserve of *SCMP*, after the handover Chinese-language newspapers gained much greater access to such stories (Law Siu-Lan 1999: 41). Given the intense competition in the Chinese sector, these newspapers had no scope for complacency in the pursuit of news; while for the government, their larger circulation meant that leaking hot stories to the Chinese press was a more effective way of communicating with the public.

The same applied to *Hong Kong Today*, the English-language RTHK morning programme modelled on BBC Radio 4's *Today*: the programme gradually declined in significance, attracting fewer movers and shakers among its interviewees and its audience following the handover. Tensions rose over international stories such as the 1999 bombing of Kosovo, when some in Hong Kong argued that RTHK should adopt a line critical of the West, rather than basing its coverage on materials from the international media. When British Foreign Office minister Derek Fatchett visited Hong Kong in April 1999, his scheduled interview on RTHK's *Hong Kong Today* was actually cancelled because of a big local story on health care – a nice illustration of the declining significance of the British in the territory.[3] In 1998, Chief Executive Tung is said to have told critics of RTHK privately that the problem would be addressed 'slowly, slowly', implying a long-term desire to whittle away the organization's independence from the government. His alleged remark caused alarm inside RTHK, but was never verified or repeated in public. RTHK staff saw Anson Chan and their Director Cheung Man-yee as key allies in maintaining the organization's integrity, but concerns about the future beyond their terms of office continued. A more compliant RTHK director might collude with the gradual watering down of the organization's political coverage.

Media changes under Tung

At the same time, some have argued that following the handover the local media assumed an important new role in scrutinizing the workings of the Hong Kong administration.[4] During the Patten era, the handover itself was the big story; now, ironically, China was less important, and what mattered more was the day-to-day scrutiny of the performance of the administration on policy matters. The media had a very important watchdog role, and arguably was tougher on the post-handover administration than it had been on the colonial administration. More was now expected of the Hong Kong government than before, whereas in the past there was a certain amount of punch-pulling. In his farewell interviews, Patten had declared that the media would start applying higher standards once Hong Kong people themselves were in charge. This reflected some of the pre-handover propaganda: 'once the colonialists are gone, we will be free to run the place' with the consequence that Hong Kong would be better 'hoisted on its own petard'. Yet Jonathan Dimbleby argues in his excellent book on Patten that the last governor knew all too well how far 'proprietors were suggestible and biddable, and, with a handful of exceptions, indifferent to the principles on behalf of which he was so agitated' (Dimbleby 1997: 270).

In the post-handover period, changes were made in the operations of the Government Information Services (GIS). Under Patten, who was the only professional politician to have run Hong Kong, GIS was rather politicized and partisan. Tung's style was to present information more in a neutral civil service mode. Hong Kong veteran Stephen Vines described Tung's office at the time of the handover as having 'the most shambolic public relations known to personkind' (Knight and Nakano 1999: 39); subsequently, Tung appointed a new official spokesman, Steven Lam, as information co-ordinator. Patten's brilliant Australian spin-doctor Kerry McGlynn was kept on – mainly writing Anson Chan's speeches – but was somewhat tainted by his perceived proximity to the *ancien regime*, and lost most of his high-level connections (Knight and Nakano 1999: 30). Tung's spokespeople were much less in the loop than Patten's had been. Privately, senior journalists expressed the view that Lam – though a 'nice guy' who briefed the press in three languages and gave out his home phone number – was not working out, and that GIS was much less willing to provide information than before. Meanwhile the Hong Kong Journalists' Association (HKJA) criticized the government's tendency to use various forms of 'spin', including disseminating articles supporting the official line to selected newspapers and giving an increasing number of unattributed press briefings (HKJA 2000: 13).

Tung was supposed to be good one-on-one or with small groups, but he disliked facing rooms full of journalists and dealing with the media himself. His technocratic and paternalistic style made him look like everyone's Chinese grandfather and did not offer good raw material with which spin-doctors could weave their webs. For many, the handover did not so much usher in a new era of freedom from colonialism as see one remote imperial master replaced with another, as suggested by opposition legislator Emily Lau (Lau 1997). The handover was accompanied by an 'unmistakable shift of political power from the legislature back to the executive', with associated implications for the media (Nip 1997: 66). Yet Patten had opened people's eyes, giving Hong Kong a little taste of what democracy might be like, and they were now using the same standards to judge Tung. Patten was very successful in creating changed conditions in which Tung would flounder. Beijing wanted Hong Kong to step backwards politically; starting a small blaze on the way out was a low-cost strategy for the British. This was the irony of the handover: colonialism began looking so much better at the very end. Positive views of Hong Kong always suggested that the territory embraced the best of two worlds, serving as a bridge between China and the West. A more negative interpretation saw Hong Kong as the worst of both worlds: an ex-colony weighed down by its peculiar history.

Ethical standards and tabloid feuds

Meanwhile, many of the greatest problems of the media in Hong Kong related not to attempts at censorship by Beijing, but to low ethical standards in the Chinese-language press. As Chris Yeung put it 'It seems ironic that two years after the handover . . . the biggest concern for press freedom is the media's own irresponsibility' (Yeung 2000: 58–9). Chinese-language newspapers in Hong Kong typically mixed elements of tabloid and quality newspapers: *Apple*

Daily, for example, contained a regular column entitled 'Fat Dragon', a consumer's guide to prostitution in the Territory. For publishers and owners, newspapers were a business in which anything goes. Sensational and ridiculous stories abound. In one notorious case in October 1998, Chan Kin-hong, a man whose wife had committed suicide by jumping out of a window just days earlier (having first thrown out their two children) posed for *Apple Daily* with a couple of prostitutes. In an unprecedented move, *Apple Daily* subsequently published a front-page apology for running the story. Such cases led to calls for a regulatory press council, but any form of regulation had grave dangers in the political context of Hong Kong (HKJA 1999: 7, 27). Bodies such as the HKJA feared that irresponsible and sensational reporting could be used to justify the creation of press regulatory bodies that might in turn suppress critical political coverage (HKJA 1999: 28). In April 2000, the government published proposals to regulate indecent and obscene articles (HKJA 2000: 13–14). In July 2000 the Hong Kong Press Council was finally established, without the support of leading newspapers, or indeed of the HKJA (HKJA 2001: 26–8). This self-regulatory body was created partly to forestall government moves to institute a statutory body to handle complaints against the press, primarily on issues of privacy. By 2001, there were some signs of a backlash on the part of middle-class readers over questionable ethical practices by Hong Kong journalists (HKJA 2001: 26). The HKJA argued that the best way forward was for individual publications to adopt better ethical practices.

Many press controversies involved the newspaper *Oriental Daily News* (*ODN*), which did not hesitate to sue or harass its critics and competitors. Between 1995 and 1999, the newspaper's owners were involved in no less than fifty-one separate lawsuits, including thirteen against Next Media (owners of *Apple Daily*), nine against *Ming Pao* Group, five against the *Hong Kong Economic Journal* and three against RTHK (HKJA 1999: 29). On one occasion, *ODN* sent paparazzi to hound a judge involved in a case against it; in consequence, the newspaper's editor in chief was ultimately given a four-month jail sentence for contempt of court (HKJA 1999: 30). While the paper rarely won its court cases, it had the financial resources to employ legal means to exhaust and deter those who might think of challenging it. *ODN* was highly partisan, but its loyalties could shift dramatically. Seen in the past as pro-KMT, the owners of *ODN* had also been behind the ill-fated *Eastern Express* (a pro-Patten, pro-democracy English-language newspaper) that eventually failed. *ODN* had then adopted a strongly pro-Beijing stance, in contrast to that of its main rival, *Apple Daily*. *ODN* consistently called for the resignation of 'pro-British' Anson Chan and Donald Tsang, two leading figures in the Hong Kong government. The paper was critical of the opposition Democrats, dubbing them 'running dogs' of the British and of Western imperialism. It also regularly criticized the (mainly Western) judiciary. Yet this stance did not extend to hostility to Tung himself.

Chan, Ma and So were critical of the increasing number of libel actions involving Hong Kong media:

> One apparent consequence of the over-use of libel suits is that media commentators hesitate to criticize other media. Those who have the financial prowess can therefore say what they like, whereas individual columnists have to shut up out of fear. Such feuds among news media organizations may set a bad example. It is worried that in the future the same legal tactic may be adopted by political or economic authorities to stop dissenting voices from criticizing social injustices.
>
> (Chan, Ma and So 1997: 464)

Legal challenges were not the only threat to media freedom in Hong Kong. Physical violence was also sometimes directed against leading figures, including well-known talk-show host Albert Cheng (who suffered a near-fatal attack by two meatcleaver-wielding assailants), *Apple Daily* owner Jimmy Lai, and Leung Tin-wai, publisher of *Surprise Weekly* (HKJA 1999: 29).

ODN and *Apple Daily* constituted a 'virtual' duoply among mass circulation Chinese newspapers, commanding around 75 per cent of the market. This dominance which was strengthened by an intense price war between the two (HKJA 1999: 22–3), which severely affected the profits of both publications. *ODN* also launched a sister paper, *The Sun*, in March 1999; there were fears that the dominance of these two newspaper groups would marginalize other publications and reduce the diversity of media ownership in Hong Kong. *Apple Daily* continued to adopt an anti-Beijing stance –

partly a function of its feverish and litigious rivalry with *Oriental Daily News*. Though lionized by the Western media as a fighter for democracy, *Apple Daily* owner Jimmy Lai argued that he was simply a businessman, and an anti-Beijing line sold newspapers. In 2000, Lai announced that he was leaving Hong Kong for Taiwan, though he would continue to publish *Apple Daily*. Lai's decision to quit Hong Kong could be interpreted as a sign of exasperation with the business and political climate in the territory.

Self-censorship and no-go areas

Lee and Chu (1998: 70) list 'three explicit noes' laid down by Beijing for the Hong Kong media:

- No advocacy for the independence of Hong Kong and Taiwan (not to mention Tibet).
- No advocacy for subverting Chinese communist rule.
- No personal attacks on Chinese leaders.

They argued, however, that the media system in Hong Kong was likely to change gradually into a more repressive one, as the region's political actors and structures were themselves transformed. They cited as an example the legitimacy accorded by the media to the selection procedures for the first Chief Executive: despite the fact that only 400 pre-selected insiders were granted the vote, the Hong Kong press covered these procedures like a normal election, so 'helping to make Chinese rule appear inevitable and just' (Lee and Chu 1998: 72).

An ongoing debate in Hong Kong surrounded the degree to which local media organizations were pervaded by a culture of self-censorship. Annual reports on media freedom published by the Hong Kong Journalists Association – in association with the London-based NGO Article 19 – frequently argued that self-censorship was a problem. Kin-ming Liu, general manager of *Apple Daily* and former chair of the HKJA, was one of the strongest advocates of this argument. Indications of a climate of self-censorship could be found from small details. How were the events of 4 June 1989 described? A 'massacre', an 'incident', or an 'event'? The word 'massacre' disappeared after the handover, not as the result of an edict from the government, but because of self-censorship – and this in a territory where one million people (ten per cent of the population) had joined anti-Beijing protests in 1989.[5] Critical articles about Tibet appeared occasionally in *SCMP*, but close scrutiny of the by-lines revealed that these items came from the wire-services, not from Hong Kong-based journalists.

Yet not everyone agreed that self-censorship was a major problem. Veteran journalist Arnold Zeitlin, director of the Freedom Forum's Asia Centre in Hong Kong, argued that 'The elusive topic of self-censorship has become an urban myth' (Zeitlin 2001a). Zeitlin was critical of a recent US State Department human rights report, which had made several references to self-censorship in Hong Kong on the basis of scant evidence. He argued that his Centre routinely checked the coverage of major stories in Hong Kong in the

> seven or eight main English and Chinese language dailies that comprise the territory's independent press . . . . Never have we seen any evidence that on these issues the English-language and independent Chinese-language press pulls punches in a way that could be interpreted as self-censorship.

He argued that many of the problems with Hong Kong media coverage related more to 'journalistic inexperience and incompetence' than to any tendency to self-censor. While self-censorship might be an issue, there was no compelling basis for the argument that the practice was endemic or harmful.

The weakness of Zeitlin's approach lay in his emphasis on scrutinizing the content of Hong Kong newspapers, rather than a first-hand knowledge of their internal processes of news-gathering and editorial decision-making. While not endorsing Zeitlin's criticisms, the 2001 HKJA Annual Report argued that the issue of self-censorship was becoming 'increasingly meaningless' and 'far more complex' (HKJA 2001: 25). Whereas in previous reports the HKJA had been able to cite specific examples of 'spiked' stories on sensitive issues,

> Certain subjects are emerging as 'no-go' areas for some media outlets and journalists – sometimes quick to pick up on what

their editors want – will never simply suggest articles on these topics. Such unwritten rules can become almost institutionalized in a news organisation's culture. Newspapers with large 'no-go' areas often find that staff who are interested in such topics drift to other publications.

(HKJA 2001: 25)

The strength of this interpretation lay in the fact that HKJA's members themselves worked at the coal-face of news production in Hong Kong; the views in their Annual Report reflected the distillation of their collective experiences. A survey of its members conducted by the HKJA in 1995 found that 90 per cent believed self-censorship existed in their industry, and one third admitted having exercised it themselves (Mak Yin-ting 1997: 88–9). At the same time, the remarkable lack of specificity in the 2001 report was disappointing, making its arguments incompletely convincing.

Most of the serious stories and editorials that appeared in the press did not engage with political questions relating to mainland China; they emphasized local economic issues and the parochial sideshow of what passed for politics in Hong Kong. For many political reporters, Hong Kong's Legislative Council was the centre of the universe. The problem lay not in what the press was writing, but in what it was not writing: the lack of serious scrutiny of Chinese affairs from the semi-detached proximity of Hong Kong. In post-handover Hong Kong, serious issues were less prominent, politics was sidelined, and down-market sensationalism was the order of the day.

Questions about self-censorship were not limited to established publications. In April 2000, it emerged that the exceptionally popular website hongkong.com was employing censorship of its chatrooms and discussion groups, deleting messages on subjects such as Tibet and Taiwan (HKJA 2000: 22). As a result of a backlash of criticism by users, the site subsequently ended the practice – but the clear readiness of its owners to engage in censorship was a disappointing discovery for those who had hoped that new media could help sustain a climate of open debate in Hong Kong.

Pressures on the Chinese-language press in Hong Kong were exerted in a variety of positive and negative ways. On the negative side, these included 'denying unfriendly newspapers access to Chinese news sources and financial support'; *Apple Daily* in particular found its reporters unable to obtain entry into China (Knight and Nakano 1999: 157; Lee and Chu 1998: 66). Financial pressures were also used by the Beijing authorities to discipline the Hong Kong media, by withholding advertising by Chinese-controlled enterprises, or leaning on banks not to underwrite businesses associated with critical publications. On the positive side, proprietors of loyal media outlets were often appointed to prestigious committees close to the Beijing government, including the important Preparatory Committee for the Hong Kong Special Administrative Region, which appointed the first Chief Executive. Editors and proprietors were wined and dined by the authorities, and during these meals 'unfriendly' journalists in their employ might be singled out for criticism by the hosts (Lee and Chu 1998: 67).

Yuen Ying Chan of Hong Kong University, argued that the 'grand narrative' of press freedom and self-censorship largely missed the point. The Hong Kong press might not be doing a good job of covering China, but this was simply a function of the lack of in-depth reporting and over-opinionated writing in all areas. For her, the core problems of Hong Kong's press concerned ownership and the structural weaknesses of the industry, problems which could be addressed through more coherent attempts to meet training needs. She argued for the development of an 'infrastructure of press freedom', building up such values with more systematic training and changes in the working culture of journalists.[6] As two other Hong Kong journalism lecturers put it, there was a serious danger that

> Journalism instructors may end up teaching people to take into consideration the consequences to themselves of what they write, and this is hardly an appropriate approach to a competent education in journalism.
>
> (Hamlett and Clarke 1997: 19)

Chan's arguments reflected her own mission to offer new journalism programmes at the University of Hong Kong, predicated upon her belief that

> The Hong Kong media can ill afford to be small-minded, parochial or corrupt... at a time when US media organizations are cutting back on international coverage, a well-trained and sophisticated journalistic corps in Hong Kong, well versed in the Chinese language and culture, could help inform the world about China, a country we must learn to understand and to work with.
>
> (Chan 1999: 89)

Despite this laudable vision, the Hong Kong media still experienced difficulty simply in informing Hong Kongers about political debates in one part of Greater China: Taiwan. Whereas a number of local newspapers had previously adopted a pro-KMT line, this became more difficult to sustain after the handover, and indeed following the KMT's April 2000 loss of control in Taiwan itself. Political changes in Taiwan were highly salient for Hong Kong: a Leninist party had relinquished its long-term grip on power, and public debate about a declaration of independence from the mainland had been intense. In April 2000, a senior Chinese official warned the Hong Kong media not to report the views of pro-independence elements in Taiwan, a remark apparently reflecting Beijing's displeasure at an interview broadcast on Hong Kong-based Cable Television with new Taiwanese vice-president Annette Lu (HKJA 2000: 6). Wang Fengchao, deputy director of China's liaison office in Hong Kong, told a journalism seminar in Hong Kong:

> The media should not treat speeches and views which advocate Taiwan's independence as normal news items, nor should they report them like normal cases of reporting the views of different parties. Hong Kong's media have the responsibility to uphold the integrity and sovereignty of the country. This has nothing to do with press freedom.
>
> (Quoted in HKJA 2000: 6)

The HKJA responded that the issue had everything to do with press freedom, and declared in an official statement:

> If the media does as Mr Wang suggests, and becomes a tool for the pursuit of national policies, the independence

and credibility of the media will be destroyed, as will press freedom.

(HKJA 2000)

While Anson Chan proceeded to issue a statement supportive of press freedom, Tung himself made ambiguous utterances on the subject, which touched on the core of debates about the role of the press. Was the job of the media to act as an agent of stability, restraint, or change? Beijing sought to bring the Hong Kong media into line, asking them to support the party line on Taiwan in the national interest, or what Lee and Chu call the 'public relations model' (1998: 75); HKJA, representing a pro-free press position, argued that the media had a duty to offer a credible, independent voice. Ironically, the nub of this issue was most clearly exposed where the Hong Kong media's coverage of a third territory (rather than either China or Hong Kong itself) was involved.

RTHK: a bellwether?

The government-run RTHK (Radio and Television Hong Kong) continued to sound very much like the BBC, featuring British presenters on its English language stations and giving over a whole channel to relaying the BBC World Service. Private television channels were more cautious and declined to show anti-Chinese programming. However, RTHK director Ms Cheung was transferred to a trade-related post in Tokyo in October 1999. While the official line was that she had chosen to make the move, many linked her transfer to an episode in July that year, when RTHK was criticized for broadcasting remarks by Taiwan's senior representative in Hong Kong, Cheng An-kuo (HKJA 2000: 6–7). The transfer prompted a letter of protest from the New York-based Committee to Protect Journalists. In the wake of the Cheng controversy, a Hong Kong deputy to the People's Congress had echoed the views of Beijing officials when he declared that '(as) a government-funded station, it ought to have self-control . . . . Mass media should not advocate secession' (HKJA 2000: 7). Ms Cheung's deputy, Chu Pui-hing, took over as director – rather than an outsider, as some RTHK staff had feared – but the future independence of the organization remained precarious. RTHK continued to cover the Taiwanese presidential election and the new policies of President Chen Shiu-bian, but the Taiwanese representative in Hong Kong had to leave after his visa was not renewed.

Conclusion

The following points have emerged from the above discussion:

- Many of the changes in the media climate in Hong Kong significantly predated the handover.
- Much of the Hong Kong media has little difficulty taking a critical line about Hong Kong politics.
- Yet the extent to which the Hong Kong media take a critical line about the inner workings of Chinese politics is much more debatable.
- The handover has seen a decline in the significance of the English-language press, especially the *South China Morning Post*.
- The real action concerns Chinese-language media.
- In the Chinese-language sector, ethical standards are often low and the main tabloids are locked in numerous feuds.
- Certain topics – notably Taiwanese independence – are generally considered off-limits for the Hong Kong media.
- Opinion was divided over whether self-censorship was a pervasive problem in the media.
- Some argued that the Hong Kong media's greatest problems were really internal: at root, lack of professionalism.

As a rare example of a Territory moving from relative media openness to a potentially more repressive media regime, Hong Kong will remain an important test case for all scrutiny of the interaction between media and politics in Pacific Asia.

6 International media and domestic politics: tales from Thailand

The international media in Pacific Asia

Although the Thai electronic media remain subject to significant state control, newspapers in Thailand have gained considerable latitude to report and comment on political developments. The Thai press is one of the freest and most outspoken in Pacific Asia. In particular, the Thai-language press frequently engages in antagonistic exchanges with political office-holders, and has often been credited with contributing to major upheavals. For example, the press was involved in the downfall of the Democrat-led government coalition over a land-reform scandal in May 1995 (Fairclough 1995) and played important roles in the demise of two subsequent governments.

Traditionally, Thai newspapers have been regarded as platforms for articulating the political views of their owners. Politicians have typically cultivated close personal ties to newspaper editors and columnists in order to further their own objectives (McCargo 2000b: 137–9). In recent years, the character of some Thai newspapers has changed. Whereas old-style newspapers such as *Thai Rath* and *Daily News* remain private family companies, newspapers such as *Matichon*, *Phujatkan* and the now-defunct *Siam Post* are part of larger corporate entities. Thai newspapers will be viewed here as essentially independent political actors, with considerable autonomy to pursue their own news agendas. It will further be argued that some politicians – such as former Prime Minister Banharn Silpa-archa – have not fully recognized the political independence of Thai newspapers, persisting in viewing them as largely passive instruments of the domestic political 'game'. This view becomes especially problematic when Thai newspapers run news stories that are in turn based upon stories about Thai politics which have appeared in the international press.

In recent years, the use of nationalist or regionalist rhetoric by Pacific Asian politicians has grown increasingly common, especially criticisms of the international media as a 'western' force. The international media have frequently been criticized for attempting to impose their own political values upon Asian states and societies in an almost neo-colonial fashion. They have also been accused of misunderstanding and misrepresenting Asian societies and cultures. In Southeast Asia, these criticisms have been most vocally articulated by Singapore and Malaysia. Garry Rodan has offered a detailed analysis of the techniques used to control the international press in Singapore, Malaysia and Hong Kong (Rodan 1998). Court cases and bans have regularly been invoked against foreign media outlets; during one week early in 2002, the Malaysian government simultaneously blocked distribution of *The Economist*, the *Far Eastern Economic Review*, *Time* and *Newsweek*.

Negative reactions to foreign coverage are by no means unknown in Thailand – though until the premiership of telecommunications magnate Thakin Shinawatra, foreign journalists were usually treated gently by regional standards. Where the story deals with social problems, especially the issue of prostitution, the general Thai reaction may be hostile.[1] Where it deals with political issues, the pattern is more complex: typically there is a clearly discernible divide between hostility from an aggrieved party – such as a politician accused of corruption – and support for the foreign story by the domestic press. Given the partisan nature of the Thai press, it is quite common for the foreign story to be given considerable prominence in an attempt to cause political embarrassment at home. Sometimes it is the foreign story that is distorted by the Thai press, rather than the Thai story which is distorted by the foreign press. In other words, far from a relationship in which the international press lords it over Asian countries in a condescending and manipulative fashion, the reality is of a mutually beneficial relationship between the international and domestic media.

The situation in Thailand has some parallels with that in Japan. Frustrated Japanese journalists have been known to tip off foreign correspondents about scandals; former *Economist* bureau chief

Nick Valery received such information about one aspect of the Recruit scandal in 1989 (Farley 1996: 141). More significantly, a grilling received by Prime Minister Kakuei Tanaka at the Foreign Correspondents' Club in 1974 was a crucial turning point in his downfall over corruption allegations. Once the Tanaka story – already published in a political magazine in Japan – was 'launched internationally', it was then picked up by the mainstream Japanese newspapers, 'bringing it back into the country' and Tanaka's demise was assured (Farley 1996: 147).

The Tanaka incident closely resembled a development in March 1992, when Narong Wongwan, a veteran politician and leader of the Samakkhi Tham Party looked certain to be nominated as Prime Minister. A Singaporean journalist asked Narong at a press conference whether it was true that the US government had denied him a visa over allegations of involvement in drug trafficking. This became a major international news story, was taken up by the domestic press, and Narong's prime ministerial hopes were dashed (see Heuvel and Dennis 1993: 173–5). During the mass demonstrations against the Suchinda Kraprayoon government that followed in May 1992, the international media were regarded by progressive elements in the Thai press as important allies in publicizing military attempts to suppress popular protests by means of violence. The international media communicated news of the protests to the outside world; this news was in turn filtered back into Thailand through satellite television, short-wave radio broadcasts, and direct fax and telephone communications from Thai living abroad. The international media offered a wider forum to publicize political problems in Thailand, a forum that could exert a positive influence over domestic developments (see McCargo and Bowra 1997). A central lesson of the May events was that the international media could be enlisted by the domestic print media to pursue their own political objectives. A similar pattern emerged in Indonesia in 1998.

Early in 1995, I was interviewing a well-known public figure in Bangkok. During the course of the interview, he asked me whether I could help him publicize an important development with disturbing political implications. He told me that taking the matter to the Thai press would not have sufficient impact; he wanted the story to appear in a British or international English-language newspaper or news magazine. In addition, he wanted the story to appear under the by-line of a Westerner, not the name of a Thai journalist employed by one of those publications. Only if the government believed that foreigners (to be more precise, in fact, Westerners) were monitoring their actions would they be sufficiently alarmed to take notice.

This conversation starkly illustrated a tendency among political and media practitioners in Thailand: the tendency to make use of the international media for domestic purposes. Stories written about Thailand by foreign publications could have a significant impact on domestic political debate. Thai newspapers (particularly Thai-language newspapers) pick up on international news stories and use them to criticize particular politicians or to illustrate particular themes. Very often, however, there are discrepancies between the tone or content of the original international stories and of the domestic stories they generate. Sometimes the international stories contain misrepresentations or distortions of domestic political developments in Thailand. Very often, the domestic stories reflect a misreading of international coverage. It will be argued that these processes of reciprocal misreading form part of a mutually beneficial dialogue between domestic and international media.

Foreign news gathering in the Thai-language press

Foreign news forms a significant part of the news content of Thai-language newspapers. Even popular mass circulation newspapers such as *Thai Rath* assign a full page for foreign news, and foreign material is also extensively used in the business, features and sports pages. However, foreign news (especially foreign political news, including Thai coverage of foreign coverage of domestic Thai politics) is gathered very differently from domestic news. Whereas domestic news is gathered first-hand by teams of reporters, the primary source of foreign news is wire service reports, supplemented by material from the international English-language press. Thai newspapers do not employ full-time, salaried foreign correspondents, though they do sometimes have stringers (often informal ones) in cities with sizeable Thai populations such as London and Los Angeles. Foreign-news staff on Thai-language newspapers are essentially translators. Nor are they professional translators:

typically, a young university graduate with a degree in a humanities or social-science subject will be assigned to the foreign desk and expected to start translating wire service reports almost immediately, with the aid of a few dictionaries.

Most Thai-language newspapers employ no more than one or two reporters or editorial desk staff with a good command of spoken English; very often, those who can speak English are not employed in a job where they can use this skill for news-gathering purposes. Some reporters with good spoken English skills working for Thai-language publications complained that other staff were jealous of their English ability, and this led them to feel inhibited about using English in the course of their work. Most such reporters quickly moved on from the Thai-language press to work for local English-language newspapers (mainly *Bangkok Post* and *The Nation*), or to international press agencies or foreign publications.

When an important foreign story breaks, Thai-language newspapers are faced with serious practical difficulties in pursuing it. There are no professional foreign correspondents already in place. Except in very rare cases, resources are not available to send correspondents abroad. In any event, very few staff possess the experience and linguistic competence to be sent off in pursuit of stories. Insofar as wire-service stories can be followed up, telephone interviews and faxed requests for documentary information are the main methods used. Requests for comment from Thai agencies involved (especially the Foreign Ministry) are another standard approach, as well as calls to the Bangkok embassies of countries concerned. In covering foreign stories, including those directly relevant to Thai interests and to domestic political concerns, the Thai-language press often operates largely in the dark, fumbling around to grasp what is really going on.

The strengths and limitations of the Thai-language press in dealing with foreign stories become especially apparent when the story concerned has an immediate domestic political impact. This chapter will examine two cases from 1995: first, the coverage of Banharn Silpa-archa and the Chat Thai Party in the international press during the early stages of the general election campaign, and the way this coverage was portrayed in the Thai press; and second, Thai coverage of an 'international' story concerning accusations by Swedish peace activists that the Chat Thai Party had accepted tainted election campaign contributions from a submarine manufacturer. It will then review relations between the Thai Rak Thai Party leader (and later Prime Minister) Thaksin Shinawatra, and the international media from March 2000 to April 2002.

Siam Post, until early 1996 the sister-paper of the English-language *Bangkok Post*, differed somewhat from other Thai newspapers in its use of foreign stories. *Siam Post* (established in 1992) quickly gained a reputation for hard-hitting political stories. As Lewis observes, the dominant newsframe for much of the international coverage in the Thai press was its relevance to domestic political concerns (Lewis 2000: 136) One of the techniques favoured by the paper was using foreign news stories with a Thai dimension as front-page leads. One senior member of the foreign-news staff was assigned to work closely with the front-page desk, constantly looking out for foreign stories with domestic political mileage. In practice, this meant looking for stories in the international press that were critical of Thailand or of Thai politicians. However, in seeking this criticism, the editorial staff of *Siam Post* were not wanting to pick a fight with the Western press. On the contrary: they were seeking to use the Western press to highlight and legitimate concerns of their own about issues such as political corruption and the low quality of many Thai politicians.

One staff member of *Siam Post* explained that they regarded the international press, and particularly well-known regional international publications such as the *Asian Wall Street Journal* and the *Far Eastern Economic Review*, as highly influential in shaping foreign perceptions of Thailand (interview notes, 24 November 1995). Thai people ought to be aware of what these publications were writing about their country. Whereas Thai newspapers were very willing to highlight the coverage of the international press, they were very unwilling to give 'credit' to issues uncovered by other Thai newspapers, including English-language papers. This resulted in a curious circulation of information. Critical stories about the government would appear in the Thai-language press. These would then be discussed in the domestic English-language press, particularly in *The Nation*. Foreign correspondents in Bangkok (only two or three of whom could read Thai in 1995) would pick up the stories from the English-language newspapers and work them into their own despatches. Thai-language newspapers such as

Siam Post would then 'pick up' the stories as an example of how Thailand's image was suffering in the eyes of the international community. Very often, *Siam Post* (and sometimes other papers) would reprint the original English story in facsimile form on its front page, with an accompanying Thai translation. Thai politicians would then read the story (very few politicians in the Banharn government could read English with ease) and be interviewed about it by reporters from the political desks of all the Thai language papers, whereupon the 'foreign attack' on Thai politics would be denounced by Cabinet ministers, and sometimes even the Prime Minister himself. In this way, the press would manufacture news stories which had virtually no kernel of factual content, pyramids of accusation and counter-accusation.

An important distinction in the context of the Thai-language press is the distinction between news and comment. 'News' especially political news, is narrowly defined as literal descriptions of actual events, plus the verbatim utterances of people involved, especially senior figures. News rarely contains background information or explanation of the significance of events or statements concerned. By contrast, the inside pages of Thai-language newspapers contain considerable amounts of political 'comment', mainly by regular columnists. Most political columns consist almost entirely of opinion, with very little factual material. Most political news consists of the comments of people 'outside' in the wider political world (mainly MPs, party leaders and ministers), while most political columns contain the comments of those 'inside' the newspaper and those closely associated with it. In other words, Thai-language newspapers are structured around a constant political dialogue between two groups of commentators, both of which have the status of 'insiders' in the Thai political system. There are often close personal ties between politicians and columnists, ties which sometimes bring financial and other benefits to the columnists concerned. The addition of foreign voices to the ongoing noisy conversation among different political commentators enhances the boisterous, 'temple fair' atmosphere. As with local voices, political commentators will rush to denounce or to support the foreign speaker, seeking to discredit him or to co-opt him. Most Thai politicians see a critical foreign commentator as a potential threat to their image and public standing. For Thai columnists, a foreign voice can lend credibility to concerns they have been voicing about the behaviour and conduct of politicians. The foreign voice is a potential maverick that does not fit into the usual Thai categories.[2] Typically, Thai politicians will try to undermine the foreign voice by arguing that it is really a Thai voice, a disguised player in the day-to-day 'game' of politics. A domestic publication wishing to criticize a Thai politician will seek to establish the credibility and international status of the foreign voice, so as to demonstrate that the foreign voice stands above the domestic 'game'.

Responding to coverage of the 1995 general election

The *modus operandi* of the Thai press in recycling foreign coverage of domestic politics was especially clear at the time of the 1995 election held on 2 July. The election was preceded by around six weeks of intensive media coverage, following the collapse of the Chuan Leekpai government in a non-confidence vote in mid-May.

On 1 June 1995, *Siam Post* led with a story based directly on a front-page article from the previous day's *Asian Wall Street Journal*. The original story by Paul M. Sherer was headlined 'Elite appear to underestimate Banharn', and sub-headed 'Observers see Chat Thai Party leader in contention to be Thai premier' (*AWSJ*, 31 May 1995). The article was accompanied by an artist's sketch of Banharn. *Siam Post* reproduced the entire front page of the *Journal* on its own front page, thereby making it clear that Sherer's article had been prominently featured in the newspaper. As its headline suggests, the thrust of Sherer's article was that Banharn's political ascent was not being taken seriously by many people in Thailand. Sherer stressed Banharn's ministerial record and his achievements in his home province of Suphanburi, and noted the tendency of many prominent and well-informed Thais to belittle both Banharn's record and his prospects of gaining the premiership. The story continued on an inside page, where Sherer mentioned Banharn's old nickname of 'Mr ATM' (the nickname satirized Banharn as a 'fixer', who could always sweeten his requests for political support with immediate cash incentives) and the fact that senior members of his party had been denied US visas on account of their alleged involvement in the drugs trade. Sherer concluded by quoting an unnamed western diplomat as saying that while it remained unclear how far

Banharn might be supported by intellectuals, he would be accepted by ordinary people if he became Prime Minister. Sherer's article was scrupulously fair to Banharn; if anything, it was a sympathetic view of him.

For *Siam Post*, though, Sherer's background details were of more interest than his main thrust. This was in spite of the fact that both the 'Mr ATM' nickname and the drug allegations were very old stories that had been extensively covered by both the international and domestic press before. The *Siam Post* headline was 'Foreigners eye Banharn, assess old poisonous wounds' (*SP*, 1 June 1995). Above the main headline was the smaller headline 'Keeping an eye on premier-to-be / Dubious ATM machine – Party members trade dust'. The story lead-in declared 'Foreigners are starting to keep an eye on Mr Silpa-archa, the leader of the Chat Thai Party; now that he might gain the position of Prime Minister people are generally starting to notice his ATM machine image and members of his party selling drugs'. The article went on to give a detailed and very restrained translation-cum-summary of the Sherer piece. There was a clear discrepancy between the content of the Sherer article (reflected in the body of the *Siam Post* story), and the *Siam Post* headlines and lead-in material. The headlines, coupled with the accompanying reproduction of the original article, suggested a critical denunciation of Banharn by a leading regional publication. This image of the *Journal* story (rather than the content of the story itself) was highly effective in embarrassing Chat Thai and the party leader, putting them immediately on the defensive. The line taken by *Siam Post* was echoed by mass-circulation *Khao Sot*, which ran the story with the headline 'Foreign newspaper missile hits Banharn'. Unlike *Siam Post*, *Khao Sot* dealt only with the negative aspects of the article. The story was also carried by *Matichon* and covered by the radio news service INN.

Chat Thai's response to the story became news for a couple of days following its appearance. Banharn himself declared that there was a conspiracy at work among his domestic political opponents, who had given information to the *Journal* in an attempt to discredit him. He was reported as saying 'Somebody here gave the information to the newspaper. This is just the beginning. More will follow' (*Nation*, 2 June 1995). Chat Thai secretary-general Sanoh Thienthong declared: 'This kind of news is likely to have some political party behind it' (*SP*, 2 June 1995). Somsak Prissanananthakul, deputy Chat Thai spokesman, called the article 'a conspiracy to destroy Chat Thai, curbing our growth and blocking our leader from rising to the premier post'(*Nation*, 2 June 1995). He went on to argue that since Chat Thai had begun to gain in popular appeal during the no-confidence debate, the party's opponents had been trying to discredit it. He believed that it must be someone of considerable political importance who had given information to the *Asian Wall Street Journal* (*SP*, 2 June 1995). Like Banharn, Somsak expected further damaging reports to appear in the foreign press in the next couple of days.

Although far-fetched in this instance, Banharn and Somsak's view that a conspiracy was at work linking foreign journalists with domestic opponents acknowledged the degree to which critical coverage in the international press could be damaging to Thai politicians. As an internationally-published newspaper report, the *Journal* article on Banharn had considerable credibility. The response of Banharn and Chat Thai was to attempt to neutralize that international credibility by characterizing the article as part of a domestic political 'game'. If the *Journal* article could be viewed in the same light as a commentary in a Thai-language newspaper such as *Siam Post* or *Khao Sot*, its impact would be minimal. In this case, the comments by Banharn and Somsak illustrate their failure to read the original article and grasp its intended significance. They interpreted the article as part of a Thai political 'game' precisely because of the game-playing of misrepresentation practised by the front-page editors of the Thai-language press. Banharn and his associates did not fully understand the way the international media operated.

At the same time, Banharn's belief in the existence of conspiracies to discredit him cannot be dismissed as mere ignorance or paranoia.[3] His view was based on two known facts: Thai reporters are employed by the Bangkok bureaux of several international publications (one such reporter worked for the *Asian Wall Street Journal*); and some Thai politicians enjoy close ties with certain foreign correspondents, sometimes supplying them with 'leads', unattributed leaks and misinformation (*ploi khao*). One such politician was Prasong Sunsiri, former intelligence chief, and Foreign Minister from 1992 to 1994. Prasong had played a part in publicizing US narcotics-related allegations about Narong Wongwan and Vattana Assawahame, two leading figures in Chart Thai. The Democrat Party also contained a couple of MPs with academic backgrounds and fluent English who maintained excellent ties with the foreign journalistic community, including party spokesman Abhisit Vejjajiva and former Deputy Foreign Minister Surin Pitsuwan.[4] Chat Thai had no equivalent figures to manage its relations with the international press. The outlines of the plot imagined by Banharn would involve either an unsympathetic Thai reporter (perhaps with links to a politician or political party) using influence with a foreign colleague to get a critical story written (or even ghost-writing it for a foreigner), or else a foreign correspondent falling under the sway of a persuasive Thai opponent such as Abhisit or Prasong. According to one source, Banharn was so concerned that he went in person to at least one Thai newspaper office (that of *Matichon*) on 1 or 2 June to explain that people were plotting against him.[5]

In its 2 June front page story on the political response to the *Journal* article, *Siam Post* noted that there was now a movement for a 'neutral person' to become Prime Minister, rather than the leader of either the Democrat or the Chat Thai parties. People who did not relish the prospect of a Banharn government were trying to generate a *krasae*, a political 'current' or 'bandwagon' for an alternative prime ministerial candidate to emerge. Was *Siam Post* attempting to build up this kind of tide of feeling, or was the newspaper simply reporting an existing sentiment (like that of middle-class distrust of Banharn)? The story described the *Asian Wall Street Journal* as 'a newspaper which has influence among the leading businessmen of the world'. This theme of 'the world is watching our politicians' was a recurrent one in *Siam Post*'s treatment of international news stories about Thailand. *Siam Post* consistently sought to invoke the wider world as a watchdog of Thai political standards and public morality.

On the same day, *Siam Post* ran as its lead a second story about supposed foreign criticism of Chat Thai. Under the headline 'Getting Banharn to clean up cast-off image of "white powder government"' – with a smaller headline above reading 'Foreign news agency takes a look at Thai politics after the election' – the story described how an Associated Press (AP) article questioned the qualifications of prospective Chat Thai ministers in the wake of the *Asian Wall Street Journal* story. The story went on to summarize the AP account, describing how Thai political scientists were speculating that Chat Thai politicians accused of involvement in drug-dealing could become ministers after the election. The AP story was based upon interviews with two Chulalongkorn University political scientists, Chaiwat Khamchoo and Kramol Thongdhammachart. But because these two academics had given interviews to AP, the story had been recycled by *Siam Post* as an example of international scrutiny of the Thai political scene. Again, however, there was a serious discrepancy between the prominence and bold headline of this front-page lead, and the substantive content of the article. A story which that only have merited a small item on the inside pages had the academics given interviews to Thai reporters became front-page news, simply because of the 'international' route by which their statements had emerged.

On 3 June, *The Nation* ran a front-page story entitled 'Rivals behind smear campaign, insists Banharn'. The story linked the *Asian Wall Street Journal* article, press agency reports, and (less plausibly and relevantly) one of *The Nation*'s own previous articles on calls by Thai academics for Banharn to clarify the issue of alleged drug-dealers in his party. Typically, the story included no new information, simply citing the latest responses of senior Chat Thai members to the criticisms being voiced in the press. One telling detail was a quotation from Prime Minister Chuan Leekpai, who pointed out that most Thais did not read English-language newspapers. The standard Thai practice of publishing 'news' stories that consisted of nothing more than comments on the comments of others made it easy to keep alive political 'issues' of no substance. The apparent objective of the media was to create pressure upon the Chat Thai Party to clean up its political act.

Siam Post – now for the third day running – ran a new front-page lead story on 4 June 1995 about coverage of Chat Thai in the international media. Using the headline 'Chat Thai evades answering, says it's a Democrat game to harm them' – the paper went on: 'The foreign media is still eyeing up the future of the "Banharn 1 government" as concerns the fact that Chat Thai won't agree to give a clear answer about the issue of public figures affiliated with it, openly stating that the Democrats are playing a game to harm them'. The peg for their story was an article in the latest issue of the *Far Eastern Economic Review* by Michael Vatikiotis, entitled 'Devils' advocate: Banharn wants to change Chat Thai's image'.

Siam Post reproduced most of the article alongside its headline, a further example of the kind of 'intertextuality' employed in the *Asian Wall Street Journal* story. However, the original story contained only one passing reference to the issue of Chat Thai figures linked to drug allegations, the point highlighted by the *Siam Post* headline. *Siam Post* gave a brief account of the *Review* article, before again referring to the *Asian Wall Street Journal* and AP pieces and their mention of the drug allegations. *Siam Post* quoted Banharn as saying that the stories were an example of *ploi khao* by political opponents. Banharn claimed Chat Thai also had information about its opponents that it might decide to release. If it did so, people would know who had deeper information about the other. Banharn's response illustrated his view of politics as a game in which all parties gathered dirt on each other; any party that threw an unreasonable amount of dirt at an opponent through the media could expect to be attacked in return. None of the interviews with various political figures dealt directly with the content of the *Review* article.

The furore over the *Asian Wall Street Journal* article subsequently died down as it gradually became apparent that the episode was the kind of storm in a teacup so beloved of Thai-language newspapers and Thai politicians. Dr Surakiart Sathirathai, then dean of the law faculty at Chulalongkorn University and a close advisor to Banharn, was one of the few Banharn aides to enjoy good relations with the international media. Surakiart made it known that Banharn now understood that the *Journal* article had not been conceived as an attack on him. A few days prior to the election, Banharn had a private dinner at an up-market restaurant in Bangkok's Sukhumvit area, with a handful of editorial staff and senior reporters from *Siam Post*. A Thai reporter from the *Asian Wall Street Journal* was also invited. One purpose of the gathering was to 'clear' the problem between Banharn, the *Journal*, and *Siam Post*. The English word 'clear' is often used in Thai to indicate this kind of conflict resolution involving politicians and journalists, a wiping clean of the slate. At the dinner, Banharn appeared to understand that the foreign newspaper had not been involved in a plot against him. A truce was called in this particular match in the long-running series of press versus politician 'games'.

The rules of the game remained the same, however: a news story that appears in the international media has more impact than a story in the local media, even if the international story came from the local media. Former government spokesman and Democrat MP Abhisit Vejjajiva expressed it like this:

> The Thai press takes a stance, the *Far Eastern Economic Review* merely reflects what the Thai press says, and it becomes big news that the *Review* says it. There is this attitude that if the *Far Eastern Economic Review*, *Time*, or *Newsweek* says it, everyone else in the world must be reading it, and it must carry weight. It's baffling even to the people who write for the *Review*.[6]

Henrik Westander and the Kockums case

In November 1995 Henrik Westander, a Swedish peace activist and independent researcher on the arms trade, published a newspaper article alleging that Kockums, a Swedish submarine manufacturer, had promised sizeable campaign contributions to the Chat Thai Party, conditional on receiving submarine orders from the Thai Navy (*Dagens Nyheter*, 26 November 1995). According to Westander: 'This information was provided by a centrally placed source with direct access to the submarine deal'.[7] Westander's article was distinctly short on details about the alleged bribery: he did not specify who was to be paid, who was to do the paying, when the payments were to be made, or how much money was involved. An AFP story that carried details of the original article was picked up by a number of Thai newspapers, including *Thai Rath*, *Matichon*, *Siam Post* and *The Nation*. For several weeks, Westander's accusations were extensively covered in the Thai press. *Siam Post* was particularly detailed in its coverage of the issue; a few days after the story broke, Chat Thai sued *Siam Post* for libel, despite the fact that other newspapers had carried the story and that coverage in the Thai press was based on Westander's claims. Despite intense media interest in the issue, no new information of a substantive nature emerged about the core allegation. Nor did Westander provide any documentary or other evidence to back up the indirect testimony of his anonymous 'centrally-placed informant'.

The Kockums case provides excellent illustrations of the *modus operandi* of the Thai press in dealing with a foreign news story that had important domestic political ramifications. The allegations by Westander came at a time when the Banharn government was facing media criticism for its alleged lack of financial and political integrity. The Kockums charges allowed the media to broaden out the attacks on Chat Thai: not only were they accused of 'domestic' corruption, but they had also allegedly been willing to sell out Thailand's national interests to a foreign arms company.

It must be stressed that no assertion or implication is being made here that Kockums, its representatives, or any Thai politician, military officer, or government official acted improperly over the submarine question.[8] Rather, the discussion is concerned solely with analysing media and political aspects of the press controversy. However, undertaking such an analysis involves first sketching out the rationale behind the media's considerable interest in Westander's accusation.

The purchase of submarines had been under consideration in Thailand for some time. The Thai Navy had long been something of a Cinderella service, lacking the long-standing political clout of the Army and latterly of the Air Force. At the same time, the public looked sympathetically upon the Navy, which had not participated in the violent suppression of political protests during the May 1992 upheavals. Military reporters for the major newspapers were overwhelmingly supportive of the Navy's desire to acquire submarine capabilities, but the Chuan government had vetoed submarine purchase on budgetary grounds in April 1995. Chuan had become Prime Minister against a backdrop of anti-military feeling following the May 1992 events, and although he had done little to curb military privilege, he had been reluctant to approve major arms purchases. There was every reason to think that a new government coalition led by senior figures in the Chat Thai Party might be sympathetic to increased spending on defence contracts, given their desire to secure military support, and their known partiality for 'commissions'.

A number of companies were interested in bidding for the submarine contract; the German and Swedish proposals were generally considered leading contenders. The Navy was believed to be very sympathetic to the Swedish bid, but in practice any decision would have to be approved by its political masters.[9] A complicating factor was the role of General Chavalit Yongchaiyudh, leader of the New Aspiration Party (NAP). Before entering civilian politics, Chavalit had been Army commander-in-chief and armed forces supreme commander. He had approved numerous arms purchases during his tenure in these positions, including that of Chinese-made frigates for the Navy. Some of Chavalit's purchases had been controversial. Chavalit was rumoured to be sympathetic to the German submarine bid. The NAP was likely to join a Chat Thai led coalition, and Chavalit was bound to take an interest in defence matters (in the event, he became Defence Minister). It was therefore highly possible that Chavalit would seek to use his influence in the new government to approve the purchase of German submarines. Thus it would have been entirely logical for Kockums to have made efforts to buy Chat Thai's support.

For the Thai-language press, covering the Westander story proved difficult. Their normal technique in dealing with a political controversy was to seek quotations from protagonists, but in this case Westander himself was accessible only by telephone, and only through the medium of English. Very few Thai journalists had the ability to conduct a telephone interview with Westander, or with other sources in Sweden such as the Kockums company, the Defence Ministry, or opposition politicians. No Thai newspaper had a stringer or correspondent in Sweden; to complicate matters, Westander himself was living in Denmark, though the offices of his organization – the Swedish Peace and Arbitration Society – were in Stockholm. Although a television crew from Pacific Intercommunications did eventually visit Sweden to make a documentary about the story (they never met Westander), no Thai newspaper sent a reporter there.

Siam Post dealt with this problem by seeking to publish material that supported Westander's account and enhanced his credibility. On 28 November, *Siam Post* ran the story as its front-page lead, accompanied by a large photograph of Sweden's ambassador in Bangkok calling upon the Thai Foreign Minister to deny the allegations. Westander's claims had been dismissed by some Chart Thai politicians on the grounds that no one would offer bribes before the outcome of the election was known. Interviewed by telephone for the article, Westander clarified the position: the campaign contributions were 'a much more uncertain form of investment', a speculative attempt to secure later support rather than an outright bribe for a specific favour. He was also asked about his track record as a peace campaigner, and he explained how in 1984 he had provided evidence concerning illegal arms exports to the Middle East by the Swedish company Bofors, which had resulted in criminal proceedings being brought; in 1989 three executives of the company were convicted in a Swedish court. This detail was included in the story's lead-in: Westander was 'the one who had been responsible for the Bofors case, resulting in company executives being jailed'.[10] He had later played a part in uncovering details of the Bofors India case, publishing a book on the subject (Westander 1992). *Siam Post* noted that Westander had been working as a full-time arms researcher for thirteen years, working solely on the Bofors and Kockums companies.[11]

Siam Post also pointed out that in addition to giving a special interview to the newspaper, Westander had also given an interview to the BBC in London, 'which is broadcast all over the world' (*SP*, 28 November 1995). In fact, however, Westander was interviewed (with translation) by the BBC World Service Thai Service, which is listened to almost solely by Thais, most of them in Thailand. This interview was important in lending additional credibility to Westander, since the BBC Thai Service plays an important role in legitimating news stories. A story which a Thai language newspaper might be hesitant about running can be covered as an account of a BBC story. News and political editors at major Thai newspapers such as *Bangkok Post*, *Matichon*, *Phujatkan*, and *Thai Rath* are in regular telephone contact with the producers and presenters on the Thai-language service, all of whom are Thai, and most of whom are themselves former journalists on Thai newspapers. Whenever Thai newspaper reporters make trips to London (as they commonly do during the March–May hot season, often on company-sponsored 'inspection tours') they drop in at the BBC Thai Service. Physically removed from the daily machinations of Thai politics – but in constant touch with events – the BBC Thai Service is an authoritative voice that acts as an external referent. A story not covered by the BBC can much more easily be dismissed as frivolous or spurious than one the BBC is taking seriously.

Siam Post supported its lead story on the submarine allegations with a second front-page story concentrating on the domestic angle, detailing the denials of Banharn and other government figures. Defence Minister Chavalit Yongchaiyudh reprimanded the Thai press for lacking caution in publishing a story that could have an impact on revered national institutions. He claimed the story was planted. Chavalit's response reflected a military mentality that saw freedom of information as a potential threat to the Thai state. For the Thai press, this line of argument was crude and transparent; in an editorial *The Nation* described Chavalit's statements as 'a gesture typical of political immaturity' (29 November 1995).

On 29 November, *Siam Post* continued its coverage of the Kockums allegations with two front-page stories. Its lead story concentrated on allegations about the role of the company's Thai 'advisor', former naval officer Supridi Sribhadung. A second story dealt with the latest government responses. The comments of Chat Thai secretary-general Sanoh Thienthong were especially telling. Sanoh declared:

> This story is a matter of national honour; we're hitting back – it's not true. I ask the media to be aware that we are living together in a Thai way. We have to be careful concerning anything which tarnishes the nation. What this is all about I don't know. Foreigners tend to like planting news to make trouble for our government.
>
> (*SP*, 29 November 1995)

Like Chavalit, Sanoh sought to present the accusations as a foreign intervention in Thailand's domestic affairs, and attempted to invoke nationalist sentiment to discredit the claims. As a leading figure in the Chat Thai Party (in most Thai parties, the secretary-general takes principal responsibility for fund-raising, lobbying and other kinds of dirty dealing), Sanoh's own 'honour' was at stake. Just as for *Siam Post* the foreign character of the allegations was evidence of their credibility – on the grounds that Westander was not involved in domestic political concerns – so for government politicians the foreign origin of the allegations was invoked as evidence that Westander was seeking to meddle in Thailand's internal affairs. There was intense speculation about the identity of Westander's 'centrally placed source', generally assumed to be Thai until Westander gave discreet assurances to the contrary.[12]

What was Westander's motive? The obvious answer was that Westander was a professional pacifist, a campaigner dedicated to opposing the arms trade. This answer made him suspect in the eyes of many Thais, who saw him as a leftist agitator pursuing his own political agenda. But it was not an explanation sufficient to discredit him altogether. Discrediting Westander would mean linking him directly to figures in the Thai business or political worlds (therefore demonstrating that he was part of the local 'game'), linking him to other vested interests involved in the submarine bidding (especially to a rival company out to disqualify the Kockums bid), or ideally linking him to some kind of wider 'plot' connected with the bidding exercise, Thai politics, or even both.

Siam Post continued its pursuit of the Kockums story the following day, again with two front-page stories devoted to the case. One was on the resurfacing of Kockums 'advisor' Supridi (who had been lying low in Chantaburi province since the story broke), while the other was on the SPAS call for the Swedish government to investigate bank records of money transfers between Sweden and Thailand to see if there was evidence to support the allegations. The first part of an SPAS press release, complete with letterheading, was reproduced on the front page. The paper gave over most of page three to transcripts of two radio interviews with Supridi, one from *Nation* radio, and another from INN. Also on page three was a translation of a commentary on submarines in Asia from the previous day's *International Herald Tribune*. In the absence of new hard information, *Siam Post* was filling its pages with any available material – from radio interviews to foreign-press stories – to keep the controversy alive. In the text of the main front-page story, *Siam Post* quoted Westander as stating that there was now great media interest in the case in Sweden itself and that opposition parties were raising questions about the actions of Kockums and of the Swedish government.

One of the issues exciting public interest in Sweden was the claim that Democrat Party secretary-general Sanan Kachornprasart had been offered money by people claiming to be representatives of

Kockums when his party was still in government. This claim had appeared in the *Bangkok Post* on 28 November. The *Bangkok Post* story was picked up by an international news agency and appeared in the Swedish newspaper *Tidnivgarnas Telegrambrya*. A piece of domestic reporting in Thailand – coincidentally by *Siam Post*'s then sister paper – created a political stir in Sweden, which then was recycled in turn for Thai consumption. On 1 December, *Siam Post* ran copies of headlines from six Kockums-related stories in the previous day's Swedish press on its front page. The stories – which no one at *Siam Post* could read – illustrated the degree of interest the issue had raised in Sweden, thereby further legitimating the story. *Siam Post* reported that Banharn had announced his intention to sue the Thai newspapers that had covered the case, and to investigate the possibility of suing the Swedish newspaper as well. In its second story, it reported that two opposition parties in Sweden had now formally called for the issue to be officially investigated. The story was now focusing on questions of litigation and investigation, relating to the core allegations. Westander had still produced no evidence whatever for his claims, and apart from Sanan's rather vague allegations, there had been no further concrete development in the case itself since the original article had appeared.

On 2 December, the Chat Thai party filed a lawsuit against *Siam Post*. Although other Thai-language newspapers had covered the story, the tone of their coverage was more mild, and the coverage itself less detailed than that of *Siam Post*, which had set aside most or all of page three for the case on five consecutive days, in addition to its extensive front-page stories. The 3 December issue of *Thai Rath* illustrated the extent of the climbdown: the weekly political analysis column on page three, one of the most influential articles in the Thai-language press, came out in strong support of the Chart Thai party. 'The source who wrote the Swedish newspaper article is from the NGO movement', and speculated that the allegations might be related to intense rivalry between competing bidders for the submarine contract. *Thai Rath*'s 'political team' urged that the interests of the country be put first, implying – like government politicians – that those who criticized Banharn over the allegations were behaving unpatriotically.

The *Thai Rath* article itself became the basis of speculation as to what had been taking place behind the scenes. During the previous week, close aides of senior Chat Thai politicians had invited a senior editor from *Siam Post* for a lunch or dinner meeting on Friday 1 December, to discuss the problem of the paper's trenchant coverage of the case.[13] The senior editor had replied that he would be happy to meet them, but that they should not expect the paper's coverage of the submarine issue to change as a result. In the event, no meeting took place and the following day *Siam Post* was sued. It seemed highly possible that Chat Thai figures had made contact with the editors of other Thai-language newspapers, and successfully induced them to 'tone down' the submarine story, leaving *Siam Post* to bear the brunt of legal action alone, on account of its noncooperation. The international character of the story meant that *Siam Post* could be implicitly criticized by both government figures and rival newspapers for betraying Thailand's national interest in pursuit of a story. According to a Chat Thai spokesman, *Siam Post* had been singled out because it had gone beyond the original wording of the Swedish newspaper story in saying that monies had been received by Chat Thai (Sherer 1995). Coalition leaders were reported as saying that *Siam Post* was being sued because of its 'aggressive, insulting, and obviously biased' coverage of the case (*Nation*, 15 December 1995). Although the Reporter's Association of Thailand issued a statement (Reporters' Association 1995) criticizing Chat Thai's decision to sue *Siam Post*, Chat Thai had sought to isolate *Siam Post* from the broader newspaper community.

In retrospect, the lawsuit brought by Chat Thai against *Siam Post* was the beginning of the end for the Westander/Kockums story, although articles on the allegations continued to appear intermittently for some weeks. The second week of the case saw several new developments, including: an official four-page statement on the case from Prime Minister Banharn Silpa-archa, a second article by Westander, the appointment of a Swedish investigating committee, and attempts by Supridi and Kockums further to discredit Westander and to defend themselves. One of the most interesting developments was the statement from Banharn, in which he claimed that he was not acting to defend himself or his party but out of higher motives: 'This matter concerns the country's prestige and political legitimacy. If it is ignored, people would think the allegations have grounds.'[14] He went on to say that he and his party 'even in opposition, never accentuated issues for publicity in other countries'. The implication was that the Democrat opposition had breached implicit 'rules' of the Thai political game by first leaking information to Westander and then corroborating his story.

Banharn found it strange that 'even our media' (*suamuanchon fai rao*) were spreading Westander's allegations without any clear first-hand evidence to back them up. He implied that he expected the Thai media to demonstrate its loyalty in the face of criticism from abroad. According to Banharn, it was obvious that the allegations 'were born of a conflict of trade linked to regional political interests', a cryptic sentence on which he did not elaborate. The accuser seemed to have been successful on account of the prompt assistance provided by Thailand's media. Like the *Thai Rath* Sunday political analysis article, Banharn pointed out that Westander was affiliated to a pacifist group that campaigned against war and the arms trade, and went on to suggest that other countries were trying to prevent 'developing countries' from acquiring the means to build up their own defences. He concluded by arguing that interest groups both inside and outside the country were trying to harm Thailand's good name and reputation. Banharn's statement was long on self-justification and insinuation but contained very little factual content.

On the same day, Westander produced a new five-page article specially for publication by the Thai press. Rather like Banharn's press release, it contained little new factual information, except to confirm that his source was not a Thai naval officer nor one of Kockums' competitors (Westander 1995). Westander argued that the onus was now on the Swedish government to investigate the allegations by checking bank transfers to Thailand. The investigation could be helped by the various agencies: by the Democrat Party revealing more information, by Swedish opposition parties pressing the Swedish government to pursue the matter, and by the Thai government putting diplomatic pressure on the Swedish government. Following a debate in the Swedish parliament, it was agreed on 6 December that the government's War Materials Inspectorate (known as KMI) would look into Westander's allegations. In the absence of any new revelations from Westander, and the continuing refusal of Sanan and the Democrats to fuel the flames of the controversy any further, the submarine issue began to die down.

In any case, *Siam Post* began running a new 'exclusive' story on 6 December, concerning allegations that Dr Surakiart Sathirathai, the current Finance Minister, had operated a company to broker arms and other deals during the 1990–91 period when he was a member of former Premier Chatchai Choonavan's Ban Phitsanulok advisory team. Kockums remained an important story but was increasingly eclipsed by the new story, which became known as the 'Dr S' case.[15]

On the evening of 14 December, Supridi Sribhadung appeared on the satellite television station Thai Sky Channel 1, in a panel discussion with Prasong Lertratanawisute (one of the front-page editors of *Matichon*), Aroon Larnlua (editor of *Siam Post*), and Phiraphan Phalusuk, a Chart Thai MP. On this programme, Supridi mounted his most trenchant defence yet of his own activities and of Kockums. Supridi criticized Westander's allegations for their lack of specific details, describing Westander as having used 'masked source' and 'big liar'[16] tactics in his attempts to discredit Kockums. He cited a series of alleged errors in previous allegations by Westander,[17] and claimed that there was a plot to block the sale of Swedish submarines to the Thai Navy. Up to six different groups were involved in the plot, including SPAS (with its ideological opposition to weapons sales), other countries which did not want to see Thailand get submarines, rival submarine manufacturers, weapons agents, and Thai government officials who want to discredit the Navy (this presumably implied military officers from other branches of the services).

However, when Supridi was pressed by the moderator he conceded that his explanation was 'theoretical', rather than based upon hard information. Not all the groups he listed had necessarily been involved in the plot. In other words, Supridi's explanation was little more than conjecture, a grand conspiracy theory with no more detailed evidence to support it than Westander's original allegations. The beauty of Supridi's argument was that Westander became not a detached peace campaigner but the front man for an elaborate plot linking commercial, geo-political, international, and domestic rivalries. Supridi implied that neighbouring countries (obvious suspects might be Singapore and Malaysia) were seeking to block Thailand's acquisition of submarines, and so might have made common cause with Thai Army or Air Force officers (who wanted to preserve the higher status of their own forces vis-à-vis the Navy), rival submarine companies (such as the German company HDW), Thai arms dealers (by implication, individuals such as Rasri Bunlert, a major Thai arms dealer said to be working for HDW (*SP*, 30 November 1995) and alleged by some sources (for example, see *BP*, 16 December 1995) to be close to New Aspiration leader Chavalit Yongchaiyudh and his wife Khunying Pankrua), and foreign NGOs such as SPAS. If substantiated, Supridi's master-plot would have undermined Westander's credibility, involving him inextricably in the Thai political 'game'. But although Supridi's theories were certainly ingenious and entertaining, to most commentators they seemed rather less probable than Westander's original allegation.

Supridi's interpretation elaborated on the conspiracy theory suggested by Banharn's reference to a 'conflict of trade linked to region political interests'. Just as he had arrived at his own notion of a domestic political conspiracy to account for what he misinterpreted as a hostile article about him in the *Asian Wall Street Journal*, so Banharn had come up with another conspiracy to explain criticism of his administration over the Kockums and 'Dr S' cases. The outlines of this conspiracy are hinted at in a *Nation* commentary by Sorrayuth Suthassanachinda (Sorrayuth 1995). Banharn had told *The Nation*: 'I know who is behind all this and I'm watching to see what he's going to do next'. Sorrayuth observed that Banharn 'seems to have sound reasons for believing his present crisis can be traced back to just one man, a dangerously ambitious one'.

Sorrayuth's article makes clear – without ever saying so – that the man in question was Defence Minister Chavalit Yongchaiyudh.[18] The suggestion was that Chavalit, with his eye on becoming the next Prime Minister, had used the Kockums allegations both to improve the prospects for the German HDW bid and to weaken Banharn's political standing. The investigative reports published in *Siam Post* on the 'Dr S' case focused upon two close Banharn aides, and clearly made use of leaked documents confiscated during the 23 February 1991 coup. Banharn believed the military sources had leaked the documents to discredit the two men, and assumed that former Army commander-in-chief and current Defence Minister Chavalit was responsible for these leaks, as well as for feeding information to Westander.

Banharn's apparent interpretation of the Kockums scandal, like his view of the *Asian Wall Street Journal* article, reflected a profoundly Thai-centric view of the world. Banharn failed to appreciate the way foreign journalists and researchers operated, not recognizing that these were professionals with their own agendas, objectives and standards. They had a wide range of sources and were not passively dependent upon unreliable Thai messengers for all their information. Banharn saw the media in traditional Thai terms, whereby politicians cultivated reporters and columnists, plying them with financial favours and giving them useful leads in exchange for sympathetic press coverage. Under such conditions, any rumours or scandals appearing in the press usually had traceable origins and predictable meanings.

The internationalization of the media had made this view of the Thai press increasingly outdated. Like the generals behind the military attempts to suppress the May 1992 popular protests, Banharn was out of touch with the realities of modern communications, which have rendered political news no longer constrained by national boundaries and thus almost impossible for individual politicians or governments to monitor, let alone control.[19] There was no necessary or probable link between a Swedish peace activist writing an article for a Swedish newspaper based on a Swedish source, and the internal problems of Banharn's own coalition administration. Nor did extensive coverage of the Swedish story by elements of the Thai press prove the involvement of rival politicians in a plot to discredit the Banharn government. In this case, they simply illustrated the refusal of newspapers such as *Siam Post* to play the government's 'game' by acceding to Chart Thai's 'lobbying' requests that the paper 'tone down' an important story. The intensity of the Kockums furore testified more to *Siam Post*'s refusal to play the domestic political game, rather than to *Siam Post*'s determination to play such a game. The Kockums case offered an opportunity to newspapers such as *Siam Post* to operate as political actors, providing them with excellent materials with which to run a campaign.

The Kockums affair rumbled on, with no clear end in sight. On 14 December *Dagens Nyheter* published new bribery allegations, saying that Kockums had given money to five different political parties in Thailand in an attempt to secure the submarine contract.

The story, by a professional correspondent rather than an activist such as Westander, lent further credence to the earlier allegations (*SP*, 16 December 1995; *Nation*, 16 December 1995). The BBC Thai Service interviewed an assistant editor at the Swedish newspaper, who confirmed that the paper would not have published the story unless it had confidence in its accuracy (*SP*, 16 December 1995).

The results of official investigations into the submarine affair were mixed, however. While the Foreign Affairs Committee of the Thai House of Representatives (chaired by an opposition MP) came out with a report criticizing the government and raising a number of unanswered questions, the Committee had been hindered by its inability to compel important witnesses to testify. Among those who had failed to appear was the Prime Minister himself (*Nation*, 5, 6 and 9 January 1996). On 15 January, the Swedish KMI reported finding no evidence of Kockums having paid bribes to Thai politicians in an attempt to secure submarine contracts (*Nation*, 16 January 1996). But like the Thai investigation, the KMI investigation was limited in scope: it had called various witnesses, including Westander, but had not investigated bank transfers between Sweden and Thailand (*BP*, 16 January 1996; *Nation*, 16 January 1996). Westander was unsurprised by the outcome of the KMI probe, but in the absence of strong political pressure from the Thai side (even the opposition Democrat Party, for all its posturing, had not formally called upon the Swedish government to investigate the bank transfers) and his own inability to reveal more, the story became a dead letter. The Chart Thai Party eventually won its libel case against *Siam Post* and its editor, Aroon Larnlua. The newspaper and Aroon were fined 100,000 baht each, Aroon received a one-year suspended jail sentence, and *Siam Post* was ordered to publish an apology (*Matichon*, 26 September 1997).

Thaksin and the foreign media

By 2000, it was becoming clear that Thaksin Shinawatra would be a strong contender to emerge as Thailand's next prime minister. The telecommunications magnate had served for a time in the police force – acquiring an American PhD in the process – before making a fortune in computers and mobile phones and becoming one of the richest men in the country (Ukrist 1998; Hewison 2001: 17). By the mid-1990s he was seeking to parlay his business success into a political career. He joined forces with the Palang Dharma Party founded by former Bangkok governor Chamlong Srimuang, serving for a short time as Foreign Minister before later assuming the leadership of the party in 1995. He then served as Deputy Prime Minister in the short-lived Banharn Silpa-archa government of 1995–96, and briefly again under Chavalit Yongchaiyudh in 1997. In July 1998 he created a new political party, Thai Rak Thai ('Thais Love Thai'), which sought to combine the more nationalist rhetoric in vogue after the 1997 financial crisis with the image of a high-tech, modern and decisive leader who could operate effectively in the global marketplace. An electoral professional party such as Thai Rak Thai[20] would depend heavily on the media to build its image with urban voters; yet surprisingly, Thaksin quickly found himself at loggerheads with elements of the international press.

Thaksin's sensitivity to criticism became apparent when *Time* magazine published a one-page article on him by Robert Horn, under the headline 'This time he's serious' (Horn 2000). The article reviewed Thaksin's track record of political failures – he presided over the demise of the once-mighty Palang Dharma Party, failed to deliver on a laughable promise to cure Bangkok's traffic jams and could not restore economic confidence to Chavalit's administration after the crisis – and pointed out that for all his claims to be a new-style 'digital' leader, he had formed alliances with many 'analogue' provincial power brokers. Leading Thai daily *Matichon* picked up the article at once, translating it in its entirety, but emphasizing the phrases and sentences most critical of Thaksin's record. One prospective parliamentary candidate immediately detected a conspiracy against Thaksin by his political enemies (*Naeo Na*, 2 March 2000). Thai Rak Thai Party deputy spokesman Suranan Vejjaijiva responded to the article in an interview with *Matichon*, declaring that the writer had not done his homework; in addition, Horn had included some of his own views and confused them with facts.[21] He cited as an example the question of Thaksin's broken promise to solve the traffic problem in six months.[22] Suranan's non-specific 'refutation' of this point had the effect of confusing the issue for anyone who did not check back to the original article or could not clearly recall political developments more than four years earlier.

Suranan also criticized the 'foreign intellectuals' who had been cited by Horn in the article. Duncan McCargo, he said, was someone with great faith in Chamlong Srimuang, and had actually written a book about him. It might be understandable, he continued, that McCargo held a negative view about Thaksin and blamed him for destroying the Palang Dharma Party, but 'Thais knew better' and were aware that Thaksin had not done this. Suranan was apparently attempting to suggest that Thais inherently knew more about issues than non-Thai academics who had researched them in depth; knowledge about Thailand was a question of nationality or ethnicity, rather than expertise.[23] In similar vein, Pongthep Tepkarnchana, deputy secretary of Thai Rak Thai, stated that Horn 'cited foreign intellectuals who did not understand Thailand enough' (*Naeo Na*, 2 March 2000).[24] In any case, the observation that Thaksin destroyed Palang Dharma was not attributed to McCargo in the original article.[25]

Thaksin was quoted in *Naeo Na* the following day comparing the case explicitly with Kockums and citing it as another example of media distortion. He complained that while the original article was headlined 'This time he's serious', in the Thai press and on radio programmes it became 'Thaksin is an analogue knight' (*Naeo Na*, 3 March 2000). The phrase 'analogue knight' never appeared at all in the original article, but was adopted by the Thai media as a kind of short-hand for its criticisms of Thaksin. The phrase is alliterative in Thai (*asawin analog*), and resonates ironically with popular discourse about 'white knights' coming to the rescue of the nation.

Subsequent coverage emphasized Thaksin's hostile reaction to the article, which predictably became a much larger story than the article itself. In *Thai Rath* and *Krungthep Thurakit*, the focus was primarily on Thaksin's response. A commentary in *Thai Post* responded that the only shortcoming in foreign coverage of Thaksin was that it was too mild, failing to highlight the potentially dangerous conflict of interest between his business and political activities (*Thai Post*, 2 March 2000). *Thai Post* also observed that leading figures in Thai Rak Thai admired Mahathir of Malaysia, and they believed that *Time* habitually sought to undermine Asian leaders such as Mahathir and Thaksin. To their thinking, criticism of Thaksin by *Time* legitimated Thaksin's image as a serious Asian leader who offered a challenge to Western hegemony.

Incensed by the article's observation that Thaksin had destroyed Palang Dharma, party founder Chamlong Srimuang issued a widely reported statement arguing that the party came to an end because of its refusal to buy votes (*Matichon*, 3 March 2000). This highly misleading statement begged one glaringly obvious question: how come Palang Dharma gained significant numbers of parliamentary seats in the March 1992, September 1992 and July 1995 general elections,[26] but only one in the 1996 election? Chamlong's explanation was too much for the residual members of the party to take, and the following day *Phujatkan* carried a story based on an interview with Nattapong Banrungrit, the secretary-general of the party. Nattapong supported the interpretation of the *Time* article, arguing that it was an incontrovertible fact that Thaksin had damaged the image of the party and destroyed its electoral credibility (*Phujatkan*, 4 March 2000).

The furore over the *Time* article continued for several days, and the phrase 'analogue knight' entered the Thai political lexicon as a result. Yet this phrase was simply invented by the Thai press. Similarly, a foreign academic who was criticized by Thai Rak Thai had only been quoted by *Time* praising Thaksin, and none of the supposed 'factual inaccuracies' of which about Thaksin and his supporters complained were actual errors. In other words, the *Time* controversy was not at all about the substance of the original article, which merely provided an opportunity and a pretext for the Thai media to highlight critical questions about Thaksin.

The situation was nicely summarized by Sorrayuth Suthas-sanachinda (Sorrayuth 2000: 9), who pointed out that all the issues raised in the article were old stories; the main feature of the *Time* piece was that it brought together all Thakin's weak points. Thaksin's claims that there was a conspiracy to discredit him, that the foreign press used only half the information he offered and that the Thai press then exaggerated the information, were over the top. Nor was the comparison with the Kockums case – suggesting that many stories are started by foreigners, then blown up by the Thai press for commercial reasons – an appropriate one. As Sorrayuth observed 'It is the nature of media; no one tried to distort the information or damage his image. He should understand that the press does does not have a duty to publish things that politicians would like us to.'

Sorrayuth predicted that this would not be the last time Thaksin would find himself in conflict with the international press. Sure enough, a year after becoming Prime Minister, Thaksin was at loggerheads with the respected weekly magazine *Far Eastern Economic Review* (*FEER*), a digest of politics and business published in Hong Kong. In February 2002, the Thai immigration authorities made the disturbing announcement that they were proposing to black-list Shawn Crispin and Rodney Tasker, the magazine's two correspondents in Bangkok – as well as the Hong Kong based editor and publisher of the magazine. The ostensible reason for these proposed actions was a short 175-word article entitled 'Right Royal Headache', which had appeared (with no by-line) in the 10 January issue. The piece discussed tensions between the palace and Government House, and specifically suggested that Thaksin had business links with the Crown Prince. It was believed that the government had long been unhappy with the critical tone of *FEER*'s coverage of Thaksin, including its reporting of the King's birthday speech of 4 December 2001. *FEER* had interpreted comments made in this speech as a personal rebuke to Thaksin. The Thaksin government's threat to banish two foreign correspondents from the kingdom was without recent precedent (no such correspondent had been banned from Thailand since 1977), and raised alarming questions about issues of press freedom in Thailand. The implicit charge against the two journalists was that they had commented improperly on sensitive matters relating to the monarchy, which is covered by strict laws of lese-majesty.

The original piece in *FEER* was read by very few people in Thailand, since an immediate ban was imposed upon its distribution. Indeed, for more than a month after the article appeared, this distribution ban (a relatively common ploy used by the Thai authorities when a foreign news publication touches on the monarchy) was the only action taken against *FEER*. But on 23 February Crispin and Tasker had their visas suspended; official letters they were handed described them as a threat to national security (*Bangkok Post*, 26 February 2002). Moves to deport them were only halted following a letter of apology from *FEER*'s publishers, when an immigration panel decided to reverse the earlier decision to expel them (*Bangkok Post*, 8 March 2002). The apology, however, was made if the article generated 'any adverse commentary concerning Thailand's highest institution'; it was not an apology to Thaksin. *FEER* declined to retract the article itself. Thaksin and his Interior Minister, Purachai Piumsombun, insisted throughout that the action against *FEER* had been taken solely by the police, without any prompting from the government – a line many observers viewed with considerable scepticism (see, for example, Thepchai 2002).

A letter from the Special Branch sent to Crispin and Tasker on 8 January explicitly asked who had written the article and who was the source of the news (*Nation*, 27 February 2002). Predictably, Thaksin claimed the article was part of a conspiracy by the opposition to defame him and suggested that the source for the story was a pipe-smoker. This was widely understood as referring to Prasong Sunsiri, a former Air Force officer and national security chief, ex-Foreign Minister and professional cold warrior, whose page-three column in the Thai-language daily *Naeo Na* was well known for its anti-Thaksin stance. The idea that Prasong had ordered the story written was taken up by some elements of the Thai press, including leading daily *Thai Rath*. In a television interview on 27 February which was mysteriously blacked out, Prasong admitted to knowing Tasker, but denied being the source of the story (*Nation*, 28 February 2002). Similarly, *FEER* editor Michael Vatikiotis insisted that the article had not been written as a favour on behalf of a Thai opposition figure (*Nation*, 27 February 2002). Like Banharn before him, Thaksin was seeking to present an international news story as part of a domestic game by his political enemies.

Reactions from the Thai press to the story were varied. Prominent journalist and senator Somkiat Onwimol came out in strong support of the *FEER*, reading out the offending article on a radio programme (which was subsequently taken off the air), faxing and e-mailing it in Thai translation to numerous people, and challenging the authorities to arrest him. However, other senators denounced the 'lenient' treatment of the *FEER* reporters, and called for Somkiat to be punished (*The Nation*, 9 March 2002). This split was reflected in the press coverage; some editorials and columns criticized the government's harsh treatment of the correspondents, while others argued that *FEER* had attempted to exploit the monarchy for political purposes. In a surprising speech, respected social critic and reform activist Dr Prawase Wasi described attacks by the foreign press on Thailand as part of attempts by 'the superpower' to dominate the world (*The Nation*, 10 March 2002). Prawase's speech testified to the growing current of nationalist sentiment into which Thaksin was successfully tapping. The debate concerning *FEER* had been compounded by a fifteen-page special supplement on Thailand in the 2–8 March issue of *The Economist*. The supplement discussed Thaksin in a critical light and also devoted five paragraphs to the issue of monarchy, touching on the delicate question of the royal succession. Again, the issue could not be distributed in Thailand.

The debate over *FEER*'s coverage of tensions between the monarchy and Thaksin was actually an opportunity for the Thai press and leading figures in Thai society to address national concerns about the future of the country. Some of these concerns related to the royal succession, others to Thailand's place in the world following the devastating experience of the 1997 economic crisis.[27] As Prawase put it:

> We have already lost our economic sovereignty. Next will be political sovereignty and the right of Thai people to chart their own future.
>
> (*Bangkok Post*, 10 March 2002)

Thaksin's use of nationalist rhetoric was much cruder: he declared that if journalists who came to destroy Thailand, then regardless of their race or nationality he would consider them *persona non grata* (*The Nation*, 28 February 2002). The *FEER* reporters responded in kind; at one point, Crispin made a speech in Thai testifying to their love of Thailand and respect for its monarchy.

The actual *FEER* story that triggered this debate was very much a secondary issue, a pretext for the indirect airing of hidden concerns and anxieties. Though not exactly innocent victims, the journalists involved were soon embroiled in a controversy far larger than anything they could have envisaged. At the same time, the controversy also clearly illustrated the illiberal tendencies of the Thaksin administration. Subsequent developments – when it emerged that outspoken Thai journalists were being investigated for alleged money-laundering, a blatant tactic of political intimidation – were to highlight the degree to which Thaksin equated criticism with slander

(Baker 2002). In a fence-mending cover story interview with *FEER* on 11 April 2002, Thaksin implausibly alluded to a plot by his enemies to topple him by stirring up trouble in the eyes of the public (Vatikiotis and Tasker 2002). He argued that because his enemies could not oust him by parliamentary means, they were resorting to dirty tricks. This was a wearily familiar line of argument, trotted out by successive Thai prime ministers when under fire.

Conclusion

The four cases examined here – Thai media coverage of an *Asian Wall Street Journal* article about Banharn Silpa-archa by Paul Sherer; media follow-up on allegations made by Henrik Westander in the Swedish newspaper *Dagens Nyheter* concerning alleged clandestine payments to Thai politicians by Kockums; the response to a *Time* magazine story critical of Thaksin Shinawatra; and the furore over the *Far Eastern Economic Review*'s allusions to issues touching on the monarchy – illustrate the ways Thai domestic politics can interact with stories appearing in the international media. Thai newspapers, especially Thai-language newspapers such as *Siam Post*, have a tendency to respect the credibility of the international press as a news source and value the corroboration of international news stories in order to support their own criticisms of politicians. In particular, they regard the foreign media as a resource they can use in order to campaign against abuses of power in the Thai political order. Sometimes this kind of campaigning involves a wilful misreading of stories in the international press, exaggerating their criticisms of domestic politics.

While politicians such as Banharn Silpa-archa are right to believe that media organizations can behave as political actors, they are wrong to assume that newspapers invariably played supporting roles to the plots and schemes of political rivals. Both the domestic and the international press were entirely capable of independent action, pursuing agendas and 'games' of their own devising. Just as military commanders misunderstood the nature of the global information order during their violent suppression of demonstrators in May 1992, so Thailand's civilian politicians have failed subsequently to appreciate the degree to which their performance is being monitored by an international media audience. Nor have politicians recognized the degree to which Thai political observers themselves have access to information that originates far outside Thailand's borders.

The considerable freedom of the Thai press in comparison with the media in most other Southeast Asian countries means that Thai patterns of interaction between domestic and international media are not widely replicated. In Malaysia and Singapore, the relationship with the foreign press is generally a more antagonistic one, in which the overseas publication tends to be seen as a hostile commentator rather than a potential ally. In Indonesia prior to the fall of Suharto, while the foreign media could be invoked by the domestic press in order to raise sensitive political issues, there were serious limits on the extent to which the local press was free to play such games. The banning of three weekly publications (*Tempo*, *Editor* and *Detik*) in June 1994 symbolized a decline in official tolerance for 'openness' in the Indonesian media. Increasingly, critical and outspoken reporting were forced into underground publications, and onto the unregulated Internet, where foreign press reports and material produced by non-mainstream sources such as the Alliance of Independent Journalists offered alternative sources of news to the heavily self-censored material to be found in the mainstream Indonesian press. Nevertheless, there was some cooperation between Indonesian journalists and foreign correspondents that parallels Thai interactions.[28] The foreign media commonly functioned as a means of first exporting, then re-importing, sensitive news stories (rather as happened in Thailand in May 1992). Another technique used by the Indonesian press was to run foreign news reports of official denials by the Indonesian government concerning controversial incidents. Covering the denial allowed the newspaper an indirect means of referring to the original incident. As David Hill notes:

> Readers can thus register what information was being carried by the overseas media, compare it with the official line, then choose the more credible interpretation.
>
> (Hill 1994: 130–1)

More complex interactions in which a foreign news story itself prompted a series of domestic political developments were less common than in Thailand.

Foreign press reports were regularly cited by critics of the short-lived governments of Banharn Silpa-archa and Chavalit Yongchaiyudh; parliamentary no-confidence debates during both administrations featured references to critical international media stories. Chavalit sought to use both domestic and international media as scapegoats for declining investor confidence during the crisis that engulfed the Thai economy during his premiership.[29] At one point he declared that foreign leaders were now treating him contemptuously, as a direct result of a hostile media campaign.[30] The Thai domestic media again made extensive use of foreign press reports to highlight and support their concerns about the parlous state of Thailand's economy and financial institutions.

Thaksin Shinawatra was at odds with the international press long before he became Prime Minister. Curiously, this Western-educated, English-speaking telecommunications tycoon seemed in some respects even more parochially Thai in his attitudes to media than his less sophisticated predecessors. Unable to tolerate critical international coverage, he resorted to giving detailed responses to a short article in *Time* magazine, and seems to have toyed with expelling two *FEER* journalists on the basis of a few sentences that practically no one in Thailand had read.

A number of important points have emerged from the above discussion:

- Some Thai politicians regard the international press simply as an extension of the domestic political 'game'.
- Politicians who believe they are being criticized by the international press readily subscribe to conspiracy theories attributing 'hostile' foreign coverage to the mischief of political opponents.
- Although some stories about Thai politics that appear in the international press may result from leaks by political opponents, the majority do not.
- The Western media does not play a hegemonic, neo-colonial role in Thailand's information order; nor can domestic plots dictate the content of international news stories concerning Thailand.
- Rather, the relationship between domestic and international political news in Thailand is based upon processes of reciprocal

misreading, and paradoxically forms part of a mutually beneficial dialogue between domestic and international media.
- International media coverage can offer useful opportunities for the Thai press to raise critical issues or allude to topics normally consider 'off-limits'.
- The most important function of international media coverage of Thai politics is arguably as a resource on which domestic media may draw, a source of agency for restraining power holders and even for promoting political change.

In future, news stories of international origin may decline in domestic importance as Thai newspapers become more politically independent and thus more credible. Yet given the endemic structural weaknesses of Thailand's electoral system and political order, it may be some time before the Thai press becomes a truly effective 'fourth estate'. Until then, the international media will probably continue to function as a valuable external ally for critical voices in the Thai media. Many of the observations made here about the Thai case have explanatory salience for other countries in the region: though sometimes presented as a foe of governments, the international press may be a useful resource for Asian citizens.

7 Conclusion

This book began with two premises: that the interplay between the media and politics is of crucial significance in Pacific Asia; and that very little systematic academic work has been done in this field. Most of the literature on politics and the media is deeply Eurocentric. Yet attempting to address that gap is an inherently unfinishable task: there are seventeen different territories in Pacific Asia, and new issues concerning media–state and media–society relations are constantly coming to the fore. Hence the task of the book has been to raise questions and problems, rather than to offer comprehensive answers.

In the Introduction, many of the ideas underpinning understandings of politics and the media were explored and challenged. It was asserted that the media are first and foremost political actors in their own right, and so not necessarily reliable allies of progressive causes or processes of democratic change. Given that the media are political actors, it has been argued that analyses of politics and media need to focus squarely on the central question of agency. In other words, what kind of political roles are the media performing? Three broad alternatives were suggested: conservative roles as supporters of the status quo (agents of stability); progressive roles as monitors dedicated to 'checking and balancing' the established order (agents of restraint); and transformative roles as protagonists at moments of transition (agents of change). These three were presented not as mutually exclusive but as alternative modes of agency that might be available to the same media outlets at different political junctures. Given that print media typically have greater scope for independent action than other media forms, the main emphasis of the book has been on newspapers and news magazines.

Other salient media issues were then reviewed and problematized. Ownership was found to be a troublesome matter in the Asian context; while formal ownership could usually be readily ascertained, in practice *de facto* control of space and air time might be 'subcontracted' to editors, columnists and even to news sources. This practice was sometimes linked to the 'polyvalence' of media outlets, a capacity to express a range of diverse views within the same publication as a means of negotiating complex relations with multiple power-holders. Partisanship was not a simple matter of long-term support for a particular political party, but an interlocking network of competing connections. Under such conditions, profitability was not the primary concern of all publications: in many parts of the region, simply owning a publication could help secure intangible political and economic benefits. Nor were profitable media businesses the most effective political actors; the more owners had invested, the more they tended to become risk-averse. Given that media reflected the business interests of their stakeholders, it was difficult to argue that they would (or even should) act consistently in the public interest.

The idea of a 'fourth estate', of media dedicated to the public interest, was an ideal rather than a description of empirical realities for most of Pacific Asia. While press freedom was an important principle and concept for understanding the role of the media, it was not a black-and-white affair. Freedoms were often a matter of constant negotiation. In any case, the state was by no means the only threat to media freedom: many other threats emanated from different elements of society, and even from within the media themselves. Corruption among news practitioners was commonplace in many countries; and often media organizations had themselves adopted restrictive or narrow journalistic practices that inhibited their effectiveness. Most media organizations were badly in need of reform.

A chapter on democratic transitions and the media in Southeast Asia reviewed a series of political movements in the 1980s and 1990s. It emerged that generalizing about the role of media in transitions was impossible; while some components supported moves for progressive change, others served the interests of the state or of other power-holders. Typically, minority elements of the print media, allied with the international media and Internet news sources, formed coalitions for change – while incumbent governments were much more successful in controlling the broadcast media. Large newspapers often waited for the political tide to turn. There was little evidence that the media could themselves initiate transitions, but the supporting role they played could be crucial. Yet alliances formed in the heat of a political transition were rarely sustained for long once a new order had been ushered in. Elements of the media could engage in transformative modes of agency, helping change the political order, but these modes of agency were inherently temporary.

During the 1990s, Japan saw significant changes in its political order that were mirrored – and even promoted – by changes in the way media engaged with politics. From a media scene heavily dominated by the major newspapers, which treated politicians reverentially and monitored their every move through 'press clubs' that functioned as information cartels, Japan changed to a media climate in which 'soft' television news made most of the political running. As a result, media-savvy politicians were able to displace old-style bagmen in front-line positions, including that of Prime Minister. Nevertheless, this apparent transformation was not supported by any real change in the way media scrutinized substantive policy debates. During a period of economic crisis, Japan remained largely in denial; the media did little to ensure that the ubiquitous rhetoric of reform was translated into reality. Ironically, changes in news presentation that appeared to engage the public more effectively with political developments left many of Japan's real power-holders untouched. While the media appeared to have adopted a more progressive form of political agency, in practice this was open to serious question.

Chapter 4 examined the politics surrounding the 1994 bannings of three Indonesian weeklies – *Tempo*, *DeTik* and *Editor* – by former-President Suharto. These magazines had attempted to change their mode of agency from promoting stability to restraining the excesses of Suharto's regime. Yet their efforts to institutionalize for themselves a progressive role as agents of restraint had foundered when the regime refused to countenance this expanded and altered role for the media. Too many of the polyvalent voices of the media were now critical ones, and Suharto was unable to tolerate hearing them. Ultimately, it was argued, the New Order's failure to open up more political space for the media helped contribute to its own demise. As political and economic conditions change, it may be impossible to limit the media to a particular mode of agency.

The case of Hong Kong saw the media participating in a different kind of transition: the 1997 change from British colonial rule to Chinese suzerainty. However, it would not be appropriate to focus unduly on the handover itself. Media in Hong Kong have undergone a gradual transformation, particularly in its ownership structure, that began long before the formal end of British administration. The Hong Kong media remain vibrant, and rarely hesitate to express critical views on local issues. Yet the form of agency practised by the Hong Kong media in relation to greater China is more conservative than the mode it practises in relation to Hong Kong itself. Sensitive issues, such as the grubby machinations of Beijing politics and the troublesome matter of Taiwan's future, remain somewhat occluded. Commentators are divided about the degree to which self-censorship is an issue for the Hong Kong media, but the intensity of this debate itself indicates the degree to which the proper form of agency for media in Hong Kong remains a matter of continuing negotiation. The hand-over has long passed, but the question of the most appropriate political role for Hong Kong's media is not yet satisfactorily answered.

Finally, Chapter 6 examined the nature of interactions between the international and domestic media in Thailand. A series of controversies have erupted since the mid-1990s, all centring on critical coverage of Thai politics in the international press, which was then 'recycled' by the Thai-language media. Typically, Thai politicians sought to claim that these international stories were part of a domestic plot by their opponents. Such claims reflected a process of mutual misreading, in which both foreign correspondents and Thai political actors would persistently misrepresent one another. Despite the nationalist rhetoric often employed by the Thai politicians concerned, these developments did not constitute foreign interference in domestic affairs. International media coverage was primarily invoked by the Thai press in order to highlight issues of existing concern to them. Thus the international media became a source of additional agency for the Thai media, a resource on which they could draw in their attempts to pursue progressive or transformative roles. The participation of international actors gave local media greater political space in which to challenge power-holders.

Isagani Serrano rightly notes that:

> (The) media have been important in deciding the outcomes of dramatic social changes in Asia-Pacific. Certainly, media played a role in galvanizing people's responses, in deterring dictators from engaging in mass slaughters in the Philippines, South Korea, Nepal, Bangladesh, Thailand, and elsewhere.
> (Serrano 1994: 62)

Several recurrent themes emerge from a close scrutiny of the media's role in times of political change across Pacific Asia. In the societal upheavals discussed, the media served as sophisticated political actors in their own right, not simply serving the agendas of the state, the public interest, or opposition movements. Generalizing about the media's role is almost impossible. However, the electronic media typically prove easier for the state to control; support for political change tends to come from minority sections of the media, often newspapers. Different forms of political agency available to the media include: aiding the stability of a regime, urging restraint, and advocating change.

Even individual publications are often polyvalent, articulating contrasting perspectives even in the very same issue. This polyvalence reflects the multiplicity of stakeholders in a given media outlet. In some cases, a simple conflict between state power and media freedom remains the central area of contestation, but in many Pacific Asian cases the picture is vastly more ambiguous and the issues are far more complex and subtle. Frequently, editors, columnists and reporters enjoy close (often financial) relationships with a range of power-holders from different elements of the elite.

The media often rises to the challenge during a political crisis, when there is an explicit 'fire-fighting' role to perform, but evidence that the media led or initiated political transitions is patchy. For the most part, the role of the media in political transitions is a supporting one. When the crisis is over, the media may decline in effectiveness as institutions of civil society. Media institutions are untrustworthy political actors, capable of supporting political liberalization at one juncture but undermining an elected government at the next.

Much more work needs to be done on the political role of the media in Pacific Asia. This field of study has been largely occluded, for reasons outlined in the Introduction. A preliminary discussion of some actual periods of political change quickly calls attention to the inadequacy of most research in this field. Media practitioners are inclined to over-state their own importance, communications specialists are inclined to depoliticize media activity, and political scientists tend to discount the media's role. Western understandings of media do not translate well to Asian contexts, and crude Third-Worldist paradigms preoccupied with images of state censorship and repression fail to do justice to the complex realities of media ownership and control in the region. Apprehending the political role of Pacific Asia's media in times of change requires a nuanced approach, based on uncovering multiple layers of ambiguity.

Notes

Chapter 2

1 For a discussion of the politics of these transitions and attempted transitions, see McCargo (2001a).
2 Suchinda has often been casually characterized as a military dictator. This is incorrect: he was appointed Prime Minister by parliament, following the March 1992 general election. Nevertheless, he did lead the 1991 military coup and was able to orchestrate the outcome of the subsequent election to his own advantage.
3 For a fuller discussion of these events, see McCargo (1993).
4 The precise number of people killed remains unclear. Officially, 44 bodies were recovered, but Kritaya *et al.* (1995: 46) suggest that a further 41 of the 80 people confirmed missing at the time of the May events may also have died. Callahan (1998: 148–56) argues that the process of counting the missing was highly politicized; in late 1992, 81 people previously considered missing were dropped from the list because their families could not be contacted. It is therefore possible that the real number of fatalities was well over a hundred. During fieldwork in Bangkok in September 1992, an eyewitness told me of seeing bodies thrown into the back of military vehicles near the City Hall during the period 17–20 May.
5 For a more detailed exposition of this argument and a case study of the role of media in contributing to the downfall of the Chuan Leekpai government in May 1995, see McCargo (2000b: 12–17).
6 Associated Press, 'Indonesian Official says Press Freedoms Inhibiting to Some Ministers', 14 August 1998.
7 The websites in question included www.saksi.com, www.freemalaysia.com, and www.harakahdaily.com. More recent launches include www.agendamalaysia.com and www.malaysiakini.com

Chapter 3

1 A useful working definition of 'civil society' is Larry Diamond's: '(The) realm of organized social life that is voluntary, self-generating, (largely)

self-supporting, autonomous from the state, and bound by a legal order or set of shared rules' (Diamond 1994: 5).
2 For an overview of these debates and an explanation of the terms 'mainstream' and 'revisionist', see McCargo (2000a), especially pp. 1–4.
3 For an up-to-date factual account of the Japanese media, see Saito (2000).
4 Circulation figures are taken from Foreign Press Center (1997: 21); these are combined figures for both morning and evening editions.
5 Interview with Hiroshi Hori, former TBS newscaster, 12 August 1994.
6 Interview with Ken Kondo, former editor, *Mainichi Daily News*, 19 July 1994.
7 On the background to the Kanemaru scandal, see Johnson (1995: 218–22).
8 In a 1997 interview with Gerald Curtis, Miyazawa admitted that he had never really expected to pass any reform legislation – it seems that he was simply attempting to 'talk out' the issue in the *Sunday Project* interview (Curtis 1999: 94, note 20).
9 See, for example, the *Daily Yomiuri* editorial 'Abuse of freedom of expression', 24 October 1993.
10 Interview, 31 August 1994.
11 For a detailed discussion, see Sherman (1994).
12 Cunningham, an NHK employee, was dismissed after writing this newspaper article.
13 For a critical view of these changes and a response from NHK, see the articles by Peter Hadfield and Koichiro Shoda, in *No. 1 Shimbun* (newsletter of the Foreign Correspondents' Club of Tokyo), 15 August 1994.
14 Interview with Takahama Tatou, Senior Fellow, Yomiuri Research Institute, 18 August 1994.
15 For a detailed discussion and full translated texts of the proposals, see Hook and McCormack (2001).
16 For a series of relevant case studies, see Cooper-Chen (1997: 33–47).
17 I am deeply indebted to Kondoh Hisahiro for his critical comments, which form the basis of this and the following paragraph.

Chapter 4

1 Endy Bayuni, managing editor of the *Jakarta Post*, argued that his newspaper was alone 'out on the front line' in the final months of the Suharto regime. Interview, 12 August 1997.
2 Indonesia is the fourth most populous nation in the world, with a population of over 220 million, and experienced very high levels of economic growth in the later 1980s and early 1990s.
3 Under the New Order, some political parties and a parliament were permitted to operate, and regular elections were held. However, in

practice parliamentary politics was almost totally subordinated to executive power.
4 Harold Crouch, personal communication, 10 November 1997.
5 Interview with Daniel Dhakidae, head of *Kompas* research department, 11 August 1997.
6 Interview with Aristides Katoppo, former chief editor of *Sinar Harapan*, a daily banned in 1986, 15 July 1997.
7 Interview with Goenawan Mohamed, former chief editor of *Tempo*, 4 August 1997.
8 'Berkeley mafia' is a term often used for a group of key economic ministers from the early period of the New Order. They all held doctorates from the University of California, Berkeley.
9 Interview with Herry Komar, chief editor of *Gatra*, 12 July 1997.
10 Interview, 12 August 1997.
11 Goenawan interview, 4 August 1997.
12 Daniel interview, 11 August 1997.
13 Personal communication, November 1997. For a similar view, see Ramage 1995, pp. 111–12.
14 Tatik Hafidz, personal communication, 10 March 2002.
15 Hefner describes this Islamic shift at the time of the bannings as 'a little-noted turning point in late New Order politics'; but it is mentioned in many of the sources cited in this chapter and was clearly spelled out in Liddle (1996b) and McCargo (1999a).
16 Aristides interview, 15 July 1997.
17 Eddy interview, 11 July 1997.
18 Goenawan interview, 4 August 1997; Daniel interview, 11 August 1997.
19 On the changing political economy of the Indonesian press, see Christianto Wibisono, 'From fighting press to money controlled media today', *Jakarta Post*, 13 July 1997.
20 Herwanto interview, 11 July 1997.
21 Herry interview, 12 July 1997.
22 Satrio Arismunandar interview, 6 August 1997.
23 Aristides interview, 15 July 1997.
24 Goenawan interview, 4 August 1997.
25 Interview with Bambang Bujono, Consulting Editor, *D & R* magazine, 10 July 1997.
26 See www.idola.net.id/Tempo
27 Goenawan interview, 4 August 1997.

Chapter 5

1 Interview with Arnold Zeitlin, Director, Freedom Forum Asia Center, 8 April 1999.
2 See also the very useful September 1998 interview with Fenby by Kathy Wilhelm of Freedom Forum, at www/freedomforum.org/international/1998/3/10fenby.asp

3 Interview with Chris Bale, political editor, RTHK, 16 April 1999.
4 Interview with Kerry McGlynn, Deputy Director, Government Information Services, 13 April 1999.
5 Interview with Kin-ming Liu, chair, HKJA, 14 April 1999.
6 Interview with Ying Chan, senior fellow, University of Hong Kong, 14 April 1999.

Chapter 6

1 An example was the 1993 Longman dictionary affair, when it emerged that a dictionary published by the British publisher Longman described Bangkok as a city known for its large number of prostitutes. For a critical view of the affair, see Suthichai (1993).
2 For a relevant discussion, see Pharr (1996).
3 For a Thai view highly critical of the Western media's coverage of the election, see Prangtip (1995).
4 When the Democrats returned to power in November 1997, Abhisit was appointed a minister in the Prime Minister's Office, and Surin became Foreign Minister.
5 Interview with Bangkok-based journalist, 2 February 1996.
6 Interview with Abhisit Vejjajiva, 31 January 1996.
7 Translation from 'What the contentious article on bribery said', *The Nation*, 29 November 1995.
8 In the interests of full disclosure, I should make clear that during late November and most of December 1995, I was undertaking fieldwork at *Siam Post* newspaper, and was therefore a participant-observer in the newspaper's coverage of the Kockums case. This included regular telephone and fax communication with Henrik Westander and SPAS. This chapter draws upon field notes from my research.
9 For background details see, for example, 'Behind the scenes . . . the submarine political torpedo: national strategy collapses because of political strategy?' *Athit Weekly*, 925, 3–9 March 1995, pp. 24–8; Surasak Tumcharoen, 'US subs find little support in bedevilled bidding war', *Bangkok Post*, 16 December 1995.
10 This was actually an over-statement; Westander said simply that the three executives were convicted in court.
11 Again, this was a slight embellishment of what Westander had said.
12 Westander made clear that his source was Swedish in a letter to the *Bangkok Post*, 16 December 1995.
13 Field notes, December 1995.
14 For full text in Thai see *Siam Post*, 5 December 1995. For an English summary, see 'Banharn blames sub allegations on trade conflict', *Bangkok Post*, 5 December 1995.
15 For a detailed discussion of the 'Dr S' case, see McCargo (2000b: 107–35).
16 Supridi used these English phrases in his explanation.

17 Many of Supridi's points had been previously mentioned in letters from Dag Tornblom, a retired Swedish Brigadier-General and by Kockums Submarine Systems President Per Johnsson, *Bangkok Post*, 9 December 1995. Westander responded to these points in a letter published in the *Bangkok Post*, 16 December 1995.
18 This was made explicit in an earlier article, 'Coalition blues: rumours of treachery', *The Nation*, 17 December 1995.
19 See, for example, 'Generals fail to come to grips with information age', *Bangkok Post*, 1 June 1992.
20 For a discussion of the 'electoral professional' party and its application to Thailand, see McCargo (1997b).
21 See McCargo (2000b), especially pp. 33–8, for a critique of the often-muddled distinction between 'fact' and opinion in the Thai media.
22 This was a curious example of an 'inaccuracy', since Thaksin's pledge was widely publicized and documented, and his appointment as Deputy Prime Minister was made specifically to address the traffic issue, apparently at his own request (see, for example, *Straits Times*, 29 May 1995, *Financial Times*, 19 July 1995, *Straits Times*, 19 July 1995). Suranan gave no indication of why he believed the statement to be inaccurate.
23 Again, however, the charge was impossible to rebut; Palang Dharma's parliamentary strength declined from 23 MPs to one MP between July 1995 and November 1996, under the leadership of Thaksin – who had taken over the party in an explicit bid to make it a stronger political force (*Economist*, 24 June 1995). The decline of the party reflected internal divisions as well as the shortcomings of Thaksin's leadership, but should be seen primarily as 'the punishment dished out – mainly by Bangkok's volatile electorate – for Thaksin's long and distasteful flirtation with Banharn and Chart Thai' (McCargo 1997a: 300).
24 These responses by Suranan and Pongtep seem to suggest Thai politicians take it for granted that foreign academics will ignore gratuitous insults made about them in the Thai-language press; their respect for accuracy is strictly a one-way street.
25 Although I was singled out for public criticism by Thai Rak Thai over the *Time* article, no criticisms of Thaksin were attributed to me in the article. Indeed, I was cited making the positive point that Thaksin had been a hero to many Thais. All the negative comments about Thaksin cited in the article were attributed to Australian academic Kevin Hewison. At the same time, I would not wish to distance myself from the general view of Thaksin presented by Horn.
26 The numbers in these three elections were 41, 47 and 23 seats respectively.
27 For a discussion of nationalist and populist rhetoric inspired by the post-1997 climate in Thailand, see McCargo (2001b).
28 For example, in July 1997 Andreas Harsono, a journalist closely associated with AJI, was attacked in his car in Jakarta. Indonesian

newspapers were reluctant to cover the story directly, but when AFP ran a story about the incident, at least one local publication published it as a news agency report (see 'Men attack journalist', *Indonesia Times*, 27 July 1997).
29 For a relevant discussion, see Lewis (1998).
30 See, for example, 'It's not my fault, it's global – PM blames media for contemptuous tone of foreign leaders', *The Nation*, 30 October 1997.

Select bibliography

AJI. (1997) *Broadcasting in Asia*, Jakarta: Alliance of Independent Journalists & Institute for the Studies on Free Flow of Information.
Alford, Peter (2000) 'Mahathir can't silence his critics', *The Australian*, 30 March.
Allot, Anna (1990) 'The media in Burma and the pro-democracy movement of July–September 1988', *South-East Asia Library Group Newsletter*, December: 17–38.
Altman, Kristin Kyoko (1996) 'Television and political turmoil: Japan's summer of 1993', in Susan J. Pharr and Ellis S. Krauss (eds) *Media and Politics in Japan*, Honolulu: University of Hawaii Press, 165–86.
Article 19 (1991) *State of Fear: Censorship in Burma*, London: Article 19.
Article 19 (1994) *The Press under Siege: Censorship in Indonesia*, London: Article 19.
Aspinall, Ed (1999) 'Opposition and elite conflict in the fall of Soeharto', in Geoff Forrester and R. J. May (eds) *The Fall of Suharto*, Singapore: Select Books, 130–52.
Astraatmadja, Atmakusumah (1998) 'After Suharto, disillusionment among young Indonesian journalists', *Free: Freedom Forum Online*, 10 July. (www.freedomforum.org/international/1998/7/10/suharto.asp)
Atkins, William (2002) *The Politics of Southeast Asia's New Media*, Richmond: Curzon.
Baker, Mark (2002) 'Dark age of repression looms', *The Age*, 23 March.
Banthuk Yiaokhao Na Samoraphum Thanon Ratchadamnoen Prutsaphakhom 2535 (1992) [Journalists' Record: Ratchadamoen Battlefield, May 1992], Bangkok: Reporters' Association of Thailand.
Baron, Cynthia S. and Melba M. Suazo (1986) *Nine Letters: The Story of the 1986 Filipino Revolution*, Quezon City: Gerardo P. Baron.
Berfield, Susan (1999) 'Fall of the house of Aw', *Asiaweek*, 12 February.

Blumler, Jay G. and Michael Gurevitch (1995) *The Crisis of Public Communication*, London: Routledge.

Bogart, Leo (1998) 'Media and democracy' in Everette E. Dennis and Robert W. Snyder (eds) *Media and Democracy*, New Brunswick, NJ: Transaction, 3–11.

Borsuk, Richard (1999) 'Reforming business in Indonesia', in Geoff Forrester (ed.) *Post-Soeharto Indonesia: Renewal or Chaos*, Singapore: Institute of Southeast Asian Studies, 1999, 135–43.

Bourchier, David (1999) 'Skeletons, vigilantes and the Armed Forces' fall from grace', in Arief Budiman, Barbara Hatley and Damien Kingsbury (eds) *Reformasi: Crisis and Change in Indonesia*, Clayton: Monash Asia Institute, 149–67.

Brasor, Philip (2001) 'Politics in entertaining TV shocker', *Japan Times*, 28 October.

Bruck, Peter A. (1992) 'Crisis as spectacle: tabloid news and the politics of outrage', in Marc Raboy and Bernard Dagenais (eds) *Media, Crisis and Democracy: Mass Communication and the Disruption of Social Order*, London: Sage, 108–19.

Brull, Steven (1994) 'NHK of Japan tries to revive a fading picture', *International Herald Tribune*, 31 August.

Budiman, Arief (1994) 'Suharto's revised New Order', *Far Eastern Economic Review*, 22 December.

Callahan, William A. (1998) *Imagining Democracy: Reading 'The Events of May' in Thailand*, Singapore: ISEAS.

Chan, J. M., C. C. Lee and P. S. N. Lee (1994) 'Fighting against the odds: Hong Kong journalists in transition', in C. C. Lee (ed.) *China's Media, Media's China*, Boulder, CO: Westview Press, 239–55.

Chan, Joseph Man, Eric K. W. Ma and Clement Y. K. So (1997) 'Back to the future: retrospect and prospects for the Hong Kong mass media', in Joseph Y. S. Cheng (ed.) *The Other Hong Kong Report*, Hong Kong: Chinese University Press, 454–81.

Chan, Ying (1999) 'Hong Kong: still a window between China and the West', *Media Studies Journal*, 13, 1: 84–9.

Christensen, Ray (2000) *Ending the LDP Hegemony: Party Cooperation in Japan*, Honolulu: Hawaii University Press.

Cook, Timothy E. (1998) *Governing with the News: the News Media as a Political Institution*, Chicago: University of Chicago Press.

Cooper-Chen, Anne (1997) *Mass Communication in Japan*, Ames: Iowa University Press.

Coronel, Sheila S. (1999) 'The information crisis', in *News in Distress: The Southeast Asian Media in a Time of Crisis*, Quezon City: Philippine Center for Investigative Journalism, 1–12.

Coronel, Sheila (2000) 'Philippines: free as a mocking bird', in Louise Williams and Roland Rich (eds) *Losing Control: Freedom of the Press in Asia*, Canberra: Asia Pacific Press, 147–68.
Crouch, Harold (1988) *The Army and Politics in Indonesia* (second edition), Ithaca: Cornell University Press.
Crouch, Harold (1994a) 'Freedom of press proves short-lived', *Canberra Times*, 25 June.
Crouch, Harold (1994b) 'Censorship has not ended the friction in Indonesia'. *Canberra Times*, 4 July.
Crouch, Harold (1994c) 'Indonesia: an uncertain outlook', in *Southeast Asian Affairs*, Singapore: Institute of Southeast Asian Studies.
Crouch, Harold (1999) 'Wiranto and Habibie: military–civilian relations since May 1998', in Arief Budiman, Barbara Hatley and Damien Kingsbury (eds) *Reformasi: Crisis and Change in Indonesia*, Clayton: Monash Asia Institute, 127–48.
Cunningham, Philip (1993) 'Staged programmes are nothing new at NHK', *Mainichi Daily News*, 10 February.
Curran, James and Myung-Jin Park (eds) (2000) *De-Westernizing Media Studies*, London: Routledge.
Curtis, Gerald (1999) *The Logic of Japanese Politics: Leaders, Institutions and the Limits of Change*, New York: Columbia University Press.
Diamond, Larry (1994) 'Rethinking civil society: towards democratic consolidation', *Journal of Democracy*, 5, 3: 4–17.
Diamond, Larry (1999) *Developing Democracy: Towards Consolidation*, Baltimore: Johns Hopkins Press.
Dieter, Miu Oikawa (1993) 'Japanese politics enters the age of TV', *Japan Times*, 26 August.
Dimbleby, Jonathan (1997) *The Last Governor*, London: Warner Books.
Dixit, Kunda (1999) 'Global media and empire', in *News in Distress: The Southeast Asian Media in a Time of Crisis*, Quezon City: Philippine Center for Investigative Journalism, 49–55.
Doronila, Amando (1985) 'The Media', in R. J. May and Francisco Nemenzo (eds) *The Philippines after Marcos*, London: Croom Helm.
Doronila, Amando (2000) 'Preface – Press freedom in Asia: an uneven terrain', in Louise Williams and Roland Rich (eds) *Losing Control: Freedom of the Press in Asia*, Canberra: Asia Pacific Press, xi–xvi.
Eklof, Stefan (1999) *Indonesian Politics in Crisis: The Long Fall of Suharto, 1996–98*, Copenhagen: Nordic Institute of Asian Studies.
Er, Lam Peng (1994) 'Urban political machines in Japan', *Asian Journal of Political Science*, 2, 2: 112–43.
Fairclough, Gordon (1995) 'Free to air: newly assertive media pique the government', *Far Eastern Economic Review*, 16 November.

Farley, Maggie (1996) 'Japan's press and the politics of scandal', in Susan J. Pharr and Ellis S. Krauss (eds) *Media and Politics in Japan*, Honolulu: University of Hawaii Press, 133–63.
Feldman, Ofer (1993) *Politics and the News Media in Japan*, Ann Arbor: University of Michigan Press.
Feldman, Ofer (1996) 'Nagatacho beat: messengers or minions?' *Japan Quarterly*, 43, 4: 20–8.
Fenby, Jonathan (2000) 'Why a top Hong Kong journalist had to go', *The Times*, 10 November.
Fenby, Jonathan (2002) 'Killing off the voice of dissent', *The Times*, 24 May.
Florentino-Hofilena, Chay (1998) *News for Sale: The Corruption of the Philippine Media*, Quezon City: Philippine Center for Investigative Journalism and the Center for Media Freedom and Responsibility.
Foreign Press Center (1994) *Japan's Mass Media*, Tokyo: Foreign Press Center.
Foreign Press Center (1997) *Japan's Mass Media*, Tokyo: Foreign Press Center.
Forrester, Geoff (1999a) 'A Jakarta diary: May 1998', in Geoff Forrester and R. J. May (eds) *The Fall of Suharto*, Singapore: Select Books, 24–69.
Forrester, Geoff (1999b) 'Introduction', in Geoff Forrester (ed.) *Post-Soeharto Indonesia: Renewal or Chaos?* Canberra: Research School of Pacific and Asian Studies, Australian National University, 1–18.
Freeman, Laurie Anne (2000) *Closing the Shop:Information Cartels and Japan's Mass Media*, Princeton: Princeton University Press.
Green, Shane (2002) 'Japan's favourite female MP turns and bites the hand that sacked her', *Sydney Morning Herald*, 19 March.
Greenlees, Don (2001) 'Indonesian media feels pressure from all sides', *The Australian*, 15 November.
Gunaratne, Sheldon (ed.) (2000) *Handbook of the Media in Asia*, New Delhi: Sage.
Hall, Ivan P. (1998) *Cartels of the Mind: Japan's Intellectual Closed Shop*, New York: Norton.
Hamilton, Walter (2000) 'Japan: the warmth of the herd', in Louise Williams and Roland Rich (eds) *Losing Control: Freedom of the Press in Asia*, Canberra: Asia Pacific Press, 93–114.
Hamlett, Tim and Judith Clarke (1997) 'The law and Hong Kong news media after July 1997', *Asia Pacific Media Educator*, 2: 4–19.
Hanazaki, Yasuo (1996) 'The Indonesian press in an era of Keterbukaan: a force for democratisation?' Unpublished PhD Thesis, Victoria, Australia: Monash University.

Handley, Paul (1997) 'More of the same? Politics and business, 1987–96', in Kevin Hewison (ed.) *Political Change in Thailand: Democracy and Participation*, London: Routledge, 94–113.

Harsono, Andreas (1995) 'Indonesia: dealing cautiously with rumours', *The West Australian*, 29 September.

Harsono, Andreas (2000) 'Indonesia: dancing in the dark', in Louise Williams and Roland Rich (eds) *Losing Control: Freedom of the Press in Asia*, Canberra: Asia Pacific Press, 74–92.

Hefner, Robert W. (1999) 'Islam and nation in the post-Suharto era', in Adam Schwarz and Jonathan Paris (eds) *The Politics of Post-Suharto Indonesia*, New York: Council on Foreign Relations Press.

Hefner, Robert W. (2000) *Civil Islam: Muslims and Democratization in Indonesia*, Princeton, NJ: Princeton University Press.

Heng, Russell Hiang-Khng (2000) 'Of the state, for the state, yet against the state – the struggle paradigm in Vietnam's media politics', Unpublished PhD thesis, Canberra: Australian National University.

Heng, Russell Hiang-Khng (2001) 'Media negotiating the state: in the name of the law in anticipation' *Sojourn*, 16, 2: 213–37.

Hernandez, Carolina G. (1986) ' Reconstituting the political order' in John Bresnan (ed.) *Crisis in the Philippines: the Marcos Era and Beyond*, Princeton NJ: Princeton University Press.

Heryanto, Ariel (1996) 'Indonesian middle class opposition in the 1990s', in Garry Rodan (ed.) *Political Oppositions in Industrialising Asia*, London: Routledge.

Heryanto, Ariel, and Adi, Stanley Yoseph (2001) 'The industrialization of the media in democratizing Indonesia', *Contemporary Southeast Asia*, 23, 2, August.

Heuvel, Jon Vandel and Everette E. Dennis (1993) *The Unfolding Lotus – East Asia's Changing Media*, New York: The Freedom Forum Media Studies Center.

Hewison, Kevin (2001) *Pathways to Recovery: Bankers, Business and Nationalism in Thailand*, Hong Kong: City University of Hong Kong, Southeast Asia Research Centre, Working Papers Series No. 1, April.

Hidayat, Dedy N. (1999) 'Mass media: between the palace and the market', in Richard W. Baker *et al.* (eds) *Indonesia: The Challenge of Change*, Singapore: Institute of Southeast Asian Studies, 179–98.

Hill, David T. (1994) *The Press in New Order Indonesia*, Nedlands: University of Western Australia Press.

Hill, David T. and Krishna Sen (1997) 'Wiring the warung to global gateways: the internet in Indonesia', *Indonesia*, 63.

Hill, Hal (1999) 'The Indonesian economy: the strange and sudden death of a tiger', in Geoff Forrester and R. J. May (eds) *The Fall of Suharto*, Singapore: Select Books, 93–103.

HKJA (1999) *1999 Annual Report: The Ground Rules Change*, Hong Kong: Hong Kong Journalists' Association (with Article 19).

HKJA (2000) *2000 Annual Report: Patriot Games*, Hong Kong: Hong Kong Journalists' Association (with Article 19).

HKJA (2001) *2001 Annual Report*, Hong Kong: Hong Kong Journalists' Association (with Article 19).

Hook, Glenn D. and Gavan McCormack (2001) *Japan's Contested Constitution: Documents and Analysis*, London: Routledge.

Horn, Robert (2000) 'This time he's serious', *Time*, 6 March.

Hutcheon, Stephen J. (1998) *Pressing Concerns: Hong Kong's Media in an Era of Transition*, Cambridge MA: Joan Shorenstein Center, Kennedy School of Government, Harvard University, Discussion Paper D-32, September.

Ishikawa Ichiro (2001) 'Koizumi's spin doctoring dazzles political opponents', *Nikkei Weekly*, 17 December.

Johnson, Chalmers (1995) *Japan: Who Governs? The Rise of the Developmental State*, New York: Norton.

Johnson, Stephen (1994) 'Continuity and change in Japanese electoral patterns: the 1993 general election in Yamanashi', *Japan Forum*, 6, 1: 8–20.

Kavi Chongkittavorn (2000) 'Thailand: a troubled path to a hopeful future', in Louise Williams and Roland Rich (eds) *Losing Control: Freedom of the Press in Asia*, Canberra: Asia Pacific Press, 219–38.

Kawamoto, Ken (1998) 'Indonesian protests used net to seek help, information', *Free: Freedom Forum Online*, 28 May. (www.freedomforum.org/technology/1998/28indonesia.asp)

Keane, John (1992) 'The crisis of the sovereign state,' in Marc Raby and Bernard Dagenais (eds) *Media, Crisis and Democracy: Mass Communication and the Disruption of Social Order*, London: Sage, 16–33.

Khin Maung Win (1999) 'The Burmese way of muzzling dissent', in *News in Distress: the Southeast Asian Media in a Time of Crisis*, Quezon City: Philippine Center for Investigative Journalism, 59–67.

Kitley, Philip (2000) *Television, Nation and Culture in Indonesia*, Athens, OH: Ohio University Center for International Studies, Southeast Asia Series No. 104.

Knight, Alan (2000) 'Fact or friction: the collision of journalism values in Asia', in Damien Kingsbury, Eric Loo and Patricia Payne (eds) *Foreign Devils and Other Journalists*, Clayton: Monash Asia Institute, Monash Papers on Southeast Asia no. 52, 1–16.

Knight, Alan and Yoshiko Nakano (eds) (1999) *Reporting Hong Kong: Foreign Media and the Handover*, Richmond: Curzon.

Krauss, Ellis (2000) *Broadcasting Politics in Japan: NHK and Television News*, Ithaca: Cornell University Press.

Kritaya Archavanitkul, Anuchat Poungsomlee, Suporn Chunhavittiyanont and Varaporn Chamsit (1995) 'Political disharmony in Thai society: a lesson from the May 1992 incident', *Asian Review*, 9: 39–56.

Kwan Weng Kin (2001) 'Japan's iron lady', *Straits Times*, 20 May.

Kyu Ho Houm (1998) 'Democratization and the press: the case of South Korea', in Patrick H. O'Neil (ed.) *Communicating Democracy: The Media and Political Transitions*, Boulder CO: Lynne Rienner, 171–93.

Lague, David (2002) 'Soft on China', *Far Eastern Economic Review*, 23 May.

Lane, Max (1999) 'Mass politics and political change in Indonesia', in Arief Budiman, Barbara Hatley and Damien Kingsbury (eds) *Reformasi: Crisis and Change in Indonesia*, Clayton: Monash Asia Institute, 239–51.

Larimer, Tim (2001) 'Japan's destroyer', *Time*, 17 September.

Lau, Emily (1997) Interview with Alan Knight, at www.geocities.com/Athens/Forum/2365/lau.html, 20 March.

Law Sui-Lan (1999) 'In character: Chinese language papers are gaining fresh clout in post-handover Hong Kong', *Asiaweek*, 8 January.

Lee, Chin-Chuan (2000) 'State, capital and media: the case of Taiwan', in James Curran and Myung-Jin Park (eds) *De-Westernizing Media Studies*, London: Routledge, 124–38.

Lee, Chin-Chuan and Joseph Man Chan (1990) 'The Hong Kong press in China's orbit: thunder of Tiananmen', in Chin-Chuan Lee (ed.) *Voices of China: The Interplay of Politics and Journalism*, New York: Guildford Press, 140–61.

Lee, Paul S. N. and Leonard L. Chu (1998) 'Inherent dependence on power: the Hong Kong press in political transition', *Media, Culture and Society*, 20, 1: 59–77.

Lent, John A. (1998) 'The mass media in Asia' in Patrick H. O'Neil (ed.) *Communicating Democracy: The Media and Political Transitions*, Boulder CO: Lynee Rienner, 147–70.

Lewis, Glen (1998) 'The markets and the media: Southeast Asia's new nationalism', *Asia-Pacific Magazine*, 9–10, March.

Lewis, Glen (2000) 'Thai reporting on the rise and fall of Pauline Hanson', in Damien Kingsbury, Eric Loo and Patricia Payne (eds) *Foreign Devils and Other Journalists*, Clayton: Monash Asia Institute, Monash Papers on Southeast Asia no. 52, 133–45.

Liddle, R. William (1996a) 'Indonesia: Suharto's tightening grip', *Journal of Democracy*, 7, 4: 58–72.

Liddle, R. William (1996b) 'The Islamic turn in Indonesia: a political explanation', *Journal of Asian Studies*, 55, 3: 631–4.

Lintner, Bertil (1990) *Outrage: Burma's Struggle for Democracy*, London and Bangkok: White Lotus.

Ma, Eric Kit-wai (2000) 'Rethinking media studies: the case of China', in James Curran and Myung-Jin Park (eds) *De-Westernizing Media Studies*, London: Routledge, 21–34.

MacLachlan, Liz (2001) 'Turning seeing into believing: producing credibility in the television coverage of the Kobe earthquake', in Brian Moeran (ed.) *Asian Media Productions*, Richmond: Curzon, 108–25.

Magnier, Mark (2001a) 'A win for (hair) style, substance', *Los Angeles Times*, 28 April.

Magnier, Mark (2001b) 'Foreign minister stumbles on her home turf', *Los Angeles Times*, 30 November.

Mak Yin-ting (1997) 'Hong Kong's media freedoms: some question marks', *Asia Pacific Media Educator*, 2, January–June: 83–9.

Marcus, David L. (1998) 'Indonesia revolt was net driven', *Boston Globe*, 24 May.

Marshall, Tyler (2000) 'Hong Kong media abuzz over rights', *Los Angeles Times*, 8 December.

Mayes, Tessa and Megan Rowling (1997) 'The image makers: British journalists on Japan', in Phil Hammond (ed.) *Cultural Differences, Media Memories: Anglo-American Images of Japan*, London: Cassell, 115–38.

McBeth, John (1994) 'Rude awakening: press bans shock the emerging middle class', *Far Eastern Economic Review*, 7 July.

McCargo, Duncan (1993) 'The buds of May', *Index on Censorship*, April 3–8.

McCargo, Duncan (1996) 'The political role of the Japanese media', *Pacific Review*, 9, 2: 251–64.

McCargo, Duncan (1997a) *Chamlong Srimuang and the New Thai Politics*, London: Hurst.

McCargo, Duncan (1997b) 'Political parties: real, authentic and actual', in Kevin Hewison (ed.) *Political Change in Thailand: Democracy and Participation*, London: Routledge, 114–31.

McCargo, Duncan (1999a) 'Killing the messenger: the 1994 press bannings and the demise of Indonesia's New Order', *The Harvard International Journal of Press/Politics*, 4, 1: 29–47.

McCargo, Duncan (1999b) 'The international media and the domestic political coverage of the Thai press', *Modern Asian Studies*, 33, 3: 551–79.

McCargo, Duncan (2000a) *Contemporary Japan*, Basingstoke: Macmillan.
McCargo, Duncan (2000b) *Politics and the Press in Thailand: Media Machinations*, London: Routledge.
McCargo, Duncan (2001a) 'Democratic consolidation in Pacific Asia', in Jeff Haynes (ed.) *Towards Sustainable Democracy in the 'Third World'*, Basingstoke: Palgrave, 141–62.
McCargo, Duncan (2001b) 'Populism and reformism in contemporary Thailand', *South East Asia Research*, 9, 1: 89–107.
McCargo, Duncan and Ramaimas Bowra (1997) *Policy Advocacy and the Media in Thailand*, Bangkok: Institute of Public Policy Studies.
McKillop, Peter, and Kay Itoi (1993) 'Japan tunes in to TV politics', *Newsweek*, 2 August.
McNair, Brian (1999) *An Introduction to Political Communication*, London: Routledge.
Nemenzo, Francisco (1986) 'A nation in ferment: analysis of the February revolution', in M. Rajaretnam (ed.) *The Aquino Alternative*, Singapore: Institute of Southeast Asian Studies, 28–53.
Neumann, A. Lin (1998a) 'Freedom takes hold: ASEAN journalism in transition', New York: Committee to Protect Journalists (www.cpj.org).
Neumann, A. Lin (1998b) 'Reformasi on the air: Indonesia's new political climate spawns a radio format', Committee to Protect Journalists website, 10 September (www.cpj.org/dangerous/9_10_98/indo_radio.html)
Nip, Joyce Y. M. (1997) 'Shifting political power in and news sources: the case in Hong Kong's political transition', *Asia Pacific Media Educator*, 3, July–December: 49–69.
Nomura Takehiko (2001) 'Koizumi media attention draws fire', *Washington Times*, 27 July.
Nurbaiti, Ati (2002) 'Press faces growing threats to its freedom', *Jakarta Post*, 15 February.
Olle, John (2000) 'Sex, money, power', *Inside Indonesia*, 61, January–March.
Pajaree Tanasomboonkit (1995) 'Nangsuephim Thai Rath kap kankamnotwarasan khwam khatyaeng thang kanmuang nai hetkan pritsapa 2535', [*Thai Rath* newspaper and the agenda setting of political conflict in the May crisis 1992], unpublished MA dissertation, Faculty of Communication Arts, Chulalongkorn University.
Palacio, Raymundo Riva (1997) 'A culture of collusion: the ties that bind the press and the PRI', in William A. Orme (ed.) *A Culture of Collusion: an Inside Look at the Mexican Press*, Miami FL: North–South Centre Press, University of Miami, 21–32.

Pharr, Susan J. (1996) 'Media as trickster in Japan: a comparative perspective', in Susan J. Pharr and Ellis S. Krauss (eds) *Media and Politics in Japan*, Honolulu: University of Hawaii Press, 24–36.

Prangtip Daorueng (1995) 'Thais like their democracy, warts and all', *Manila Chronicle*, 13 July.

Raboy, Marc and Bernard Dagenais (1992) 'Introduction: media and the politics of crisis', in Marc Raboy and Bernard Dagenais (eds) *Media, Crisis and Democracy: Mass Communication and the Disruption of Social Order*, London: Sage, 1–15.

Ramage, Douglas E. (1995) *Politics in Indonesia: Democracy, Islam, and the Ideology of Tolerance*, London: Routledge.

Rampal, Kuldip R. (1994) 'Press and political liberalization in Taiwan', *Journalism Quarterly*, 71, 3: 637–51.

Randall, Vicky (1993) 'The media and democratisation in the Third World', *Third World Quarterly*, 14, 3: 625–46.

Reporters' Association of Thailand (1995) Press Release, 5 December (published in *Siam Post*, 6 December).

Rivera, Temario C. (1996) *State of the Nation: Philippines*, Singapore: Institute of Southeast Asian Studies.

Robison, Richard (1999) 'Indonesia after Soeharto: more of the same, descent into chaos, or a shift to reform', in Geoff Forrester and R. J. May (eds) *The Fall of Suharto*, Singapore: Select Books, 219–30.

Rodan, Garry (1998) 'Asia and the international press: the political significance of expanding markets', in Vicky Randall (ed.) *Democratization and the Media*, London: Frank Cass, 125–54.

Saito, Shinichi (2000) 'Japan', in Sheldon Gunaratne (ed.) *Handbook of the Media in Asia*, New Delhi: Sage, 561–85.

Sandeen, Rod (2000) 'Indonesian editor promotes press councils to resolve media disputes', Freedom Forum Online, 17 November (www.freedomforum.org).

Sanger, David E. (1993) 'Japanese politics moves into era of talk shows', *New York Times*, 21 July.

Santoso (1997) 'Into Cyberspace,' *Index on Censorship*, 2.

Schidlovsky, John (1996) 'Grim prospects for Hong Kong', *Media Studies Journal*, Fall.

Schultz, Julianne (1998) *Reviving the Fourth Estate: Democracy, Accountability and the Media*, Melbourne: Cambridge University Press.

Schwarz, Adam (1999) *A Nation in Waiting: Indonesia's Search for Stability* (second edition), St Leonards: Allen and Unwin.

Seagrave, Sterling (1996) *Lords of the Rim*, London: Corgi.

Sen, Krishna and David T. Hill (2000) *Media, Culture and Politics in Indonesia*, Melbourne: Oxford University Press.

Serrano, Isagni R. (1994) *Civil Society in the Asia-Pacific Region*, Washington DC: Civicus.
Sherer, Paul M. (1995) 'Scandal pits Thai leaders against media', *Asian Wall Street Journal*, 5 December.
Sherman, Spencer (1994) 'NHK TV Japan: East meets West in the newsroom', *Columbia Journalism Review*, March/April: 32–6.
Shirk, Martha and William F. Woo (1998) 'Hong Kong Handover: Impact on the Press. A Report to the International Center for Journalists'. Photocopy: no place of publication, 6 May.
Smith, Desmond (1996) 'Democracy and the media in developing countries: a case study of the Philippines', Unpublished PhD thesis, University of Leeds.
Smith, Martin (1991) *Burma: Insurgency and the Politics of Ethnicity*, London: Zed.
Sng, Jeffrey (2001) 'Wahid victim of prejudiced press', *Bangkok Post*, 25 March 2001.
Soeharto, Mohamed (1989) 'The role of the press in national development', in Achal Mehra (ed.) *Press Systems in ASEAN States*, Singapore: AMIC.
Sorrayuth Suthassanachinda (1995) 'Plot thickens in Kockums bribery scandal', *The Nation*, 18 December.
Sorrayuth Suthassanachinda (2000) 'Khae botkhwam khong khon khon nung' [It's only one person's article], *Nation Weekly*, 6–12 March.
Stanley (1994) 'Shattering the myth of the press industry', in Ayu Utami (ed.) *Banning 1994*, Jakarta: Alliance of Independent Journalists.
Sugiyama, Mitsunobu (2000) 'Media and power in Japan', in James Curran and Myung-Jin Park (eds) *De-Westernizing Media Studies*, London: Routledge, 191–201.
Suthichai Yoon (1993) 'A case of misplaced Thai aånger', *The Nation*, 12 July [reprinted in Suthichai Yoon (1995) *Thai Talk: a Collection of Writings from The Nation*, Bangkok: Nation Publishing, 233–5].
Tahara, Soichiro (1993) Account of Miyazawa interview, *Bunshun Weekly*, 1 July: 56–8.
Tase, Yasuhiro (1994) *Seiji Janarizumu no Tsumi to Batsu* [Crime and Punishment of Political Journalism], Tokyo: Shinchosha.
Thepchai Yong (2002) 'Thaksin can expect foreign media backlash', *The Nation*, 26 February.
Ubonrat Siriyuvasak (1994) 'The development of a participatory democracy: raison d'etre for media reform in Thailand', *Southeast Asian Journal of Social Science*, 22: 101–14.
Ukrist Pathmanand (1998) 'The Thaksin Shinawatra group: a study of the relationship between money and politics in Thailand', *Copenhagen Journal of Asian Studies*, 13: 60–81.

Vatikiotis, Michael and Rodney Tasker (2002) 'Prickly premier', *Far Eastern Economic Review*, 11 April.
Vogel, Ezra (1979) *Japan as Number One*, Cambridge, MA: Harvard University Press.
Westander, Henrik (1992) *Classified: the Political Cover-up of the Bofors Scandal*, Bombay: Gentleman Books.
Westander, Henrik (1995) 'Article on the "Sub-Affair"', Press release, SPAS, 4 December. [Published in Thai translation, *Siam Post*, 6 December].
Westney, D. Eleanor (1996) 'Mass media as business organizations: A US–Japan comparison', in Susan J. Pharr and Ellis S. Krauss (eds) *Media and Politics in Japan*, Honolulu: University of Hawaii Press, 47–88.
Williams, Louise (1994) 'Soeharto sails into battle for minister', *Sydney Morning Herald*, 25 June.
Williams, Louise and Roland Rich (eds) (2000) *Losing Control: Freedom of the Press in Asia*, Canberra: Asia Pacific Press.
Wolferen, Karel van (1989) *The Enigma of Japanese Power*, London: Papermac.
Wong, Kean (2000) 'Malaysia: in the grip of the government', in Louise Williams and Roland Rich (eds) *Losing Control: Freedom of the Press in Asia*, Canberra: Asia Pacific Press, 115–37.
Yamazaki, Kazutami (1994) 'Broadcast views: TV newscasters and their role in shaping public opinion', *Japan Scope*, Summer: 58–61.
Yeung, Chris (2000) 'Hong Kong: a Handover of Freedom', in Louise Williams and Roland Rich (eds) *Losing Control: Freedom of the Press in Asia*, Canberra: Asia Pacific Press, 58–73.
Zeitlin, Arnold (2001a) 'Press self-censorship: a myth in Hong Kong', *The Correspondent* (Foreign Correspondents' Club of Hong Kong) June–July.
Zeitlin, Arnold (2001b) 'Abrupt staff cuts may signal muzzling of critical Hong Kong media voice' (www.freedomforum.org) 24 September.

Index

Abdurrahman Wahid 39, 42, 44
Abhisit Vejjajiva 127, 130
Abraham, Thomas 104
Adil 40
AJI *see* Alliance of Independent Journalists
Alliance of Independent Journalists (AJI) 40, 41, 42, 92–5, 150, 163n, *see also* journalists
alternative press 46, 93, 94–5, *see also* Chinese-language press; free press; local press; newspapers; print media; regional press; tabloid press; Thai-language press; vanity press
Altman, K.K. 56
Amien Rais 38
Anan Kalinta, Air Chief Marshal 28
Anwar Ibrahim 46
Apple Daily 105, 107–10, 113
Aquino, Cory 20, 21
Aquino, Ninoy 20, 21
Aroon Larnlua 142
Asahi Shimbun 57
Ashadi Siregar 93
Asian Wall Street Journal 122, 124, 125, 126, 127, 128–9, 140, 149
Asiaweek 47
Aspinall, E. 38
Associated Press (AP) 127–8
Atkins, W. 5, 31, 36, 37, 39, 47
Aum Shinrikyo 69
Aung San Suu Kyi 45
Aw, Sally 101

Baker, M. 149
Ban Phitsanulok 139
Bangkit 40
Bangkok Post 26, 30, 121, 122, 133, 136
Banharn Silpa-archa 33, 117, 121, 124–9, 137–8, 140–1, 143, 149
Banyat Tasaniyavej 26, 30
Baron, C.S. and Suazo, M.M. 20
BBC World Service 28, 31, 45, 47, 67, 115, 133–4
Becker, Jasper 104
Berfield, S. 101
Bhumipol, King 31
Blumler, J.G. and Gurevitch, M. 10
Bogart, L. 14–15
Borsuk, R. 98–9
Bourchier, D. 39
Brasor, P. 71
broadcast media 5; censorship of 27–31; control over 24–5, 27–8; Japanese 51–2; ownership of 25; reality/reporting gap 28, *see also* radio; television
Bruck, P.A. 48
Budiman, Arief 83
Burma 45–8
Burma Socialist Programme Party 45

Callahan, W.A. 31, 159n
Camdessus, Michael 95
censorship 4–5, 9–10, 52–3; of broadcast media 27–31; by Astro satellite 47; crudity of 31–2; formal/informal 34; hands-off approach 101; and the Internet 47; legitimacy of 40; of print media 30–2; and self-censorship 5, 53, 79, 103, 110–15, 150

Center for Strategic and International Studies (CSIS) 35, 84, 85
Center to Promote Participation in Democracy 29–30
Cha, Louis 101
Chaiwat Khamchoo 128
Chamlong Srimuang 24, 28, 30, 31, 143
Chan, Anson 106, 109, 115
Chan, J.M. 102, 103, 112–13; *et al.* 100, 109
Chan Kin-hong 108
Chan, Yuen Ying 113
Chat Thai Party 121–2, 125–9, 130, 132, 134, 136–7
Chatchai Choonavan 24, 139
Chavalit Yongchaiyudh 33, 132, 140, 143
Cheng, Albert 109
Cheng An-kuo 115
Cheung Man-yee 105
China 12, 100–2; criticisms of 102, 103; hands-off approach to media 103; and lack of scrutiny by press 111–15; and press ownership 101; and rise of Chinese-language press 102–5; suggestions to Hong Kong media 110; and Tianamen Square incident 100, 101; as untrustworthy 100
China Daily 103
China Now 66–7
Chinese-language press, controversies in 108–9; ethical standards in 107–8; legal challenges to 108–9; and physical violence towards 109; pressures on 112–13; rise of 102–5; self-censorship/no-go areas in 110–15; tabloid/quality newspaper mix 107–8, *see also* alternative press; local press; newspapers; print media; regional press; tabloid press; Thai-language press; vanity press;
Christensen, R. 61
Chu Pui-hing 115
Chuan Leekpai 124, 128
Chulalongkorn University 30, 32, 128
civil society 44, 159n–60n
clandestine press *see* alternative press
CNN 28, 31, 47, 67

Committee to Protect Journalists 43, 115
control *see* ownership/control
Cook, T.E. 1, 2, 77
Cooper-Chen, A. 8, 160n
Coronel, S.S. 13, 21, 22
Crispin, Shawn 146–7, 148
Crouch, H. 39, 83, 85, 86, 160n
CSIS *see* Center for Strategic and International Studies
Cunningham, P. 67
Curran, J. and Park, 1
Curtis, G. 160n

Dagens Nyheter 141
Daily News 25, 117
democracy summer 45–6
demonstrations, non-effect of 46; reporting of 25, 27–31; student 35, 37, 44; support for 35; violence of 24, 28–30, 31, 45, 95, 96
Deng Xiaoping 101
Detektif & Romantika 43, 77, 93
DeTik 40, 79, 86, 89–90, 98, 150, 155
development journalism 3, 43, 77–8
Dhakidae, D. 80
Diamond, L. 46, 159–60n
Dieter, M.O. 60
Dimbleby, J. 106
Dixit, K. 4–5
Doronila, A. 16, 21
'Dr S' (Surakiart Sathirathai) Case 139, 140

e-mail 37, 70–1, 147
Eastern Press 109
The Economist 118, 148
Editor 79, 89, 90, 92, 98, 150, 155
Eklof, S. 35
electronic media 21, 32, 33, 37, 40, 45, 47, 56
Enrile, Juan Ponce 20
Er, L.P. 60
Eros Djarot 89–90

Fairclough, G. 117
Far Eastern Economic Review (FEER) 47, 104, 118, 122, 129, 146–9, 151
Farley, M. 54, 119

FEER *see Far Eastern Economic Review*
Feldman, O. 2, 53, 56
Fenby, Jonathan 103, 104
Feng Xiliang 103
Fengchao, Wang 114
Fikri Jufri 85
Florentino-Hofilena, C. 22
Foreign Correspondents' Club 119
Foreign Press Center 50
Forrester, G. 36, 39
fourth estate 15, 154
free press 5, 46, *see also* alternative press; Chinese-language press; local press; newspapers; print media; regional press; taboid press; Thai-language press; vanity press
freedom 15–17, 150, 154; attack on 80; constraints/curtailment 52–6, 78–9; dedication to 78; increased 39, 87; reports on 110, 111–12; rhetoric/reality gap 43; and state power 48; support for 114–15; threats to 25–7, 48, 113–14; warnings on 100; as Western concept 16; as zero-sum game 16, 48
Freedom Forum 111
Freeman, L.A. 2, 53, 55

Gatra 81, 91, 96
Gittings, Danny 104
globalisation of communication 36–9
Goenawan Mohamad 9, 80–1, 82, 85, 89, 91, 94, 98
Government Information Services (GIS) 106–7
Grafiti Pers 93, 94
Green, S. 73
Greenlees, D. 43
Gugati 40
Gunaratne, S. 6
Gus Dur *see* Abdurrahman Wahid

Habibie, B.J. 39, 41–2, 83–7, 96
Habibie-*Tempo* antagonism theory 87–8
Hall, I.P. 54, 55
Hamilton, W. 52, 64, 68
Hamlett, T. and Clarke, J. 112
Hanazaki, Y. 2, 34, 78–9, 84, 87–8

Handley, P. 12
Harakah 47
Harmoko (politician) 78, 88, 90, 96
Harsono, A. 36, 42, 163n–4n
Hasan, Bob 91, 92, 96, 97
Hashim Djobohadikusumo 91
Hefner, R.W. 38, 88
Heng, R.H.-K. 2, 16, 38, 88
Hernandez, C.G. 20
Herwanto, Eddy 90
Heryanto, A. 95; and Adi, S.Y. 42–3, 44, 91
Heuvel, J.V. and Dennis, E.E. 119
Hewison, K. 142
Hidayat, D.N. 91
Hill, D.T. 34, 78, 79, 90, 150; and Sen, K. 94
Hill, H. 36
HKJA *see* Hong Kong Journalists' Association
Hong Kong 118; changes in media 106–7; ethical standards/tabloid feuds in 107–10; handover of 100–1, 106–7, 156; lack of criticism by media in 111–15; media in 101–2; regulation of media 108; rise of Chinese-language press in 102–5; RTHK as bellwether 115–16; self-censorship/no-go areas 110–15, 156; and use of wire-services 111
Hong Kong Economic Journal 105, 108
Hong Kong Economic Times 105
Hong Kong Foreign Correspondents' Club 104
Hong Kong iMail 103
Hong Kong Journalists' Association (HKJA) 107, 108, 110, 111–12, 114–15
Hong Kong Press Council 108
Hong Kong Standard 103
Horn, R. 143
Hosokawa Morihiro 61
human rights 37, 38, 39, 44
Hutcheon, S.J. 101

ICMI *see* Indonesian Muslim Intellectual's Association
iMail see Hong Kong iMail
Independen 92

Index on Censorship 100
Indonesia 1; alternative media/politics in 92–5; and collapse of Suharto regime 34–44, 95–6, 97–9; demonstrations in 35, 37, 44, 95, 96; and Department of Information 39–42, 78, 80; domestic pressures on 43–4; domestication of media in 78; economic situation 34–5, 44, 83–6; elite conflict in 86, 87; foreign interest in 36–8, 43, 44, 84, 85; irresponsibility of press in 41; media as business in 79; media resistance to pressure in 89–91, 94; military involvement 35, 39, 79, 83, 84, 86; as 'nation in waiting' 94; nationalism in 82–3, 84; New Order regime 34, 37, 39, 43–4, 77, 78, 81, 82–7, 96, 98, 155–6; and outcomes of bannings in 89–90; and political economy of bannings 91–2; population of 160n; power struggles in 96–7; press in 78–92; *reformasi* movement in 39–41, 46, 47, 48; structural corruption in 83; technology in 83–6; and theories of bannings in 87–8; and warships story 85–6, 87–8
The Indonesia Times 84
Indonesian Democratic Party (PDI) 34, 89, 95
Indonesian Muslim Intellectual's Association (ICMI) 38, 84
information cartels 54–6; and credentialing of information 55; and homegenization of news/opinion 55; and limiting of agenda-setting process 55; and weakening of political auditing function 55
INN 125, 135
International Herald Tribune 135
international media 5, 6, 37, 43, 46, 49; as allies 119–20; and conspiracy theories 125–30; control of 118; criticism of 118; domestic coverage of 120–4; interaction with 118–19, 149–52, 156; political sensitivites concerning 142–9; pressure from 44, 54–5; pressure on 47–8; and Westander/Kockums case 130–42, *see also* media

International Monetary Fund (IMF) 33, 43, 44, 84, 95, 98
Internet 5, 37, 43, 44, 47, 93–4
Ishikawa Ichiro 73
Ito Kunio 62

Jakarta Post 43, 77, 84, 90, 102
Japan, constraints on freedom of information in 52–6; criticism of press in 50–1; and downfall of LDP 57–61, 75; growing political clout of television in 56–7; lack of independent media sector 68; little change in 155; media in 51–2, 74; media/politics after fall of LDP 64–5; one-party dominance in 50; and political realignment 67–9, 75; and politician strike back 61–4; and politics of 'wide show' 69–74, 75–6; and role of NHK 65–7; structure of media in 51–2, 74
Japan Business Today 66, 67
Japan Renewal Party (JRP) 58, 62
Johnson, C. 68, 160n
Johnson, S. 59, 61
journalists 18; and alliance with audience 15; blacklisting of 146, 148; boldness of 38; and cash receipts/benefits 8; competence of 121; *de facto* ownership of 8; foreign 36, 54, 68, 118–19, 120–1; freelance 68; intimidation/harassment of 25–6, 27–8, 43, 46, 97, 104, 142; jailing of 48; licensing of 41, 91; obectivity/standards of 54; and politics 2–3, 25, 32, 61–2, 77, 82, 157; protests by 26; relationship with military/intelligence services 81; treatment of 118; and use of pen-names 23; and visa restrictions 36, 43, *see also* Alliance of Independent Journalists

Kanemaru Shin 58
Katoppo, Aristides 79, 80, 89
Kavi Chongkittavorn 33
Kawamoto, K. 37
Keane, J. 98
Khalil Yaacob 47
Khao Sot 125, 126

Khin Maung Win 46
Khunying Pankrua 140
kisha clubs 53–5
Kitley, P. 79
KMI *see* War Materials Inspectorate
KMT 101
Knight, A. 16; and Nakano, Y. 103, 106, 112
Kockums affair 130–42, 162n–3n
Koizumi Junchiro 69–74, 75
Komar, Herry 81, 92
Kompas 40, 79, 84
Kramol Thongdhammachart 128
Krauss, E. 2, 51, 58, 65, 66, 71
Kritaya Archavanitkul *et al* 159n
Krungthep Thurakit 144
Kume Hiroshi 57
Kuok Hock Nien, Robert 101, 103–4
Kyo Ho Houm 8

Lague, D. 104
Lai, Jimmy 109, 110
Lam, Steven 106
Lam, Willy Wo-Lap 103–4
Larimer, T. 72
Latief, Abdul 12, 90, 92, 96, 97
Lau, E. 107
Law Siu-Lan 105
Lee, C.-C. 14; and Chan, J.M. 101
Lee, P.S.N. and Chu, L.L. 10–11, 103, 110, 112, 115
legislation 41, 48, 52
Lent, J. 13–14
Lewis, G. 164n
Liberal Democratic Party (LDP) 50, 57–61
licensing 5, 34, 41, 78, 90, 91
Liddle, R.W. 84, 94
Lintner, B. 46
Liu, Kin-Ming 110
local media 37, 110, 114
local press 6, 37, *see also* alternative press; Chinese-language press; free press; newspapers; print media; regional press; tabloid press; Thai-language press; vanity press
Lu, Annette 114
Lu Siqing, Frank 102
Lukman Harun 88

Ma, E.K.-w. 13
McBeth, J. 80, 81
McCargo, D. 2, 9, 11, 13, 14, 17, 23, 24, 26, 34, 57, 65, 117, 159n, 160n, 162n, 163n; and Bowra, 119
McGlynn, Kerry 106
McKillop, P. and Itoi, K. 60
MacLachlan, L. 68
McNair, B. 3
Magnier, M. 70, 72
Mahathir Mohamed 19, 46–8, 144
Mak Yin-ting 112
Malaysia 45–8, 118
Manager 133
Manit Sooksomchi 30
Marcos, Ferdinand 1, 19, 20–3
Marcus, D.L. 37
Mar'ie Muhammad 85
Matichon 7, 13, 25, 117, 130, 133, 139
May events 19, 24, 32, 159n
Mayes, T. and Rowling, M. 54
media, as agent of change 4, 43, 153; as agent of restraint 3, 43, 77, 98–9, 153; as agent of stability 3, 43, 77–99, 153; ambivalent role of 46–7; apalling coverage by 69; and campaigns against repression 42; categories of 5; and challenging of regimes 22; changes in 101, 106–7; corruption in 16–17, 22; crackdown on 47, 94; difficulties for 114; diversionary tactics 34–5; and empowerment 13, 76; firefighting role of 157; foreign interest in 115; as independent 21, 68, 86; indirect influence of 43–4; inertia in 67–8; and management/coverage of crises 19–48; marketing of 32; model–based approach 5; as multidimensional 4; new alignments of 102; new enemies of 49; and new technology 93–4; new ventures 40; openness of 40; oppositional responses 35; in peacetime 50–76; as political actors 2–3, 157–8; as polyvalent 43, 157; privatization by repression 22; problematizing 5–6; problems/debates concerning 110–15; and public interest 14–15; public relations model 115; as

media (*continued*)
: regulator 4–5; restrictions on 41–2; role/rights of 18, 42–3, 44, 49, 50; as servants of political establishment 50; as spectator, watchdog, servant, trickster 11; and structural reform 17; in time of transition 100–16; vision for 113–14; weaknesses of 63–4, *see also* broadcast media; international media; media/politics relationship; new media; print media

Media Dakwah 35
Media Monitoring Centre 33
media/politics relationship 77, 149, 153; analysis of 1; complicity in 29, 36, 52–5; and difference between news and comment 123–4; and influence 1; and institutions 2; and international pressures 43–4; and journalists 2–3; public awareness of 26; and resolution of conflict 129–30; tensions in 79; as twilight zone 2; and use of 'spin' 107; weaknesses in 64–5, *see also* media; politics
Megawati Sukarnoputri 34, 42–3, 89, 95
Ming Pao 101, 105, 108
Mirsky, Jonathan 102
Miyazawa Kiichi 58–60, 160n
Mohamed, G. 9
mosquito press 12–13
Mr ATM *see* Banharn Silpa-archa
Multimedia Super Corridor project 47
Murdani, Benny 85, 87
Murdoch, Rupert 14

Naeo Na 31, 32, 144
Narong Wongwan 119, 127
The Nation 27, 30, 31, 32, 121, 122, 128, 130, 134
National Human Rights Commission 38
Ne Win 45
Nemenzo, F. 20
Neumann, A.L. 19, 40
New Aspiration Party (NAP) 132
new media 5, 37, 49, *see also* media
New Straits Times 46–7
News Station 57, 58

newspapers 18; banning of 34, 78, 79–91, 150; boycott of controlled 21; circulation 51, 79, 85, 105, 109; classification of 101; closure of 24, 33; commercial links 51–2; conservative stance 52; critical reporting by 101, 102; criticisms of 50–1; and editorial policy 103, 104; and employment of stringers 102; influence of 23, 101; litigation against 41–2; new business strategies of 52; as opinion-leaders/focus points 69; oppositional line 52; as outspoken 102; as political actors 84, 141; and privatization of repression 42; privileged status of 56; profitability of 20; and reporting of criticisms 36, 38; resignations in 47; slump in 47; subsidies for 20–1; and training 17; translations in 102; types of 5–6, *see also* alternative press; Chinese-language press; free press; local press; print media; regional press; tabloid press; Thai-language press; vanity press
Newsweek 118
Next Media group 108
NHK 51, 56, 65–7, 160n
Nip, J.Y.M. 107
Nomura Takehiko 70, 71

ODN *see Oriental Daily News*
Olle, J. 40–1
Opposisi 40
Oriental Daily News (ODN) 105, 108–9, 110
ownership/control, breakdown in 36; by business 95, 103; by media proprietors 40–1, 93; by the military 23, 95; changes in 49; decentralization of 9; diversity of 109; formal/informal 78–9, 154; free–for–all press 5; levels of 8; licensed 5; as means to advance power/influence 24, 33–4, 92, 117, 153; political 4–5, 39–40, 42, 44, 78–9, 91–2; reasons for 12; shareholders 7, 78–9, 90; shifts in 100–1; surrogate/*de facto* 7–8
Ozawa Ichiro 58, 62

Pacific Asia 6–7
Paisal Sricharatchanya 30
Pajaree Tanasomboonkit 32
Palacio, R.R. 9
Palang Dharma party 24, 143, 144, 145, 163n
partisanship 9–11, 25, 32–3, 49, 103, 118, 154
Patten, Chris 100, 106–7
PDI *see* Indonesian Democratic Party
People Power movement 19, 20–3, 45
Persatuan Wartawan Indonesia (PWI) 34, 41, 42, 78, 89, 92
Pharr, S.J. 11
Philippines 20–3
Phiraphan Phalusuk 139
Phujatkan 31, 32, 117, 145
Piya Malakul 29
politics, 'explosion of free expression' 36; and internal power 46; liberalization of 76; nationalist/regionalist rhetoric 118; openness of 79; paranoia in 87–8; and recycling of foreign coverage 122–9; reporting of 105; role of media in 3–4; and transition to democracy 18, 19–49, 154–5; of wide show 69–74, *see also* media/politics relationship
Pongthep Tepkarnchana 144
Pos Kota 79
Power-holders 9–11
Prasong Lertratanawisute 139
Prasong Sunsiri 126–7, 147
Prawase Wasi 147–8
press associations 40
press clubs *see kisha* clubs
print media 5; aggressiveness of 40; as business 12–14; as first choice 6; and legislation 48; new/lively publications 46; as outlet for personal/political views 4–5, 12; as outspoken 78; and placement of articles 5–6; and state control/propaganda 4–5, 9; subsectors of 6, *see also* alternative press; Chinese-language press; free press; local press; newspapers; regional press; tabloid press; Thai-language press; vanity press

profit 11–14, 20, 92
public interest 14–15
PWI *see* Persatuan Wartawan Indonesia

Raboy, M. and Dagenais, D. 48
radio 47, 119, 135; as bellwether 115–16; censorship of 30; control of 27; harassment of 42; local 37, 40; outspokenness of 40; political watering down of 105; and reinforcement of opposition 35–6, *see also* broadcast media
Radio and Television Hong Kong (RTHK) 105, 108, 115–16
Radio Thailand 27
Radio Veritas 1, 20–3
Ramage, D.E. 84
Ramos, Fidel 20
Randall, V. 19, 33
Rasri Bunlert 140
RAT *see* Reporters' Association of Thailand
regional press 6, *see also* alternative press; Chinese-language press; free press; local press; newspapers; print media; tabloid press; Thai-language press; vanity press
Reporters' Association of Thailand (RAT) 25, 26, 137
Republika 38, 84
Reuters 25
Rivera, T.C. 21
Robison, R. 39
Rodan, G. 118
RTHK *see* Radio and Television Hong Kong

Safari FM 40
Sagawa Kyubin 62
Sanam Luang 29
Sanan Kachornprasart 135, 138
Sandeen, R. 42
Sanger, D.E. 60
Sankei Shimbun 62
Sanoh Thienthong 125–6, 134
Santoso, 94
Satrio Arismunandar 92
Sawat Amornwiwat 31
Schidlovsky, J. 100

Schultz, J. 14, 15
Schwarz, A. 83, 85, 98
Self-censorship *see* censorship
Sembiring Meliala 86
Sen, K. and Hill, D.T. 35–7, 39–40, 41
Serrano, I.R. 4, 157
Sherer, P.M. 124–5, 137
Shima Keiji 66–7
Shirk, M. and Woo, W.F. 103
Siam Post 32, 117, 122–3, 124–9, 132–7, 142, 149
Siam Rath 25
Simponi 90
Sing Pao 101, 105
Singapore 118
Sino-British Declaration (1984) 101
SkandaL 40
Smith, D. 21–2, 45
Sng, J. 42, 47
Somask Prissananantakul 126
Somkiat Onwimol 29, 147
Sorrayuth Suthassanachinda 140, 145–6
South China Morning Post (SCMP) 102–5, 111
SPAS 139, 140
Stanley, 92
State Law and Order Restoration Committee (SLORC) 45
student protests *see* demonstrations
Suchinda Kraprayoon 23–33, 119, 159n
Sugiyama, M. 63, 68
Suharto, President 3, 19, 34–48, 78, 80, 82, 83, 86, 87–8, 94–6
The Sun 109
Sunday Project 57, 58–9
Supridi Sribhadung 134, 135, 139
Surakiart Sathirathai 139
Suranan Vejjaijiva 143–4
Surin Pitsuwan 127
Surprise Weekly 109
Suthichai Yoon 27, 30, 162n
Suthin Wannabovorn 25–6
Syarwan Hamid 41

tabloid press 40–1, 41, 103, 107–8, *see also* alternative press; Chinese-language press; free press; local press; newspapers; print media; regional press; Thai-language press; vanity press
Tahara, S. 59–60
Tanaka Kakuei 119
Tanaka Makiko 71, 72–3, 75
Tasker, Rodney 146–7
Tekad 40
telephones 29–30, 35, 45, 119
television 18, 114, 119, 139; access to 31; attempts at closure 35; ban on foreign 36; as bellwether 115–16; censorship of 28–9, 30; change/conflict in 66–7; commercial 57, 61; control of 25, 27; crews as objects of derision/disbelief 29; critical presentations on 57; failures of 64–5; interviewing style on 56–7; limited effectiveness of 63–4; local 37; and non–coverage of opposition 47; and politics 56–7, 61–4; pressures on 79; private 51–2, 56, 60; semi–governmental 51; threats/warnings made to 35–6; training for 56; ultra-cautious stance of 67, *see also* broadcast media
Tempo 40, 41, 98; banning of 79, 80, 81, 150, 155; as mainstream publication 80; as polyvalent publication 80–1, 82; as questioning/critical 81–2; reasons for banning 82–7; relationship with Habibie 87–8; replacement of 91–2; results of banning 89–91; as support of government 81
Thai Post 144
Thai Rak Thai party 143–5
Thai Rath 25, 30, 117, 120, 130, 133, 136, 144, 147
Thai Sky Channel 1 139
Thai-language press, and articulation of conflict within the elite 23–5; and circulation of information 122–4; and conspiracy theories 126–30, 140; and coverage of general election (1995) 121, 124–30; curtailment of 33–4; financial/professional vitality of 32; and foreign news gathering 120–4; foreign news staff on 120–1; harassment/closure of 21; as independent political actors 117–18;

intertextuality in 129; *modus operandi* of 119–20, 121–2, 127–30, 131, 132–42, 149, 150–1; news/comment difference in 123–4; as outspoken 23, 25; ownership of 117; as parallel political universe 23–4; partisanship of 32–3; as pro-government 23; and purchase of submarines 121–2, 130–42; and reaction to foreign coverage 118–19; recession in 33; and recycling of foreign coverage of domestic politics 119–20, 122–4; resistance to pressure 32; and resolution of political/media conflict 129–30; and storms in a teacup 129; strengths/limitations of 121–2; trustworthiness of 33; and use of wire-services 121, *see also* alternative press; Chinese-language press; free press; local press; newspapers; print media; regional press; tabloid press; vanity press

Thailand, and submarine affair 130–42; bringing down of Suchinda in 23–34; electronic media in 117; foreign monitoring of 149–52; and negative reactions to foreign coverage 118–19; press in 23–5, 117–18, 121–30; and response to general election (1995) in 124–30; and Thaksin debate 142–9; and use of foreign press 119–20

Thaksin Shinawatra 33–4, 118, 122, 142–9, 151, 163n
Thinnawat Marukapitak 29
Tidnivgarnas Telegrambrya 136
Time magazine 72, 118, 144–5, 149, 151
The Times 102
Tin-wai, Leung 109
TIRAS 12, 90, 92, 96
Trisakti University 35
Tsang, Donald 109
Tsubaki Sadayoshi 61–4

Tung 105, 106–7
TV Asahi 1, 28, 57–61, 61, 62–4

U Nu 45
Ubonrat Siriyuvasak 32
Ukrist Pathmanand 142
Ummat 38
underground press *see* alternative press

Valery, Nick 119
vanity press 12, *see also* alternative press; Chinese-language press; free press; local press; newspapers; print media; regional press; tabloid press; Thai-language press
Vatikiotis, Michael 147
Vattana Assawahame 127
videotapes 31
Vines, Stephen 106
Visnews 25, 28
Vittachi, Nury 103
Vogel, E. 74
Voice of America 45
voter persuasion paradigm 1

War Materials Inspectorate (KMI) 138, 142
websites 93–4, 112, 159n, 161n
Westander, Henrik 130–42
Westney, D.E. 52
Williams, L. 83, 84; and Rich, R. 6
Wolferen, K. van 10, 50, 71
Wong, K. 47

Yamazaki, K. 64
yellow revolution *see* People Power movement
Yeung, C. 107
Yomiuri group 63
Yunus Yosifah 41

Zaharom Nain 47
Zeitlin, A. 103, 111
Zhu Ronghi 101